SEA POWER
and the Nuclear Fallacy

SEA POWER

and the Nuclear Fallacy

a reevaluation of
global strategy

Robert E. Walters

Holmes & Meier Publishers, Inc.
New York

Published in the United States of America 1975 by
Holmes & Meier Publishers, Inc.
101 Fifth Avenue, New York, New York 10003

First published by Penguin Books Ltd.
Harmondsworth, Middlesex, England

Original Title: *The Nuclear Trap: An Escape Route*

Library of Congress Cataloging in Publication Data

Walters, Robert E.
  Sea power and the nuclear fallacy.

  First published in 1974 under title: The nuclear
trap.
  Includes bibliographical references and index.
  1. Strategy. 2. Sea power. 3. Atomic weapons.
4. Geopolitics. I. Title.
U162.W35 1975   355.4'307   75-15754
ISBN 0-8419-0214-3

Printed in the United States of America

Contents

Introduction

This book attacks the foundations of Western strategy since the Second World War. It argues that strategy has to a large extent determined policy and that as a result of this anomaly a mistaken strategy has produced a wrong policy. It sets out the basis for an alternative strategy which is very much more in accordance with the needs of policy and with the geopolitical realities of the world. This study of strategy involves an examination of the global geopolitical map, and this examination leads in turn to the replacement of the West's established world outlook by a new and very different one.

Geopolitical features can be defined as the geographical facts regarded in terms of their political relevance in a global context. They include such factors as geographic position, resources, movement and transportation, and technological changes. This book evaluates the present and future significance of these features of the world environment, and relates them to the foreign policies of states. A global view presupposes a set of geopolitical ideas. Foreign policy in turn is shaped by the global view. Diplomacy and strategy, in turn, should be dependent upon foreign policy.

Familiarity, supported by the emotional grip of anti-communism, has kept one set of ideas in our minds long after they have lost plausible validity. The independence of mind which was called for has not been lacking in Western countries, but unfortunately those who have displayed it with regard to policy have not been concerned with problems of strategy; nor have they even recognized that a flexible military force is a necessary factor of power and policy in the age of nuclear armaments. Those who were dismayed at the course of Western policy should have been concerned to view strategy in its place, to see it with detachment and see it comprehensively. The more radical left has excluded itself from trying to espouse a rational and realistic strategy for Western states; the liberals have been mesmerized in matters of strategy by sanctifying received doctrine with scientistic and idealistic pretensions and confounded their liberal minds by ignoring the relation of ends and means; and the conservatives, who are probably the most critical element in the formation of strategy in a democracy, have shown a complete absence of constructive thought over this period. The professional strategists themselves have been bemused by their specialism and by their paymasters. At the same time, ironically, since the introduction of nuclear weapons, more attention than ever has been given to strategy by both professionals and a wider public.

The starting point of this book is that the West has based its strategy on the assumption that the Soviet Union, with its immense territory, population and resources, together with its central position on the Eurasian land mass, has a superior strategic position. The view that the area of Russia and Siberia, together with certain adjacent regions, has potentially a geopolitical advantage has often been called the Heartland theory. It can be shown by analysis and by authority that the Heartland theory has been the basis of the Western concept of the nuclear deterrent. Nuclear arms seemed necessary in order to redress this supposed imbalance of power.

Chapters 1 to 4 are devoted to an exposition of the Heartland theory and the development of a nuclear strategy in Western thinking. The next five chapters, 5 to 9, examine certain key premises of the Heartland theory and conclude that they are now quite mistaken. This points to the significance of other factors, which provide the foundation for a new world outlook. The last chapter brings the themes of the argument together and anchors them in the political world of the 1970s, indicating their broad implications for policy among the Western countries. The first six chapters are largely concerned with a criticism of the current state of Western strategic thinking. Chapters 7 to 10 look to the future, and develop a constructive contribution to geopolitics. The central element in this is that the world is entering a new maritime era in which there will be a great revival of maritime power, and in which the oceans of the world will become of vast economic concern. The importance of the seas is growing for military reasons and reasons of trade and transportation, and they are becoming a sphere of resources and wealth.

There are two principal theses in this book. One we can term the nuclear fallacy; it states that the place of nuclear arms in Western strategy has severely distorted military thinking, and has had a disastrous effect on policy. The other thesis is the place of the seas. The new prospects for maritime power arise from another application of nuclear energy. The undersea riches are an additional factor, and these two factors provide such a fundamental transformation in the global outlook that we can term the coming decades, without any hyperbole, a new oceanic age.

In a general sense, this book strikes a traditional note. Western civilization has owed much of its strength to sea power. The invention of the 'tall ships' enabled Europeans to explore the rest of the world, and it was through the development of sea power that Western civilization extended overseas. In recent decades, it seemed to the West that the importance of the sea was losing ground, and the global view from London and Washington saw the old security based on the sea as at an end. The influence of Western civilization has been considerably denigrated in recent years, and it is customary to adopt a cynical attitude to the future. European influence has indeed often been as destructive and inhumane as that of other civilizations. But it has much of value to contribute to the world. It has within it both the strength and the ideals to offer hope for the future. It has one saving grace to a unique degree – the capacity for self-analysis and criticism. Its lease of history will be honoured for long to come if it can now relate the instruments at its disposal to a realistic and worthwhile purpose.

The scope of this analysis has been restricted to what is essential to it. Other factors which can play a considerable part in the equations of power have been left out. They do not invalidate the arguments; they are additional factors which have, of course, to be taken into account by the politician and statesman in practice. There need be no contradiction between practice and the theory propounded here; the geopolitical framework exists, and it would obscure the essential points which are made if other factors were taken into account in these pages.

Two omissions, however, need a brief comment. Though this book is very much concerned with the genesis of a Western strategy based on nuclear armaments, it does not at all concern itself with the inner workings of the so-called 'strategy of deterrence'. There is a voluminous literature on this. The fact that the author makes virtually no reference to these studies indicates merely that they are outside his purpose. In the event of nuclear war, they could be relevant; they may be of help in clarifying some aspects of how not to start one. No disregard for the many valuable and necessary contributions in that field of nuclear strategy is implied.

It is recognized that nuclear weapons would have been – and were in the first place – developed regardless of the Heartland theory. There is no doubt that this is a very special and important consideration. The point made in this book is that they would never have occupied their place in Western strategic thinking without the Heartland theory; nor would they have been looked upon as instruments of policy without a fundamental confusion of thought. They were regarded almost as a means of salvation for the West. In truth, they are weapons which carry the highest possible risks but achieve the minimum practical effect in promoting Western interests or applying positive policies. Their main value now is as bargaining counters on matters solely related to limitation of nuclear arms. They have become a monstrous and self-contained fact which has little relevance for all other broad or specific aims of policy. This book makes a conscious departure from the determining place given to nuclear weapons in recent thinking. It turns back – or forward – to a kind of strategic consideration which has been largely ignored in the shadow of the bomb, but which cuts deep in terms of the real application of power. It is indeed concerned with power in the nuclear age – but it deals with an indirect use of nuclear power.

The other omission concerns the origins of the Cold War. It is outside the scope of this book to analyse that history; it is rather concerned with the manner in which the West's response developed. This was determined by the Western view of the Heartland threat, and, of course, the most critical area was Europe, since Russian power made deep inroads into Eastern Europe in the closing stages of the Second World War. In recent years there has been a reappraisal of the origins of the Cold War, especially by the 'revisionist' school in the United States. Among other views, these historians maintain that the Russians had no intention of trying to overrun Western Europe. The author takes a middle view between the revisionists and the former orthodoxy. Twenty million Russians had died in the war with Germany; the avowed policy of the Hitler régime towards the Slavs amounted to genocide, and at times the fate of Russia seemed to hang in the balance. Under these circumstances, any realistic Russian leader would have wanted to take as much German territory as possible as an insurance for the future. Other countries knew so little about Russia that ideas of her military strength at the end of the war were extremely speculative. There was a genuine fear of the Soviet Union, and there was initially some basis for this fear.

But through the 1950s and the 1960s – and even into the 1970s – this fear of a Russian blitzkrieg in Europe has occupied the minds of Western military experts. This cannot be reasonably justified. Europe itself had recovered from the ruins of war. All the evidence showed that a 1940 kind of blitzkrieg was not possible. Once the method of the blitzkrieg was understood, the attack no longer had the advantage. This case was argued by Sir Basil Liddell Hart, and contemporary strategists are reluctant to use the word 'blitzkrieg', perhaps out of deference to Liddell Hart's authority. Instead, it is claimed that in the age of nuclear weapons Liddell Hart's thinking is out of date. But this is begging the question; nuclear weapons have been introduced into NATO because of Russia's superiority in *conventional* arms.

We are not suggesting that the Heartland theory caused the Cold War. But, consciously or unconsciously, the set of ideas which comprise the Heartland theory became part of the global outlook of the West, and strategy was made to fit them. Even if we did not subsume these ideas under the name 'Heartland theory', the arguments in the following pages would be equally relevant: it is one map of geopolitical features compared with another. But it is more straightforward to carry out our analysis in relation to a systematic statement of the Heartland theory. The intellectual premises of Western defence doctrine are not clear without it.

The premises of power lie in geopolitics. This is clearly so in the case of strategy; it is also the case to a considerable extent in international political and economic life. We must not under-estimate such factors as social organization or even psychology – which can perhaps be seen in Japan's spectacular economic success – but for any understanding of power in the world we must first clearly delineate the geopolitical features, for it is on this background that other human characteristics exist.

Some have suggested that the place of geopolitics has diminished in the nuclear age. In fact, the place of the nuclear deterrent itself has resulted from certain geopolitical assumptions, and Western strategy as a whole has been imprisoned inside a global outlook which closed the doors to reasonable alternatives. Others have suggested that the importance of geopolitics has been overtaken by modern technology, which theoretically has appli-cations throughout the world. But technological developments themselves have profound geopolitical significance, and it is now being realized that world resources are limited. There is, for instance, the threat of a crippling fuel crisis. In a world which is one world, in that what happens in one part has more reper-cussions than ever in other parts, geopolitical considerations have a force and a range of applications which is greater than ever before. The very interdependence of the world community, in terms of trade, communications, industry, political activity and military moves, means that the tremors caused by geopolitical changes are potentially stronger in their effects.

Since the end of the Second World War, the strategy of the West has been in theory a defensive strategy, reacting to threat, though in practice – and indeed because of this – it has often ap-peared aggressive. The United States in particular has often been cast in the role of bully, determined to impose its will at all costs – and unable to do so. This is a sorry accompaniment to those acts of far-sighted statesmanship which began immediately after the war with the Marshall Plan. It has been a strategy for crisis, and is self-fulfilling in that it is bound to generate crises. This book shows the way to a strategy which is neither defensive nor aggres-sive in character, but which we can call an open strategy. It is one which is much more conducive to making strategy a partner of diplomacy, as it should be; in this way too the book strikes a more traditional note. Both diplomacy and strategy are simply ways and means of effectively carrying out policy – but if those ways and means can be flexible in operation and adaptable to changing circumstances, then this permits a wider choice of policies.

The United States obviously has the dominant part to play in Western strategy. An open strategy, in the sense to which the argument of this book leads, requires some traditional virtues in which the American psychology has not excelled, especially in international affairs. It requires finesse and a tolerance of ambiguity. It requires a certain detachment and composure, an open and objective mind. There is something of an aristocratic style to these characteristics, at least intellectually; but they are also necessary to the smooth working of democratic institutions.

Democracies, however, have their own special problems in the conduct of foreign affairs. The mechanisms of democratic institutions which, in principle, should provide appropriate adjustments of the balance of interests in domestic affairs give the citizens no special knowledge or experience of other parts of the world. But in foreign policy political leaders are still subject to public opinion, to the pressures of sectional interests and the play of domestic politics.

The trouble in the United States in particular is that, whereas the world is complex and issues not clear-cut, the American mentality looks for simple, direct solutions. Liddell Hart wrote: 'I have found myself that life becomes an unavoidable series of compromises between one's ideals and one's circumstances. It is a vain hope to seek solutions for our problems in any direct way, but the indirect approach turns out to be a philosophy as well as a strategy.' A successful foreign policy requires skilful adjustment of a large number of interacting balances. A reasonable equilibrium, in which countries have a chance of working out their own salvation as best they can, is not the sort of thing to present to spectators who want to cheer on their own side to victory in a contest which they can easily follow. The spectators may be the citizens, and therefore voters, of America. It is true that foreign policy in a democracy should be within a framework which the public can understand. Certainly, however, it is possible for the United States to have a foreign policy which is comprehensible, which can be seen to be enlightened and which can be seen to protect American interests. But it must be a policy which is not committed to a forced and straightforward 'win or lose' situation. Freedom of action is part of the essence of good strategy and diplomacy.

Though there are some disadvantages to this role of public opinion in democracies, in the long run it should be for the better. If it often distorts policy, it can also provide some check on the biases of those in power. But it makes it vitally important that there should be a politically significant element among the public which is well informed about the world, which can see the issues of policy and power realistically in a global perspective, and which has an understanding of strategy.

Strategy concerns all of us. It must not be the prerogative of any élite or expert group, whether they are professional, military or academic theorists. In modern democratic societies military matters are very much the concern of the civilian, and he should not be afraid of looking any general in the eye – and none more so than those who tell him, 'Keep out'. Strategy itself rests on assumptions which are outside purely military expertise; in fact, one of the misfortunes of the post-war period is that military thinking has been so concerned with military hardware, or rather with means of destruction, that it has neglected the essential elements of its nature.

It is quite untrue, said Liddell Hart, that if one wishes for peace one should prepare for war: but if one wishes for peace one should understand war. Peace, justice, the orderly development of man's tenure of the world, depend upon the realities and uses of power, employed with skill and wisely understood.

1. The Darkness and the Light

> It was the best of times, it was the worst of times, it was the age of wisdom, it was the age of foolishness, it was the epoch of belief, it was the epoch of incredulity, it was the season of Light, it was the season of Darkness, it was the spring of hope, it was the winter of despair, we had everything before us, we had nothing before us . . .
>
> Charles Dickens (*A Tale of Two Cities*)

It is the strategy of the deterrent which has formed the basis for Western strategy since the end of the Second World War, and it must be stressed that the nuclear deterrent has been coupled with readiness and willingness to use nuclear arms even though an opponent might choose to use only conventional weapons.

Repeated assaults have been made upon this strategic concept of the nuclear deterrent by well-meaning, but often muddled-minded, opponents. Usually these attacks have concentrated only on the issue of the unspeakable horror of nuclear and thermo-nuclear war. In spite of these striking and alarming frontal charges, the strategy of the deterrent has survived and even flourished. The growth of nuclear weapons has proceeded almost unabated, and the number of nations armed with them has risen to five. When the public in the West has been admonished to value the bomb, there have been many grave doubts concerning these weapons, even among some of those responsible for their development and deployment. Both Robert McNamara and McGeorge Bundy, for example, have noted that nuclear arms cannot be considered as realistic instruments of policy. McNamara wrote in 1968:

In strategic nuclear weaponry the arms race involves a particular irony. Unlike any other era in military history, a substantial numerical superiority of weapons does not effectively translate into political control or diplomatic leverage. While thermonuclear power is almost inconceivably awesome and represents virtually unlimited potential destructiveness, it has proved to be a limited diplomatic instrument. Its uniqueness lies in the fact that it is at the same time an all-powerful weapon and a very inadequate weapon.[1]

This is an extraordinary comment on twenty years of American military strategy. The purpose of war, in Clausewitzian terms, is the pursuance of political control and influence. McGeorge Bundy, in the Stevenson Memorial Lecture at Chatham House in December 1971, made much the same point. Bundy said he was convinced that after the confrontation between Russia and China '. . . China now recognized that nuclear war could never be a continuation of politics'.[2] The important fact is that Bundy himself had made this discovery.

If one considers war in its Clausewitzian sense as an instrument of policy, then one is faced with the conclusion that nuclear arms can serve no useful function for the statesman unless his policy is one of complete and utter destruction of an opponent – that is, genocide. The belief that nuclear arms, once used, can be controlled finds little support. It involves a contradiction in trying to obtain limited aims with unlimited means. Nuclear arms are unique in that a policy, and indeed one policy only, is implied in the weapons themselves.

David Halberstam noted this difficulty in a profile of Robert McNamara: 'We had sold the idea of nuclear retaliation to the Europeans, our whole budget was based on it, and yet here was a Secretary of Defense who did not believe it. If the word got out of his doubts, it would mean in effect that the US was virtually disarmed, and he would not be able to stay in office.'[3] This gives rise to an exceedingly curious situation, since Western military doctrine has rested upon the position of nuclear arms. Yet such a revelation has produced no great upheaval in defence thinking, no significant revolution in doctrine. It is startlingly clear that Western military philosophy has been caught upon the horns of a dilemma. In the misty but recent past the necessity for nuclear arms was agreed upon and accepted as more or less an article of faith. But the Clausewitzian definition of war implies that this cannot make sense, unless the policy is one of total annihilation of the enemy.

The obvious question at this point is why does the West 'need' nuclear arms? What in fact was the origin of this basic decision? Searching back into the past one finds the answer readily enough: it was the belief that the Soviet Union, emerging from the war victorious over the hitherto invincible Wehrmacht and with a vast territory in a central position stretching from Eastern Europe over 6,000 miles to the Pacific Ocean, occupied a strategically superior position in relation to any other state in the world, including the United States. It was this idea which formed the foundation for the deterrent – it was the keystone of thinking in the military sphere and it also implied a policy of containment. If the Soviet Union had a superior geopolitical position, then the 'need' for nuclear arms was axiomatic. This dovetailed with the extreme anti-communist sentiment in the West, which had accepted the idea that Russia wanted to destroy Western capitalistic society.

The idea that the Soviet Union had an advantage because of its geographical position and size was not casually picked up as the result of the emotional atmosphere of the Cold War. Rather, it seems that the reverse was true. The emotional fervour of the Cold War did not start immediately after the Second World War, but was gradually built up. The decisions of the interim period were made in the relative calm and optimism marking the end of the war.

Senator Arthur Vandenberg, the Midwestern internationalist, told President Truman that if he wished to obtain aid for Greece and Turkey, then he'd have to scare hell out of the country. And this Truman proceeded to do, with the end result that, given the American temperament which goes from one extreme to the other, his own Democratic party was caught up in the emotional fire which he had started. Senator Vandenberg recorded in his diary how within six months the whole atmosphere in Washington had completely changed. It is true that there were extreme right-wing groups in the United States, particularly in the South and Midwest, which were ready to go on anti-communist crusades, but the point is that high-level decisions unleashed these primitive forces which had been relatively dormant. The belief that the Soviet Union, despite its exhaustive and bloody conflict with

Germany, was ready for new adventures and could achieve new conquests by virtue of its superior strategic position had an intellectual basis. And although liberals and left-wing elements in the United States and Britain campaigned against the obsession with nuclear arms, even they were forced in the end to accept the nuclear deterrent. A strategic doctrine which was based on nuclear arms was bound to prevail, simply by default, if no realistic alternative was offered by its critics. It was left unchallenged to provide the one, all too easy, answer to the threat posed by the Kremlin's vast dominion.

The idea that Russia was potentially the strongest nation in the world by virtue of unique geopolitical considerations was a view put forward by the eminent British geographer, Sir Halford J. Mackinder. He had first presented this theory in a paper read before the Royal Geographical Society in 1904 with the title 'The Geographical Pivot of History'. This was later expanded into a book entitled *Democratic Ideals and Reality*, which was published in 1919. In the next chapter the ideas of Mackinder on this matter will be discussed at greater length, but a brief outline of his thinking is necessary at this stage.

The areas approximately covered by Russia and Siberia, with certain adjacent regions, were given the name of the pivot area, which was later called the Heartland. Mackinder reasoned that this area was potentially the strongest position on the face of the earth. It was rich in mineral resources and agricultural potential, and in a secure position safe from attack. Its central location on the Eurasian land mass would enable it to threaten the existence of every nation in Europe, Asia and Africa – which Mackinder termed the World Island. In time, this Heartland region could swallow the World Island and a world empire would be in sight. This was a heady theory, and it formed the foundation for the strategy of the deterrent.

But how was it possible that a man writing in 1919, and who is now little known, could have had such a profound influence upon the modern idea of the deterrent? The answer to this question is that Mackinder had formerly been extremely influential, but his personal contribution had been almost forgotten; his concepts of 1919 had, however, been tacitly accepted into modern defence thinking. The ideas of Mackinder were of great interest in Hitler's Germany in the 1930s and in the United States in the 1940s. It was in this latter period that the foundation for the deterrent was established.

Mackinder's Heartland theory had a great influence in Nazi Germany and a marginal impact upon Hitler himself. The prime mover of Mackinder's ideas in Germany was General Doctor Karl Haushofer. He was the only person in the German Army to possess a doctorate, and with this curious background Haushofer formed a school of thought at the University of Munich to foster his geopolitical concepts. Of Mackinder's 1904 paper, Haushofer wrote: 'Never have I seen anything greater than these few pages of a geographical masterwork.'[4]

In the United States a great interest in geopolitics arose in the early 1940s. There was a sudden torrent of books and articles on the subject, and in almost every case due regard was given to the ideas of Mackinder. Professor Hans W. Weigert, an American geographer and an adviser to the US government, was the author of one book entitled *Generals and Geographers*, published in 1942, in which he acknowledged: 'The reader will discover that this author stands in great awe of Sir Halford J. Mackinder's genius.'[5] In 1943 there appeared a book which was to have a great impact in the United States, *Makers of Modern Strategy*, edited by Professor Edward Earle, of Princeton. It was regularly reprinted even into the 1960s. In many of these essays the ideas of Mackinder are apparent and quite accepted.[6]

A number of American geographers and political scientists pointed out in the 1950s what they considered a loop-hole in the Heartland theory, though they regarded the existence of a Heartland as a fact. They saw that Mackinder, using the Mercator map of the world and looking at the globe from Britain, presented a distorted view of the inaccessibility of the Heartland. The pivot region, they maintained, was not secure from air power. Long-range bombers flying across the Arctic Ocean from bases in North America could strike at and destroy the source of power in the Heartland.[7] This was an extension of the air power doctrine which was being formulated in the same period. However, air power without nuclear arms would be quite impotent against the Heartland; this became clear in the later era of ICBMs and Polaris missiles.

The essential point should be noted again at this stage. It is the acceptance of Mackinder's view of the world: that there exists an Asiatic Heartland which could conceivably dominate the World Island. This world view was the foundation for the strategy of the deterrent. So one might say that the Heartland theory stands as the first premise in Western military thought.

This view is implied by Professor John Spanier in his book *American Policy Since World War II*, which has been widely used in American colleges and universities as a textbook. Spanier begins his volume by stating:

> Following World War I, the English geopolitician Halford Mackinder wrote: 'Who rules East Europe commands the Heartland (largely Russia and China, plus Iran and Afghanistan): who rules the Heartland commands the World-Island (Eurasia and Africa): who rules the World-Island commands the World.' Some years later, an American geopolitician, Nicholas Spykman, paraphrased Mackinder in a reply to his thesis: 'Who controls the Rimland (the peripheral areas of the Eurasian continent) rules Eurasia: who rules Eurasia controls the destinies of the World.'

Spanier then concludes by stating: 'No two maxims could have summed up the history of the post-World War II era more aptly.'[8]

Essentially what Spanier means is that these ideas have formed the foundation for US foreign policy thinking, for the American view of the world in the post-war period. While one might agree with Spanier about Mackinder, it is difficult to see how the views of Spykman had much influence. Spykman's ideas do not support the concept of the nuclear deterrent and they are inconsistent with Mackinder's Heartland theory.[9]

The fear of international communism was, and still is for many, a factor of great importance in forming the attitude towards Russia, but even if Russia were still controlled by the Tsars or, by some trick of fate, democratically controlled, a similar geopolitical problem would face Western statesmen. It has been geopolitical realities, as much as ideological differences, which have been the determining factor in the Cold War.[10] The main criteria for dispute in international politics have been governed by the geopolitical situation. The great tragedy is that the Western countries have been obsessed by the issue of communism in the same way that they have maintained an *idée fixe* on nuclear arms. And, indeed, these two obsessions are mutually supporting. As P. M. S. Blackett noted, 'Once a nation pledges its safety to an absolute weapon, it becomes emotionally essential to believe in an absolute enemy.'[11] Even the critics have unfortunately failed to ask the question why a nation should 'pledge its safety to an absolute weapon'. Nuclear weapons imply a policy of annihilation; therefore, as Blackett noted, it was necessary to accept the psychological framework to support such a policy.

It is a curious fact that if the Heartland theory forms the foundation for the deterrent, it has been ignored even by contemporary academic strategists; the explanation appears to be that it has been so implicitly accepted that it has seemed the only possible view. Professor W. T. R. Fox, Director of the Institute for War and Peace Studies at Columbia, wrote on this subject:

> The annihilation of distance for some purposes but not for others, which are the consequence of the new military technology as it pertains to a possible World War III, means that every exercise in strategic theory is at least in part an exercise in geopolitical thinking. However, our habit of thinking in geopolitical terms is so completely assimilated into the thought patterns of the typical contemporary student of international relations that the word 'geopolitics' itself seems almost to have dropped out of sight, and people speak in geopolitical language while thinking quite incorrectly that geopolitics died with Haushofer and Mackinder.[12]

In addition, the subject of geopolitics in the period immediately after the Second World War had a distinctly distasteful air about it because of its association with the Nazis. The outward attitude towards communism and Russia was cloaked in the righteous mantle of a crusade of goodness against evil. But foreign policy, like an iceberg, has much below the surface. Sometimes this has been more or less visible. General Omar Bradley stated in 1951, when he was Chairman of the Joint Chiefs of Staff: 'If Soviet Russia ever controls the Eurasian land mass, then the Soviet-satellite imperialism may have the broad base upon which to build the military power to rule the world . . .'[13] This was in the period when the idea that Moscow controlled China was accepted in Washington. It unquestionably reflects the influence of the Heartland theory.

We come back to the beginning of our story. If Mackinder's Heartland theory is accepted, we are forced to admit that this region occupies the strongest strategic position in the world; therefore the West needs nuclear arms. But if war is viewed as an instrument of policy, nuclear arms have no use. It is a case of admitting contradictory propositions: nuclear weapons have no place in policy and nuclear weapons are essential in policy.

One answer to the dilemma is obvious – a re-examination of the ideas of Mackinder. It must be recalled that Mackinder first wrote his Heartland theory at the turn of the century, basing it upon the geopolitical view of the world at that time. Geography changes with developments in technology. Weigert and others have stressed how the development of air transport had changed the meaning of the Heartland. In the last few decades there have been major developments of a more subtle nature, the significance of which has escaped attention. They will have a profound influence on the future, which will be considered in later chapters.[14]

There is one principal concept which points to the centre of gravity for such a re-evaluation of Mackinder's ideas. Ortega y Gasset once remarked that if man were immortal, then the motor car would be meaningless. Since he is not, movement is of great significance in the practical affairs of life – in commerce and in war. All the great captains of industry and war have known that transportation (or, in the soldier's terminology, mobility) is a factor of vital importance; movement has often been called the soul of war. This element of movement changes the geographical shape of the world. Mackinder remarked of the relationship between history and geography: '. . . The true geographer thinks in shapes. Might we not complete the idea with the statement that the true historian thinks in movements – movements upon the shapes of the geographer? Both of them see with the mind's eye.'[15]

The two major geopoliticians who are of interest here are Mackinder and the American naval writer Alfred T. Mahan. The essential difference between them (and they agreed on many basic ideas) revolved around the mode of transport or means of movement. Mahan was the great apostle of sea-borne transport, and Mackinder foresaw the tremendous possibilities in land transportation with the steam locomotive and the internal combustion engine.

Mahan, in stating the case for sea power, wrote:

> Communications dominate war; broadly considered, they are the most important single element in strategy, political and military. In its control over them has lain the pre-eminence of sea-power – as an influence upon the history of the past; and it will continue, for the attribute is inseparable from its existence. This is evident because . . . transit in large quantities and for great distances is decisively more easy and copious by water than by land. The sea, therefore, is the great medium of communications – of commerce.[16]

Mackinder made the counter-attack on the sea power theory with the observation that the long superiority of sea transport, and hence sea power, was largely due to the technological lag between land and sea communications. It is hard for the modern mind to realize that for several centuries the sailing ship was the most complicated machine in existence. It had enabled men, who had been relatively land-bound and on sea forced to stay near the shore, to span the oceans of the world. Since three-fourths of the earth's surface is made up of water and all the major seas are contiguous one with another, this gave man (at first European man) almost unlimited movement over the face of the earth. It was by virtue of this sea mobility that Europeans were able to 'discover' the rest of the world. The unchallenged supremacy of sea movement lasted for almost four hundred years, from the time when Vasco da Gama and Columbus made their historic voyages until well into the nineteenth century. At the time when Mackinder was writing, in the early 1900s, great improvements had already been made in land transport and more were just on the horizon.[17]

Air movement has since developed as an alternative means of transport. The flexibility of the internal combustion engine, on land and in the air, has had immense consequences. However, the internal combustion engine has one great disadvantage: it needs a constant supply of fuel to maintain the momentum of movement. A nuclear-powered engine does not have this disadvantage; it is free from the need for refuelling. The question presents itself: what geopolitical implications does the nuclear engine have for the future?

It is now necessary to give some definition of what is meant by the term 'geopolitics'. For the purposes of this volume the term means the influence of geography, economics, demography, technology, and strategic possibilities on shaping foreign policy for a country. Geopolitics, then, is a tool for the determination of a realistic policy for a country or coalition. It is the starting point for foreign policy – the first premise. Thinking on policy should begin with fundamental principles, and these are statements of geopolitical factors.

The main contention put forward here is that Western doctrine has rested upon the geopolitical views expressed in Mackinder's Heartland theory. If this is not true, then there must be some other geopolitical theory which does provide the basis for Western thinking. Every system of thought must have its fundamental premises, whether or not these are stated or even recognized.[18]

If it can be shown that Western doctrine rests upon the Heartland theory, and if it can be further demonstrated that these ideas are not valid today, this will lead irrefutably to the conclusion that Western strategic doctrine is incorrect and far out of date. The idea has been suspected by many, but as yet no one has produced a solid refutation or come up with an alternative concept. Western cerebral soldiers have been content merely to toil away at their appointed tasks of erecting a gigantic body of defence knowledge and have paid scant heed to the essential validity of the entire structure. They have scarcely been encouraged to give independent analysis of the type which is so desperately needed. The thought that the 'emperor might not have on any clothes' is furthest from their minds, and is not an idea which can safely be put forward. The foundations for Western strategic thinking were laid down in the later 1940s and 1950s and no one dares to tamper with them. They stand as an article of faith.

And through the years layer upon layer of complicated studies and theories have been added, growing into an enormous structure. Each floor contains countless rooms and chambers and obscure passageways with intricate patterns of carefully woven thought, each more ingenious than the prior rooms and floors. Praetorian guards armed with a specialized jargon deter the novice from any close examination of the soundness of the structure. On and on the tower of Mars has risen – almost with a life and will of its own and all based upon these fundamental ideas – upon this shaky foundation. A slight push – a bit of a tremor – and this leaning tower of Mars could come crumbling down.

The decision to base Western strategic doctrine upon nuclear arms certainly opened up the Heartland for possible attack, but, correspondingly, it ended the historical invulnerability of the Anglo-American regions of the globe. It is true that in time the Chinese and Russians would develop nuclear weapons, but the point is that this fact by itself need never have forced Western statesmen to accept the belief that security and defence were primarily dependent upon a nuclear strategy. The Russians and the Chinese have never given the slightest evidence that they accepted the non-Clausewitzian view that these arms could be considered as useful instruments of policy. This historical invulnerability was not something which should have been lightly tossed away. A secure base is the starting point for any sound strategic doctrine, and probably an important factor for the growth of democratic institutions.

If the thesis put forward is valid, it means that the decision to base Western strategy upon nuclear arms must rank as one of the great blunders of history. It could well have been disastrous and still may be so, not only for the West, but for mankind. Moreover, the reliance upon nuclear arms has had a profound sociological impact upon society. It has produced an atmosphere of nihilism and it has been a major factor in forming some features of the permissive society of the West.[19] The public in the West has been told to 'love the bomb', and one must wonder at the effects of living with it, let alone loving it. It is not surprising that in 1964 a NATO diplomat made the remark, 'I'm sure that future

historians will think we were quite mad.'[20] We are just beginning
to understand the extent of this madness.

Notes to Chapter 1

1. McNamara, Robert S., *The Essence of Security*, Hodder &
Stoughton, 1968, p. 59. McNamara also wrote: 'One cannot fashion
a credible deterrent out of an incredible action' (p. 60). In other words,
force must be consistent with policy; political goals must determine the
level of violence and not the reverse. McNamara was not too happy
about tactical nuclear weapons. He stated in testimony before the
House Armed Services Committee that 'nuclear weapons, even in the
lower kiloton range, are extremely destructive devices and hardly
the preferred weapons to defend such heavily populated areas as
Europe. Furthermore, while it does not necessarily follow that the
use of tactical nuclear weapons must inevitably escalate into global
nuclear war, it does present a very definite threshold, beyond which
we enter a vast unknown' (10 January 1963).
2. *The Times*, 2 December 1971. It could be assumed that a man as
sagacious as Mao Tse-tung – a scholar familiar with the classic
Chinese military writer, Sun Tzu – would have taken twenty minutes
to reach this conclusion, not twenty years. It is curious that the West
has been so reluctant to credit the Chinese with much intelligence in
strategic thinking. Robert Payne, in his book *Portrait of a Revolution-
ary: Mao Tse-tung* (Abelard-Schuman, New York, 1961), wrote:
'Meanwhile it should be remembered that Mao is among the most
intelligent of living political leaders . . . Because he is a scholar first,
the soldier afterward, he will always be able to defeat soldiers' (p. 289).
This seems closer to the truth.
3. Halberstam, David, 'The Programming of Robert McNamara',
Harper's Magazine, February 1971.
4. Weigert, Hans W., *Generals and Geographers*, Oxford University
Press, New York, 1942, p. 116. Haushofer was also influenced by the
Swedish political scientist, Rudolf Kjellén, and the German geographer, Friedrich Ratzel, but the influence of Mackinder on his
thinking was paramount. Haushofer thought that Germany should
seek an alliance with Russia so that together these nations could
dominate the World Island and the world. Hitler, of course, had other
ideas. In Western countries the influence of Haushofer on Hitler was

grossly exaggerated. For example, the popular American magazine *Reader's Digest* published an article in July 1941 entitled 'The Thousand Scientists behind Hitler'. It stated: 'Haushofer and his Institute in Munich with its thousand scientists, technicians and spies are almost unknown to the public even in the German Reich. But their ideas, their charts, maps, statistics, information, and plans have dictated Hitler's moves from the very beginning . . . Haushofer's Institute is no mere instrument for Hitler's use. It is the other way round. Dr Haushofer and his men dominate Hitler's thinking . . . It is Haushofer who now tells the German General Staff whom to attack and when, as well as the exact strategical and psychological results of their actions . . .' Fortunately for the world these German 'whiz kids', like their American counterparts in later decades, did not quite live up to this exuberant build-up of their image.

5. Weigert, op. cit. This tribute appears in the acknowledgements. Vilhjalmur Stefansson, the Arctic expert, wrote extensively on the subject in the United States. At the same period Professor Nicholas J. Spykman at Yale put forward a theory opposing that of Mackinder. In January 1942 *Time* magazine published an article entitled 'Geopolitics in College', and during 1941 and 1942 articles on geopolitics and Mackinder appeared in many other American journals, such as *Atlantic Monthly*, *Newsweek*, *Fortune*, and *New Republic*.

6. *Makers of Modern Strategy*, ed. Earle, Edward, Princeton University Press, 1943.

7. Weigert, Hans W., and others, *Principles of Political Geography*, Appleton-Century-Crofts, New York, 1957. In support of the global view in the air power theory, they wrote: 'However, we find it difficult, if not impossible, to visualize this relation to the Heartland to a surrounding inner and outer crescent if we exchange the Mercator map for the globe or any azimuthal-equidistant map. The concept of North America as part of a chain of insular powers distant from the Heartland now becomes a geographical myth. In terms of air-geography the Heartland and North America appear in destiny-laden proximity. As viewed over the top of the world, the Heartland assumes a location different from that which Mackinder assigned to it, plotting it from Britain, and with the destinies of Britain foremost in his mind. While time has verified Mackinder's concept of Russia's growing importance as a land power in a pivotal area, and while the political and military control of the U.S.S.R. over the Heartland and Eastern Europe are at present more firmly established than ever, the skyways of the Arctic Mediterranean gave validity to a new way of regarding the geographical relations of North America and the U.S.S.R. The in-

accessibility of the vast inner inland spaces of the Heartland became evident when the Heartland power was attacked by Germany in the west, where the Heartland opens itself to invasion. But seen from North America, and in terms of new communications reaching out from many points on the far-flung "perimeter of defence", inaccessibility and vastness no longer conceal the Heartland. It no longer lies behind an impenetrable wall of isolation' (p. 217). The reader might note that the key words 'air geography' in this quotation highlight the connection between a new means of transportation and geographical and strategic views.

8. Spanier, John W., *American Foreign Policy since World War II*, Praeger, New York, 1968, p. 3.

9. Others have written in the United States about the ideas of Mackinder and Spykman with the inference that their views were consistent. Spykman looked upon the Rimland regions as of greater importance than the Heartland. However, Spykman made little reference to the means of communication, which is a crucial factor in geopolitical analysis. Hanson Baldwin, in his book *Strategy for Tomorrow* (Harper & Row, New York, 1970), wrote: 'The Mackinder–Spykman geopolitical concept of the world divided into a vast continental "heartland" of Eurasia, surrounded by Eurasian "rimland", or maritime, countries, bordering the seas, with North America as a kind of continental island, will still be essentially valid in the years to come' (pp. 44–5). Spykman, who was a political scientist at Yale, died before his views were formulated in any systematic manner. Although he used the terminology put forward by Mackinder, his thinking is vastly different.

A number of people have recognized that the ideas of Mackinder have formed the basis for the Western view of the world and so for the deterrent. Professor S. B. Cohen, an American geographer, stated in 1964: 'But when all is said and done, most Western strategists continue to view the world as initially described by Mackinder. American foreign policy of containment in the postwar era, with overseas alliances peripheral to the Eurasian land mass, is an attempt to head-off Soviet-controlled Heartland's dominion over the World Island' (*Geography and Politics in a Divided World*, Methuen, 1964, p. 40).

10. Professor Herbert Butterfield, writing in 1949, pointed out: '... There is hardly reason for regarding the problem of contemporary Russia as radically different for the diplomatist from what it would have been if the regime had been a Tsarist one, or if that country had even been democratically governed' (*Christianity and History*, Bell & Sons, 1949, p. 142).

11. *New Statesman*, 5 December 1959.
12. Letter from Professor W. T. R. Fox to the author, 26 May 1970.
There has been recently a quiet renewal of interest in geopolitics.
Robert Strausz-Hupe, for example, who had been a professor at the
University of Pennsylvania, and whose book *Geopolitics* was published
in 1945, was appointed as ambassador to Ceylon. Dr Henry Kissinger,
Nixon's adviser, has shown great concern with geopolitics. The term
'geopolitics' is being used more extensively; the *Spectator*, 3 October
1970, commented somewhat jocularly: 'Geopolitics are very big in
Washington these days, I believe they were invented by Dr
Kissinger . . .'
13. U.S. Senate, *MacArthurHearings*, 1951, p. 732.
14. Professor Gordon East wrote, 'Indeed, "geography changes as
rapidly as ideas and technologies change"; we continually have to
make new maps and newly evaluate the geography of the land and
sea areas . . . Notably our whole conception of mobility and accessibility, considerations to which Mackinder attached prime importance,
have been revolutionized by the internal-combustion engine and the
aeroplane. No less, too, have science and technology in their applications to industry and to the art of war wrought changes to which no
end can be seen. The advent of new offensive weapons, notably the
atom and hydrogen bombs, in themselves make it evermore necessary
to re-examine time-honoured assumptions of geopolitical thinking'
('The Soviet Union and the "Heartland"', in *The Changing World*,
ed. East, W. G., and Moodie, A. E., Harrap, 1956, p. 434).
Another geographer, Professor David J. M. Hooson, wrote: 'The
most fundamental of all elements of national power is sheer location on
the globe. Although this is often regarded as absolute and immutable,
it is in reality relative to the other parts of the world and its significance changes as they change, and therefore has to be constantly
reassessed' (*A New Soviet Heartland?*, Van Nostrand, New York, 1964,
p. 117). Such a reassessment is long overdue from the Mackinder
Heartland theory.
Indeed, H. J. Mackinder had pointed out the importance of re-
evaluation from time to time. 'Each century has had its own geographical
perspectives', he once wrote (*Democratic Ideals and Reality*, Norton,
New York, 1962, p. 29). This is the most recent edition of Mackinder's
1919 book, and it also includes the 1904 paper, 'The Geographical
Pivot of History', and an article for *Foreign Affairs* entitled 'The
Round World and the Winning of the Peace'.
Some people, notably the Sprouts at Princeton in books and in
conversation with this writer, have pointed out that it appears that

Mackinder later actually rejected his views concerning his Heartland theory. There is some evidence for this, but it is inconclusive. In the new introduction to the Penguin edition, published during the war in 1944, Mackinder gave no indication that he had altered his views. Though the point is of some interest in relation to Mackinder himself, it does not alter the matter here, as regardless of whether or not he recast his own thinking, the original Heartland theory has become the core of the Western global outlook.

Professor Anthony J. Pearce, a Columbia University political scientist, wrote in the introduction to the 1962 edition of *Democratic Ideals and Reality*: 'At first thought, Mackinder's work might seem superseded, just as developments in continental communications enabled Mackinder to supersede Mahan. But since the American and Soviet governments have committed themselves – by action and by words – to an indefinite stalemate in strategic weapons, the direct conflicts in the cold war have been waged by carefully limited land, sea, and air forces in the peninsulas of the World Island. Far from being outdated, *Democratic Ideals and Reality* appears to be more relevant than ever.' The same thought has been expressed by other writers. And although Professor Pearce noted that Mackinder had superseded Mahan, the theorist of sea power, this is a position which could be reversed as geography changes.

15. Mackinder, H. J., 'The Geographical Pivot of History', *Geographical Journal*, Vol. 23, 1904.

16. Mahan, A. T., *The Influence of Sea Power upon History*, Methuen, 1965, p. 200.

17. Of this Mackinder wrote: 'Today's armies have at their disposal not only the Transcontinental Railway but also the motor car. They have, too, the aeroplane which is of a boomerang nature, a weapon of land-power as against sea-power. Modern artillery, moreover, is very formidable against ships' (*Democratic Ideals and Reality*, p. 111).

18. The only other candidate seems to be the ideas of Spykman. It is also quite possible that the real basis is neither the Heartland theory or Spykman's Rimland theory, but has been left unstated. After all, the British sea power doctrine was used for centuries before someone stated what exactly was happening.

19. We live in the age of the bomb and it has inevitably influenced virtually every aspect of our lives. Modern society has been founded upon the belief in the idea of progress. There had been doubts about it in the past expressed by intellectuals such as Jacob Burckhardt and Henry Adams, but now, quite suddenly, these doubts have impressed themselves upon the ordinary man in the street and, most notably,

youth. J. B. Bury, in his book *The Idea of Progress* (Macmillan, 1920), wrote: 'If there were good cause for believing that the earth would be uninhabitable in A.D. 2000 or 2100 the doctrine of Progress would lose its meaning and would automatically disappear' (p. 5). This generation is growing up in a world in which the possibility of the extinction of human society in its life-time is real. In the 1950s and 1960s, the use of nuclear weapons seemed to many only a matter of time. In a book aptly entitled *Bomb Culture* (MacGibbon & Kee, 1968) Jeff Nuttall noted that the so-called 'generation gap' started at the time of the bomb. 'The people who had not yet reached puberty at the time of the bomb were incapable of conceiving life *with* a future' (p. 22).

It is remarkable that weapons such as nuclear arms, which have had such a profound sociological impact upon society, can be considered as the means for the preservation of Western civilization. Though they cannot now be discarded entirely, it is possible to have a different view of them. It is surprising how the fervour of the anti-bomb movement has evaporated; Nuttall noted that 'The decline of the anti-bomb movement in 1962 left us stranded in the unbearable' (p. 113). Admittedly the active protesters were a minority who, although they affected the conscience of other citizens, were not able wholly to convince the majority. Intellectually the protest movement, despite wide support from the intelligensia, was flabby. It never quite got to the heart of the matter, because it failed to consider the basic ideas at the root of the problem and provide a reasoned alternative to nuclear arms. Though the 'Ban the Bomb' movement itself has lost its impetus, it would obviously be a mistake to infer that now nuclear arms are more accepted; but the energies that went into that protest have since been channelled into other areas.

20. *Observer*, 20 December 1964.

2. The Fortress

> Besides, it was only too easy to answer him, the
> Castle always had the advantage.
>
> Franz Kafka (*The Castle*)

As the British Empire had been a great sea empire, it may seem
strange that it should have been an Englishman who formulated
a geopolitical theory for land power expansion. In fact, Mackinder's writings on the Heartland theory were essentially
warnings to his countrymen that sea power might not always be
of prime importance. The title of his book of 1919, *Democratic
Ideals and Reality*, indicates the essence of this warning. The
volume was published just as the First World War had ended, and
Mackinder noted the geopolitical importance of that war. 'We
have been fighting lately, in the close of the war, a straight duel
between land-power and sea-power, and sea-power has been
laying siege to land-power. We have conquered, but had Germany
conquered she would have established her sea-power on a wider
base than any in history, and in fact on the widest possible base.'[1]

Mackinder's Heartland theory was widely accepted in the
United States and Germany. During his lifetime, 1861–1947, his
influence in Britain was also considerable. He was highly regarded
not only in academic circles, but also in the Government. He was
a Member of Parliament, a Government Minister and a Director
of the London School of Economics. As a lecturer he was extremely popular, and he was responsible for establishing geography as a scholarly study at Oxford University.

The central assertion at the outset of this book's argument is
that the idea of the deterrent has depended upon the acceptance
of the Heartland theory – a theory which implies that Russia is
in a strategic position superior to that of the West. In order to
understand the geopolitical thinking of Mackinder, it is necessary
to review the global balance of power in the early 1900s, when
Mackinder began to write on the subject. Spykman has claimed,
quite rightly, that Mackinder was the first person to try to en-

compass the whole world in a system of thought in this manner. He had been preceded by Mahan, but the sea power theory of Mahan was centred upon Europe, since that area of the world was the dominant source of power for several centuries. Although many European nations had overseas empires, the centre of their power rested in Europe. For the past four hundred years, world history had meant essentially European history. Mackinder called this period the Columbian era. It was inevitable that the colonies of the European countries should in time break away and a new structure of power evolve. The question was: what would be the shape of this next world power structure?

Mackinder was writing when the Mahan sea power theory was prominent. Mahan had written his first book, *The Influence of Sea Power upon History, 1660–1783*, in 1890 and it was immediately accepted as a classic work, especially in Britain where it made a tremendous impact.[2] Since the writer was an American naval officer using chiefly French sources, his book was viewed as impartial by the British. The subject was the Royal Navy, which had been a great success story. People had written works on naval strategy and tactics before, but this was the first time anyone had tried to analyse in a systematic way the relationship between the Royal Navy and Britain's rise to power. Mahan's own motives for writing the book were very different. Mahan was writing at a time when steam and steel were replacing wooden sailing ships, and the major theme of his work was whether or not the age of sailing ships had any meaning for the emerging era of steam warships. Mahan claimed that the naval history of this previous period was still important for the standpoint of the strategy of his day, since overall strategy did not change. It is natural to wonder whether a present-day Mahan will arise to answer the question whether or not the age of surface ships has any meaning for the developing era of nuclear-powered undersea ships.

The English in the late Middle Ages '. . . were the most backward of the significant peoples along the Atlantic littoral on the fairway to the New World'.[3] Mahan provided an explanation of how it was possible that this fairly tiny island nation could build and maintain over such a long period a vast and mighty empire. Although the rise of Europe had been due to sea power, the

European nations were more or less dominated by the landsman's point of view. In the First World War era, Colonel Repington, the military correspondent of *The Times*, suggested that the British Navy was worth 500,000 bayonets to the French. The French generals Joffre and Foch replied that they did not consider it worth more than one bayonet. This was obviously a parochial view, but natural.

The continental European powers had to maintain their strongest defences at home, even if they had colonies scattered all over the world. The great source of danger came not from overseas, but from their European rivals. Concentration of force is one of the first principles of war. Therefore, if the greatest danger came from rival armies on the continent, it meant that the European countries were forced by geographical circumstances to concentrate their power in land armies. Mahan had put forward the theory that no country could be equally strong on land and sea. To do so implied a division of energy and attention. (It was also likely to start rivalries between services to the detriment of the interests of the country.)

The geographical position of Britain was very different. Since she was an island nation off the shore of Europe, she could not be attacked across land frontiers. Land forces were no great direct threat to her security. The only threat could come from the sea. So the Royal Navy was looked upon as the senior service, and the budget for the army could be cut to the bone while funds were lavished upon the upkeep of the navy. No other country at the time had such a favourable geographical position.

Because of this geographical location Britain was able to dominate the trade routes between Europe and the rest of the world. Since three-fourths of the earth's surface is water, this meant that in time of war Britain was able to exert an influence out of all proportion to her size. She could deny the resources of the rest of the world to her continental opponents and provide economic and financial aid to her allies. Sea power provided access to the rimlands of Europe, Asia and Africa and to the other satellite regions of the world. Any country with a coastline which could be approached freely from the sea could be threatened by sea power. In a war with a seafaring nation such as Britain, every mile of such coastline added to the difficulties of defence for a land power by stretching its resources further. The strength of land armies ended at the shoreline – they could not attack sea power, nor the country behind the sea power front.

The European countries were forced to maintain large standing armies in order to protect themselves from their rivals on the continent. Danger could arise for Britain if the European nations were to be united either by force or by a powerful coalition. If they were no longer afraid of being challenged on land, then the resources of the continent could be turned towards building a mighty navy. Since this potential threat always existed, the age-old policy of Britain towards Europe was to side with the underdog in order to maintain a balance of power. It was a policy which grew from the special geopolitical situation of Britain. It was never her aim – at least until recent years – utterly to destroy the more powerful coalition or country in Europe, since that would have upset the balance in another way. It was a policy which fostered an insular attitude towards Europe and the rest of the world, and it was a national aim which went hand in hand with the need to keep the Royal Navy as the first line of defence. Indeed, the object of the policy was to maintain the unchallenged strength of the British fleet. As the British naval writer and strategist Vice Admiral Sir Herbert Richmond noted:

The Balance of Power was a means by which to maintain this country's naval strength. It was not a means for preventing war; it was not one for dividing into two equal camps the forces of the various Powers; nor had it an altruistic aim such as supporting the weak against the strong. It aimed at obliging our continental rivals to maintain such large forces that they could not at the same time afford to maintain a navy that threatened our strength. No country can afford for long great armaments in all elements.[4]

In the late nineteenth century doubts began to arise which suggested that even the mightiest empires cannot endure for ever. It was natural to compare the British Empire with Imperial Rome. Both had endured for almost a thousand years. Now there were signs of decay. Some saw it as spiritual – a matter of energy – while others saw it as the passing of conditions favourable to the ascendancy of Britain. It seemed foolish to believe that with the continuing development of technology the same set of geopolitical conditions would exist for ever. A change was destined to occur.

The British sea power system required a concentration of force in European waters. If a strong sea power arose outside the European region, then Britain would be forced to divide her fleet and her attention. The United States existed as a potential rival, but the policies of the two countries coincided. Another threat existed in the Far East with the rise of Japan. In this case, Britain adopted a policy which might be regarded as appeasement. Mahan commented: 'It seems possible, even probable, that Great Britain made a mistake of policy in more ways than one in crippling Russia by her alliance with Japan.'[5] Eventually, Britain was forced to face this challenge to her power in unfavourable circumstances in 1941. Britain had no fleet in the Far East which could counter the threat of Japan and, as Richmond ruefully pointed out, 'It was the illusion that a Two-Hemisphere Empire can be defended by a One-Hemisphere Navy that sealed the fate of Singapore.'[6]

Mackinder thoroughly understood the basis of sea power and reasoned that it might be possible in the future for the entire land mass of Europe, Asia and Africa to serve as a mighty base for sea power. Britain was an island off the coast of Europe, but in a real sense the three joint continents together could be considered as an island. It would be the largest island in the world; hence Mackinder termed it the 'World Island'. He wrote: 'The joint continent of Europe, Asia, and Africa, is now effectively, and not merely theoretically, an island. Now and again, lest we forget, let us call it the World Island in what follows.'[7]

Mackinder saw the other continents and islands – the Americas, Australia, etc. – as satellites of this larger island. From the standpoint of geography it was natural to call the continents of Europe, Asia and Africa an island, since most of the surface area of the world is sea and only one fourth is land. It would be more apt to call the planet 'Oceans' rather than 'Earth' in view of the great disparity between the two. As it is seen from outer space this is now fairly obvious, but when Mackinder wrote the idea had not been fully appreciated. The geography of the world was summed up by Mackinder: 'Thus the three so-called new continents are in point of area merely satellites of the old continent. There is one ocean covering nine-twelfths of the globe; there is one continent – the World Island – covering two-twelfths of the globe; and there are many smaller islands, whereof North America and South are, for effective purposes, two, which together cover the remaining one-twelfth.'[8]

The chief difference between Mahan and Mackinder centred around the method of securing command over the World Island. The theory was that control of this area, either direct or indirect, would make it possible to dominate the satellite regions of the world and, hence, the world. The method depended upon the best means of mobility or movement. It had been Mahan's view that the usable sea lanes surrounding a large portion of the World Island were, strategically speaking, the interior lines of communication, because of the inherent superiority of sea transport over land movement. It was far easier to move forces, and goods, by sea than by land. Sea transport has traditionally been far cheaper, especially for bulk freight, than other forms of transport, although not always as convenient. One of the principles of war has been economy of force and sea power enabled the easy and rapid concentration of force at the optimum point.

Mackinder did not dispute that this had been the case in the past, but he warned his countrymen that it might not be true in the future. Technology had favoured sea transport for decades, but, as he was writing, the gap between land and sea transport was rapidly being closed. At the turn of the century, railways were being extended further and further across the continents. In North America a number of railway lines spanned the length of the continent–a distance of approximately 3,000 miles. The Trans-Siberian line was even longer – 6,000 miles. Mackinder envisaged that the Heartland region would be criss-crossed by railways. 'True, that the Trans-Siberian railway is still a single and precarious line of communication, but the century will not be old before Asia is covered with railways.'[9] (In fact, this has not yet occurred.)

The introduction of the internal combustion engine added another great dimension to the efficiency of land movement. It is possible to read into Mackinder a prophecy of the use of tanks and other armoured vehicles in war. The historical analogy between the Mongol horsemen of Genghis Khan and the more modern blitzkrieg, dependent upon the internal combustion engine, seems obvious. Indeed, Mackinder wrote: 'The eastward sweep of the horsemen across Asia was an event almost as pregnant with political consequences as was the rounding of the Cape, although the two movements long remained apart.'[10] The overland route across Eurasia was the natural rival, in war or peace, to the long ocean journey around the perimeter of the World Island.

In terms of efficiency, Mackinder thought that land movement could rob sea transport of some of its traditional superiority. 'In the matter of commerce it must not be forgotten that ocean-going traffic, however relatively cheap, usually involves the fourfold handling of goods – at the factory of origin, at the export wharf, at the import wharf and at the inland warehouse for the retail distribution; whereas the continental railway truck may run direct from the exporting factory into the import warehouse.'[11]

Mackinder also noted the vital factor that sea power was dependent upon a secure base. Britain, as a sea power, was secure from attack as long as she could prevent any power from striking at the British Isles themselves. 'We talk of the mobility of ships and the long arm of the fleet, but, after all, sea-power is fundamentally a matter of appropriate bases, productive and secure,' Mackinder wrote.[12] The 'long arm of the fleet' must be attached to a secure body or base. It took someone with the imagination of Mackinder to see that the roles could be reversed – that it was possible that in the future the World Island itself could become a mighty bastion of sea power. The 'long arm of the fleet' would then be attached to a different, and far larger, body.

Within the World Island itself Mackinder saw the possibility of a secure base for land power, centrally located, inaccessible from the influence of sea power, and rich enough in mineral and agricultural potential to ensure that sea power could not starve it into submission. It would be, in other words, a great fortress or castle – the greatest natural fortress area in the world, which he termed the 'Heartland'. The definition of the Heartland region varied in his writings, but just as Britain had been the secure base for sea power, so the Heartland was looked upon in Mackinder's theory as the secure base for land power. 'The Heartland is the region to which, under modern conditions, sea-power can be refused access, though the western part of it lies without the region of Arctic and Continental drainage.'[13] The word 'modern' in this quotation is a key qualification. Mackinder wrote these lines in 1919, and needless to say the conditions which were 'modern' in 1919 might not be so fifty years later. None the less, the supposedly up-to-date idea of the nuclear deterrent is based upon this 'modern' view of the inaccessibility of the Heartland by sea power.

The possible expansion of the Heartland seemed to be a matter of great importance. Moreover, there was the possibility of a union of Germany and the Heartland – of Teutonic energy and Russian resources. This was a fear which many felt independently of the geopolitical ideas of Mackinder. An alliance between Germany and Russia had attracted Haushofer and he urged this course of action to Hitler. In 1904 Mackinder wrote: 'The over-setting of the balance of power in favour of the pivot states, re-sulting in its expansion over the marginal lands of Euro-Asia, would permit of the use of the vast continental resources for fleet-building, and the empire of the world would then be in sight. This might happen if Germany were to ally herself with Russia.'[14] Such an alliance is still possible; since Russia dominates Eastern Europe, including East Germany, and has a strong enemy in the Far East in China, there would be grounds on both sides for such an alliance. It seemed possible at one time that an outside power, notably Germany, could conquer the World Island. The failure of the fierce German effort in the Second World War to conquer Russia naturally reinforced the idea that the Heartland was impregnable.

Mackinder looked upon the aeroplane and submarine as new instruments of land power directed against sea power. Certainly seamen regarded the submarine as an enemy of sea power – a raider on commerce, intent upon denying the use of the sea to the oceanic powers. Aircraft, dependent upon land bases, could be used to destroy surface ships.

The American geographer Hans Weigert saw the decline of British sea power, and the empire, as linked to these factors. 'It is a truism that the history of Britain since the Norman conquest and her political and military decisions have been clearly based on her island fortress position; her world power in the Victorian age and the decline of this power since the advent of the submarine and aircraft are linked to this geographical fact.'[15] The impression given here is that the air and submarine campaigns directed at Britain in the two world wars were successful or, at any rate, bound to succeed in time. However, it is by no means certain that air power and submarine warfare could have been decisive factors against Britain. Admittedly they caused great damage and apprehensions, but in the end they were defeated.

Weigert turns the argument around to look at the United States when pitted against the Heartland. In this case he noted that air power could be used as a means of striking out at the source of power in the Heartland. This is clearly a reversal of the way in which Mackinder saw air power in his original Heartland theory, as an adjunct to land power. But now Weigert and others were looking upon aircraft as a replacement for sea power and as a means of striking at land power. In point of logic, it appears that Weigert is inconsistent. If land power used submarines and aircraft to reduce the power of Britain, then why cannot the Heartland do the same against North America? Clearly the geographical positions are similar. Britain is an island off the coast of Europe and North America is an island off the coast of the World Island.

Another plausible idea, which indeed has been accepted, is that the aeroplane represents a rival form of transport which creates a new geopolitical picture of the world. This was suggested as early as 1904 after the reading of Mackinder's paper, 'The Geographical Pivot of History'. L. S. Amery, who later became First Lord of the Admiralty and then Secretary of State for India, commented: 'Both the sea and the railway are going in the future – it may be near, or it may be somewhat remote – to be supplemented by the air as a means of locomotion.'[16] Here was the suggestion that air power might be a form of mobility independent from land or sea movement. In the years between the two world wars the idea gradually grew in Britain that air power could be an effective instrument to strike at land power. It could supposedly deter the threat of land movement; indeed, the term 'deterrent' as applied to air power seems to have originated in this period. According to Ian Colville, in a biography of Lord Vansittart, 'The idea of a British air deterrent, which could protect the British Isles from surprise attack and deter aggression elsewhere in Europe, was discussed by British statesmen as early as November 1932.'[17] The war-winning capacity of bombers was greatly exaggerated by the exponents of air power, and it was not clear whether air power would support land power or sea power.[18]

In the post-war period air power was looked upon as an independent arm, equal with the other services and representing land and sea power. The defeat of the German Army by the Russians gave the Red Army the appearance of invincibility. Just as Hitler's Panzers had sliced through France in 1940, it was assumed that the Red Army could easily drive across Western Europe to the English Channel. The aeroplane was looked upon as a means of striking out at the Heartland. It seemed that air power was the means of countering the ominous warnings of Mackinder that the Heartland could seize control over the World Island.

In the West, particularly in the United States, the ideas of Mackinder had great meaning after the war. Mackinder's Heartland theory had been given great publicity in the United States in the 1940s, even on the popular level. The fear of Russia was double-barrelled – fear that the Red Army would sweep over Western Europe and a morbid fear of an international communist conspiracy. The Heartland theory gave an intellectual basis for the first fear and the subsequent triumph of Mao Tse-tung in China reinforced the belief that the Heartland could take over the World Island.

The Heartland came to be looked upon as a great fortress or castle. In the event of war between East and West, which for many seemed only a matter of time, the only recourse appeared to be to lay siege to the castle – lobbing missiles and flying bombers over the Polar regions. The Iron Curtain, cutting off any information from the world beyond, seemed dreadfully ominous. The silent castle, epitomized by the Kremlin itself and by the Heartland, loomed overpoweringly in the dark recesses of the mind. It is no wonder that the writings of Kafka seem to reflect the atmosphere of the Cold War. 'The Castle, whose contours were already beginning to dissolve, lay silent as ever; never yet had K. seen there the slightest sign of life – perhaps it was quite impossible to recognize anything at that distance, and yet the eye demanded it and could not endure that stillness.'[19] The only answer to the terror of the imagination seemed to be the counter-horror of the thermonuclear deterrent.

Notes to Chapter 2

1. Mackinder, H. J., *Democratic Ideals and Reality*, Norton, New York, 1962, p. 62. In a book entitled *Sea Power*, edited by E. B. Potter and C. W. Nimitz (Prentice-Hall, New York, 1960), Mackinder's Heartland theory is summed up in this manner: '(1) Contrary to the implications of Mahan's writings, sea power and land power have been alternatively decisive in the long periods of history. (2) When land power has been ascendant, it has often been able to defeat sea power by taking its bases in land campaigns. (3) England's effective control of the seas gave her world hegemony until the 20th century, but now the steam and gasoline engines and rail and highway networks are depriving the sea of its monopoly of bulk transportation; therefore England's inherent relative power has declined as compared to continental power. (4) Once it has achieved adequate communications and a high level of economic development, the centre of the greatest land mass will be in a position to exert the greatest power. This "Heartland" comprises Western Siberia and European Russia. (5) A vigorous people, armed with modern technology, may through control of the Heartland come to control the entire "World Island", i.e. Eurasia and Africa. (6) The superior resources and population of the World Island may well ultimately make possible domination of the fringe lands, i.e. Great Britain, Japan, Australia, and North and South America (p. 489).' One editor of this book, Nimitz, was the American Admiral Chester Nimitz.

2. Alfred Thayer Mahan was born at West Point, New York, in 1840, and died in 1914. He served in the US navy for forty years. After graduation, he saw service in the American Civil War, and he was one of the few to notice that the naval phase of this war was of a decisive nature. He was an unusual officer in the American navy: he knew French very well, and subscribed to the *Manchester Guardian*. In 1894 he was awarded honorary degrees by both Cambridge and

Oxford Universities. His writing began when he was assigned to the newly formed Naval War College in Newport, Rhode Island. *The Influence of Sea Power upon History* was originally prepared as lectures for his fellow officers. In the succeeding years Mahan produced about twenty books, and his reputation as a great authority on naval strategy never diminished. Robert Strausz-Hupe noted of Mahan that he was '. . . a geopolitical thinker long before the expression had even been coined . . .' (*Geopolitics*, Putnams, New York, 1945, p. 244). Haushofer in Germany had also looked upon Mahan as one of the great Anglo-American writers in the new field of geopolitics.

3. Rowse, A. L., *The Expansion of Elizabethan England*, St Martin's Press, New York, 1955, p. 158.

4. Richmond, Herbert, *National Policy and Naval Strength*, Longmans, 1928, p. 19.

5. Mahan, A. T., *The Interests of America in International Conditions*, Little, Brown, Boston, 1910, p. 143. One of the difficulties with the balance of power policy and an extensive empire was in determining the priority of dangers. The growth of potential sea rivals should have been a principal concern.

6. Richmond, Herbert, *Statesmen and Sea Power*, Oxford University Press, 1946, p. 328.

7. Mackinder, H. J., *Democratic Ideals and Reality*, p. 62.

8. ibid., pp. 64–5.

9. Mackinder, H. J., 'The Geographical Pivot of History', *Geographical Journal*, Vol. 23, 1904.

10. ibid. It was the superiority, i.e. cheapness, of sea transport which allowed Europe to rise to power. As Mackinder noted in *Democratic Ideals and Reality*, 'The seamen of Europe, owing to their greater mobility, have thus had superiority for some four centuries over the landsmen of Africa and Asia (p. 52).' Brooks Adams wrote on this matter: 'Movement is the law of nature. Venice fell through the energy of the very maritime genius she had fostered. In 1497 Vasco da Gama discovered a cheaper route to India than by the Levant. The arrival of his fleet at Calcutta was the signal for exchanges to pass at a leap from the Adriatic to the North Sea; prostrating Venice, Genoa, Pisa, and Florence, raising Antwerp and Amsterdam, and heaving up the great convulsions of the sixteenth century' (*America's Economic Supremacy*, Harper's, New York, 1947, p. 77).

11. Mackinder, H. J., 'The Geographical Pivot of History'.

12. Mackinder, H. J., *Democratic Ideals and Reality*, p. 15.

13. ibid., p. 110. 'The spaces within the Russian Empire and Mongolia are so vast, and their potentialities in populations, wheat, cotton,

46

fuel and metals so incalculably great, that it is inevitable that a vast economic world . . . will there develop inaccessible to ocean commerce' ('The Geographical Pivot of History'). Over forty years later, the inability of sea power to get at the vast industrial capacity of the Soviet Union behind the Urals was at the back of the minds of Western strategists. Air power, too, could not effectively destroy these industrial regions with aircraft carrying conventional bombs.

14. Mackinder, H. J., 'The Geographical Pivot of History'.

15. Weigert, Hans W., and others, *Principles of Political Geography*, Appleton-Century-Crofts, New York, 1957, p. 15.

16. Mackinder, H. J., 'The Geographical Pivot of History'.

17. Colvin, Ian, *Vansittart in Office*, Gollancz, 1965, p. 132.

18. Britain's leaders came to view air power as an answer to the growing threats of land power. The question arose of whether air power should be an independent force, or be divided so that the army and navy had aircraft under their control; this became a point of bitter debate between the exponents of the pure air theory, i.e. those who thought that strategic bombing could be a war-winning strategy, and the more orthodox thinkers. In Britain air power was concentrated in the RAF and, at least until shortly before the start of the war, the Royal Navy was without effective air strength. The idea of an economic stranglehold or blockade, as it were, within the country was used as a modern example analogous to the traditional role of sea power in blockade of the coastal regions. In pre-war days the epitome of land power was Germany. While the German blitzkrieg was bolting across France in 1940, the RAF was striking at industrial targets which were one hundred miles or more behind the battle and which had no influence whatsoever upon the outcome of this battle.

19. Kafka, Franz, *The Castle*, Knopf, New York, 1954, p. 128.

3. The Nuclear Deterrent and the Projectile Cycle

'Believe me, 'arold, our trouble is that the
Russians are frightened and the Yanks bomb-
minded.'
Ernest Bevin, British Foreign Minister

The idea of the deterrent seemed to rise up phoenix-like after the
end of the Second World War even before the ashes from that
titanic struggle had the chance to cool. The firm conviction soon
developed that the Russian army could easily seize Western
Europe and that nuclear arms were needed to prevent this move.
In 1948 Sir Winston Churchill, who was regarded by many in
the United States as an oracle, stated: 'I hope that you will give
full consideration to my views. I have not always been wrong.
Nothing stands between Europe today and complete subjugation
to communist tyranny but the bomb in American possession.'[1]

Some have even maintained that the dropping of the first
atomic bombs on Hiroshima and Nagasaki in August 1945 represented not the closing act of the Second World War but essentially
the beginning of the Cold War, acting as a warning to Moscow.
Whether or not this was in the minds of those who made the decision, US military leaders gradually began to take an interest in
formulating policy, rather than merely carrying out policy, and
nuclear arms did in fact become the dominant element in the
deterrent.

If the Western hawks believed that the Soviet Union was in a
strategically superior position, then the problem they faced was
to frame a defence theory to prevent Russian expansion and contain her ambition. The military answer contained two elements –
air power and nuclear arms. Both were needed, since it was
immediately realized that long-range bombers would be in-
effective weapons against the Heartland if armed only with
chemical bombs, as flying such long distances would reduce the
weight of the bombload. In addition, the efficacy of strategic
bombing in the Second World War was by no means proven. Air

power was now looked upon as the means of delivery for nuclear arms. The essential aspect of the deterrent was not air power *per se*, but nuclear weapons.

Since the nuclear deterrent involved air power, this produced a major shift in the viewpoint of the original Heartland theory. Air power now became a substitute for sea power; it was thought to be the means whereby the fringe powers, such as Britain and the United States, could threaten, or if necessary destroy, land power. Implicit in this view was the idea that air power was a function neither of land power, as Mackinder had suggested, nor of sea power, but an entirely new dimension as far as world power was concerned. The Air Force in the United States became effectively the senior service. Belief in air power had been growing before and during the Second World War. Air power striking at the economic source of enemy power seemed to be the best weapon – partly because it seemed to be the only sufficiently formidable weapon available. The decision to place faith in air power was taken very early in the war by Churchill, so that the lion's share of the defence budget, and consequently most of the war effort, was devoted to building aircraft, mainly in the form of bombers. The long-range bomber was looked upon as the means to victory. There followed an awesome consequence: the concept of strategic bombing using conventional bombs was the embryo of the nuclear deterrent.

The great bogey of the fifties, and even to some extent of the sixties, was that Russia, together with the Warsaw Pact countries, possessed superior manpower and conventional land strength. The belief was readily accepted that the Russians could overwhelm the West. The so-called 'loss' of China, as it was termed in the United States in the late 1940s, reinforced this view. In the dark days of the Cold War, especially in the United States after the start of the Korean War, the expansion of the Heartland over the World Island seemed to be in the Kremlin's power.

The Western powers saw their only recourse as lying in their superior technological capability. This implied air power – strategic bombing and nuclear arms. Nuclear arms, that is, the deterrent, now seemed to be the best weapon the West possessed – in fact, the only weapon which would be really effective against the great Eastern bloc.[2] Ballistic missiles were soon to replace the aeroplane as the means for nuclear attack. It has been suggested that this finally made the role of geopolitical considerations relatively unimportant. Professors Harold and Margaret Sprout wrote:

What the events of the 1950s more forcefully suggest is that geopolitical configuration – the global layout of lands and seas – has become very much less politically significant today than formerly. When ballistic missiles armed with thermonuclear warheads can be fired from nearly any point upon the earth's surface, either from land or from ships at sea, with a range and accuracy that enable them to devastate whole cities at nearly every point upon the earth's surface, we shall have reached the end of the line for geopolitical concepts and theories which purport to explain and to forecast the overall design of international politics by reference to the configuration of lands and seas.[3]

This is, of course, quite true, if we believe nuclear arms can be used as instruments of policy, but they cannot really be considered useful in terms of the Clausewitzian definition of war. Though they cannot be discarded entirely, as instruments for the statesman their value is nil.

At the beginning of the century, L. S. Amery predicted: 'A great deal of this geographical distribution must lose its importance, and the successful powers will be those who have the greatest industrial basis. It will not matter whether they are on the centre of a continent or on an island; these people who have the industrial power and the power of invention and science will be able to defeat all others.'[4]

At approximately the same time, a Polish banker, I. S. Bloch, was making a remarkable study in depth on the future of war. Although his writings were dismissed in his day, many of his predictions have been confirmed by events. Bloch believed with Amery that industrial strength would be the most important aspect in war, but he went much further in projecting this into the future development of tactics and its influence upon strategy. In doing so he perceived that a stalemate would result from such a contest between opposing industrial giants. Rather than one side winning, Bloch more accurately saw that both sides would be exhausted and economically ruined. Warfare such as Bloch foresaw is purely a matter of attrition – the wearing down of an opponent's manpower and material resources. It produces the type of battlefield in which generalship counts for little. Wars in this case are not decided by great battles but rather become '. . . a long period of continually increasing strain upon resources'. 'The soldier is going down and the economist is going up,' Bloch wrote.[5] This type of conflict is essentially siege warfare, in which one endeavours to attack at the weakest point and the projectile weapon is the most important arm. Bloch predicted the stalemate which occurred in the First World War and the place of trenches in it. After the first phase of the war, continuous fortified trenches, backed by artillery, ran from the English Channel to the Swiss border. In all previous wars, generals had the option of hitting an opponent on his flanks or the centre. Now there were no flanks. The only method of attack was to try to blast a hole in the opposing entrenchments with artillery and then send in infantry. This, however, never proved to be an entirely successful method of attack.

In theory, this is where sea power offered an advantage. Every mile of coastline held by an enemy without naval strength was a potential front line and troops had to be in position to protect the sea flank. At Gallipoli, efforts were made to exploit the sea advantage of the Allied Powers in the First World War. Unfortunately, the attempt was badly managed. If the British had initially put in as much force and skill as they eventually did, then there is no doubt that Turkey could have been cut off from Europe. The Turkish forces were dependent upon German munitions since they had only one small munitions factory in Constantinople. If this city had fallen to the Allies, the remaining Turkish troops in the Middle East would have been forced to surrender. (It has been suggested that even if this operation had been successful, the Allies, in any case, had no munitions to send to the Russians, which was the ultimate purpose of the operation. However, there were a million or more Allied troops fighting the Turks in the Middle East. If the Turks had surrendered, as they would have been forced to do, then the munitions for these Allied troops, or indeed the Allied troops together with the munitions, could have been sent to the Eastern Front.)

A notable defender of the attrition theory in the First World War was Mr John Terraine. In a military biography of Sir Douglas Haig, the British commander on the Western Front, he sums up the essence of his point of view:

The commonest trap for later students has always been the confusion of strategy with tactics. Because the fighting on the Western front was so costly and so apparently barren for so many years, the strategy of 'Westernism' has been discredited. Contemporary statesmen fell into the same trap. The strategic issue, as Haig saw it, was this: the diversion of large forces to another theatre 'seems a violation of a sound strategic principle which in my opinion is to concentrate at the decisive point, namely against Germany's main army. *We cannot hope to win until we have defeated the German Army.* The easiest place to do this is in France, because our lines of communication are the shortest to this theatre of war'. The key to the whole matter was communication. If it had been possible to win swift and overwhelming victories on other fronts by sudden blows, that would have been a different matter. But it was not.[6]

It must be pointed out that while the lines of communications were short for the British Army, they were even shorter for the Germans. Moreover, if one accepts the principle stated by Haig, then it must have applied equally to the German point of view. The Germans could not hope to win until they had defeated the main Allied armies. For Britain in particular, fighting in France was allowing the enemy to dictate which battlefield would be the decisive theatre of operations. In doing so, Germany was awarded a tremendous strategical advantage.[7]

The connection between the type of warfare of the First World War and the strategic bombing of the Second World War has been noted by General J. F. C. Fuller. He wrote: 'Douhet [the first air strategist] was looked upon as a futurist; but actually he was a tactical reactionary, because he harked back to the great artillery bombardments of World War I, which were purely destructive operations, and tilted them from the horizontal into a vertical position.'[8] Douhet looked upon a squadron of bombers as merely flying artillery, which was to lay siege to the entire enemy country. Fuller also maintained that bombardment alone could not defeat an enemy.[9] General Fuller, writing in the 1930s, viewed warfare in a historical perspective which has not been attained since the Second World War. His insight into military events stands up remarkably well forty years later. Fuller noted that in Western civilization there had been three cycles in tactics. They are related to the type of weapon used in a particular period, which appears to be associated with the phase of civilization. Shock warfare is an attempt to come to grips with an enemy in close combat using cutting or thrusting weapons (as in the classical period of Western civilization). Projectile arms, on the other hand, are intended to keep an enemy at a distance, using projectiles or missiles of some type. There is no clear demarcation line between periods and it is always difficult to perceive the transition from one period to another.

The phases of these cycles depend upon what Fuller called the constant tactical factor, which is the fighting man's desire to close with an enemy in order to destroy him and his natural fear which holds him back. Projectile weapons were developed when nations had the time and resources to conceive and build sophisticated arms. Fuller wrote:

As regards the origins of artillery, the most important fact is that whilst thrusting and cutting weapons, and in some cases slings and bows, are weapons of the field men, artillery is the weapon of the city dwellers, because these folk fear the brawn of the peasant soldier, live behind walls and are consequently imbued with a defensive spirit and possess the wealth and the leisure wealth creates wherein to invent cunning machines. Jerusalem, Tyre, Carthage and Syracuse, all wealthy cities, produced artillery in abundance.[10]

Modern industrial countries are psychologically suited to projectile tactics, and their wealth and leisure have made it possible for them to invent and manufacture a huge array of various types of projectile weapons, the apogee of which is the missiles which the United States has produced in astronomical numbers.

It is fairly obvious that we live in a projectile cycle and have done so for many decades. In the post-Second World War period, the West has lived in fear of the 'hordes' of Asians. There is no great desire to close with such people in shock tactics in which the West would be assumed to be at a disadvantage. The result has been to rely upon the greater technological capability of the West 'to invent cunning machines' so as to keep the brawn of the peasant soldier at a distance. The development of firearms and their continuous improvement marked the beginning of the present projectile cycle. Fuller wrote: '. . . The existing projectile cycle, which began to take definite form about 1850, should last 200 years, that is to 2050, completing its transitional stage by 1950.' This has been an accurate prediction so far. Long-range bombers or flying artillery were developed in the Second World War, and this course reached its peak around 1950 with the development of the intercontinental ballistic missile. The ICBM, which is the ultimate development of the missile – and as much a means of suicide as of offence – suggests the approaching end of the present projectile cycle.

The emphasis in projectile warfare is upon destructiveness rather than movement. Strategic thinking in terms of nuclear weaponry is obviously a simple calculus of destruction; and modern projectile tactics and battles of this period have also become essentially a matter of the computation of destruction. It is a type of warfare more suitable to the special talents of the scientist and the technician. The extent of destruction is a measurable quantity, whereas the psychological impact of mobility, or the surprise effected by movement, is a factor outside the limits of scientific measurement. The cerebral soldier assumes an important role, and the soldiers themselves increasingly take on the characteristics of technicians whose emotions of hate, fear, and tension have little meaning.

Fuller showed remarkable insight into the development of future weapons, essentially predicting the arrival of ICBMs.

Turning back to the law of military development, and remembering that the present tendency of civil science is towards the existence of an electrically constituted universe, and that industry and civil life are becoming daily more influenced by electricity, and the many applications of this energy, it is conclusive that the military organization will follow suit, and will develop what I will call, for want of a better name, the 'robot' cycle. The weapon may be primarily a land one, or a sea one, or an air one; but more likely it would seem that it will be one which can equally well operate on land, at sea, and in the air. It may be chemically propelled and electrically directed . . . It is not

54

beyond the realm of possibility to imagine that a general may be seated in some farmstead in Kent, or in a flat in London and yet be fighting a manless battle in Central Asia in which the civil population is the target ... Heroism will be dead; war will become as ridiculous a solution to human quarrels as the burning of witches eventually became to the extermination of witchcraft. It will exterminate itself, for it will have lost its glamour.[11]

Almost forty years later, in 1970, General William Westmoreland announced to a Congressional Committee:

On the battlefield of the future, enemy forces will be located, trapped and targeted almost instantaneously through the use of data links, computer assisted intelligence evaluation and automated fire control ... I am confident the American people expect this country to take full advantage of its technology – to welcome and applaud the developments that will replace, wherever possible, the man with the machine.

What General Westmoreland or the American people had to applaud, as Vietnam was used as a laboratory for this kind of warfare, is not clear, since the attempt to replace men by machines proved remarkably unsuccessful. I. F. Stone observed that the effort to solve a political problem by military means was hopeless from the start; but the military means were also unfitted to meet an opponent able and willing to use shock tactics. The great sophistication of technological hardware and software was no substitute for the different sophistication of the human will of the flesh-and-blood combatants.[12]

The elimination of the human aspect in fighting a war is achieved at a double cost: the military and economic cost of warfare which is less effective and disproportionately expensive when the enemy is fighting another kind of war; and the moral cost of annulling concern for the human consequences on the battlefield. If one of the first principles of war in classical theory is the economy of force, American tactics were moving in the inverse direction – overkill with an open-ended expenditure of force. No wonder the military means bore no relation to the political aims. 'We had to destroy it in order to save it,' an American officer was reported as saying in the ruins of Ben Tre, which had just been devastated by US aircraft during the 1968 Tet offensive.

Fighting a war in this manner leaves open only one course in the attempt to win: to increase and increase again the level of destruction. That destruction has not been the most important aspect of warfare should be apparent to the most superficial student of military history; to accept this attitude to war would obscure the relationship between aims and means. The gap between the extent of destructive force employed and the military objectives achieved widens at each stage when war is fought over underdeveloped countries as in Indo-china. An even more important factor is that the relationship between the level of force employed and the political goals becomes increasingly disproportionate, until there is no realistic connection between the two; the gap between the genuine interests of national policy and the means used to pursue them finally assumes insane dimensions. This is the logic of what is supposed to be 'limited war' fought by these tactics, and the consequence is illustrated by the Vietnam War. (That war was of course a limited war in that theoretically means were available to accomplish a level of destruction above what was carried out; but this would have been politically impracticable and at the same time destroyed the meaning of 'victory'. 'Winning the war' is an empty concept without considering what is won or lost.)

In the case of Vietnam, it was also impossible to divorce military from political factors in the conduct of the war. Trying to separate warfare, especially guerrilla operations, into watertight military and political compartments is self-defeating. War is a contest of wills and naked force is only one means of influencing those engaged in it.[13] In estimating the effect force will have on people, or the significance of body counts, the professional soldier is often completely naïve. Fundamentally the basis of war lies in the human heart – in the emotional impact upon the individual within society. Central to the Vietnam War was the emotional impact which it produced upon millions of living Vietnamese and, also, upon the American public. But not only Vietnamese realities counted; from the point of view of American interests, the impact of the war in the rest of the world mattered, and the United States' direction of the war was equally myopic in this respect. The force employed to safeguard American credi-

bility severely damaged it. This was a devastating misjudgement.
President Nixon declared his intention to command respect for
America through 'strength and resolution', but the truth is that
the United States in Vietnam never had a strategy adapted to
global realities or tactics suited to local conditions. American
strength became translated into American weakness.

There is a static-mindedness which is implicit in battles fought
in the projectile cycle. This attitude towards tactics has permeated
the military establishments in Western countries. Despite the
fact that these armies have superiority in modern transport over
their rivals, they have been unable to use it to the best advantage.
In the Vietnam War it has been admitted that the Viet Cong and
North Vietnamese were capable of quicker movement than
American forces, although the latter had helicopters, aircraft,
modern ships, tanks and so on. Walter Lippmann has pointed out
that American military leadership in the Vietnam War was far
below the standard of that in the Second World War and this is
incontestable.[14]

Bloch had predicted that increasing reliance upon more and
more force in the projectile cycle would lead to the bankruptcy of
nations; indeed, this has been the case. Although technically a
victor in the First World War, Britain faced bankruptcy as the
result of it; as it was, she obtained $4,074,800,000 from the
United States in loans which were never repaid. 'Without these
grants she would have been nearly as badly off in 1919 as in
1947.'[15] In both world wars Britain tended to rely upon siege
warfare tactics. The strategic bombing, which absorbed tremendous amounts of energy, was a logical successor to the artillery
'blitz' tactics of the previous war. The tremendous air strikes
against German cities had little influence upon the course of the
war. The bombing of Hamburg, Dresden, and other cities
counted for next to nothing as far as the actual battles on the
Eastern and Western fronts were concerned. Britain had gained
her historical position by her ability to apply measured force at
the most vital points. Trying to meet an opponent head-on in a
war of attrition proved to be the surest way to lose everything.[16]

The United States followed a similar course in Vietnam. It
has been calculated that it cost half a million dollars to kill one

Viet Cong soldier. No nation, no matter how rich, can afford such lunacy. The futility of the kind of generalship induced by the present projectile cycle is well illustrated by the observation of Senator Symington. 'We have an over $800 billion gross national product; the Vietnamese have practically none. We have 200 million people; the Vietnamese some 17 million. We have been escalating the fighting out there for over 4 years. We have had nearly 300,000 casualties, but are now in the process of acknowledging a stalemate, or passing over some kind of defeat.'[17] Professor Noam Chomsky recorded that in a visit to North Vietnam he 'was shown a bridge, still standing uneasily, that was attacked daily from 1965 until the termination of the regular bombing, with 99 American jets lost – the cost in planes alone must be on the order of half a billion dollars, to destroy one bridge'.[18] Finally, as a result of the Vietnam war, the United States was forced to devalue the dollar. Attrition warfare is an expensive business. One must also consider the moral decay induced by attrition tactics, which cannot show up on a balance sheet.[19]

The amount of destruction rained upon Vietnam is the greatest in the history of war by a vast margin, and the figures are even more shattering in relation to the modest size of the country it was directed against. By the end of 1972, the United States had discharged more than 7,000,000 tons of bombs and rockets on Indo-china since the start of its military engagement in Vietnam. This is considerably greater than the total amount of all the bombs the United States had dropped in all previous wars – that is, in Europe, Africa, Asia and the Pacific in the Second World War, and in the Korean War.

The mere survival of Vietnamese society under such a tremendous weight of firepower indicates that the projectile cycle has reached a peak and is on the downward slope. Fuller conjectured that the present projectile cycle would last until 2050 (following which a period of universal peace might ensue), but it appears that we will be going into a shock cycle much earlier than could have been anticipated. Great attention is now given to research and invention, which has not been so in previous eras. The fear of bombing, and particularly of the enormously powerful explosive devices developed by the United States to devastate wide areas, has forced soldiers to think in terms of movement and dispersion of force. Light weapons and equipment have made this possible. In the Vietnam War, the United States was unable to win against a small and poor country. The American leaders did not understand the close relationship between force and military action, but, in addition, they were fighting essentially in a projectile cycle while the North Vietnamese and Viet Cong were in a shock-projectile cycle.

The guerrilla soldier represents a newly emerging shock cycle. Increasingly the individual soldier will have the means to shoot down expensive jet aircraft. Already this has taken place on a large scale in Vietnam, and the trend will accelerate in the future with new developments which are bound to take place. It is theoretically possible to give the individual rifleman bullets with built-in micro-circuits which can home in on aircraft. With a dozen or so such ground troops in action, life would be extremely difficult for the jet aircraft which is now the foremost vehicle of the projectile era. It would be far less expensive to supply and train such ground soldiers than it would be to train pilots. Thus, the economic scales are weighted heavily against the aircraft for the future. Even now jet aircraft must fly very low in order to avoid being shot down by missiles or anti-aircraft fire.[20] The decline of the military aircraft will also mark the waning of the last phase of the projectile cycle.

The deterrent was meant to be the answer to the geopolitical imperatives implied in the Heartland theory. The deterrent concept itself seems to be part of the projectile cycle which Fuller described so well, and the evidence indicates that this projectile cycle has run its course, or very nearly. The deterrent has played itself out by its own continued development: its proliferation in numbers, its increased might and ever more sophisticated delivery systems have put it beyond credible use as an arm of the projectile cycle, if not unfortunately putting beyond question the possibility of some nightmare holocaust. The idea of all-out warfare between super-powers has eliminated itself (except for that final runaway scenario); and the fact is that this type of total war should never have arisen in both the world wars. We are faced with the prospects of so-called limited war; even here, it is doubtful whether any major power will ever repeat the course the Americans have taken in Vietnam, as it is becoming clear to the most obtuse that it is both tactically and politically inept. The dispersion of force over a wide area, as with guerrilla warfare, reduces the effectiveness of bombardment – that is, siege warfare tactics. In general, the cards seem now heavily stacked in favour of the return of a shock cycle in warfare.

It is of course still possible to escalate the amount of force to the *n*th degree, and the ultimate point would be the use of nuclear arms. But here another important, and neglected, element comes into play. When a nation increases the level of force employed, then it increases the political stakes, since war relates to policy and of necessity interacts with policy. The use even of tactical nuclear weapons would be crossing a threshold the political repercussions of which would be enormous and unknown; they would not only apply to the combatants, but extend to a country's interests and influence throughout the world, and bear heavily on the viability of all its policies in the international sphere. Western soldiers in the past several decades have concentrated so much upon the means of waging war that the end has been completely overlooked. As the British naval writer Sir Julian Corbett wrote: 'Thus, the political object of the war, its original motive, will not only determine for both belligerents reciprocally the aim of the force they use, but it will also be the standard of the intensity of the effort they will make.'[21] So if the war is escalated by degrees, then the political aims must also escalate. It cannot be otherwise and history demonstrates that this has been true.

The emphasis upon destruction has had a disastrous influence upon policy. The relationship between policy and military force is one of vital importance, and Western leaders have failed to see clearly the relationship between aims and means. This chapter has been concerned mainly with tactics. Policy can be considered to be the whole objective or ultimate goal of a nation; strategy is the method of carrying out the goal – the plan of action which may take the form of military force or of a combination of actions; tactics refers to the tools used to carry out the plan. The decision to rely upon nuclear weapons has been due to a confusion between

the terms 'policy' and 'strategy'. Many writers have called
deterrence a policy. This is not correct; it can only be a strategy.
Since this matter is of such importance, the next chapter will be
devoted to it.

Notes to Chapter 3

1. Churchill, Winston S., *Europe Unite*, ed. Churchill, Randolph S.,
Cassell, 1950, pp. 412–13. This comes from a speech given on 9
October 1948 at a Conservative Party mass meeting. Churchill also
stated: 'If it were not for the stocks of atomic bombs now in the
trusteeship of the United States there would be no means of stopping
the subjugation of Western Europe by Communist machinations
backed by Russian armies and enforced by political police . . . Of one
thing I am quite sure, that if the United States were to consent to
reliance upon any paper agreement to destroy the stocks of atomic
bombs which they have accumulated, they would be guilty of murder-
ing human freedom and committing suicide themselves' (p. 412). It is
interesting to note the comment of Owen Lattimore on Churchill's
Fulton, Missouri, speech. 'The Truman Doctrine originated more in
out-of-date British thinking than in up-to-date American thinking.
It is a child of the Fulton, Missouri, speech at which President Truman sat on the platform while Winston Churchill rang down the iron
curtain' (*The Situation in Asia*, Atlantic, Boston, 1950, p. 218).
2. Sir John Slessor, who has often been regarded as one of the
leading exponents of the deterrent theory, wrote in 1955: 'The heavy
long-range bomber is a weapon of hot war; it is only used in major
war between Great Powers. As a matter of fact it is, in my view, the
decisive instrument in cold war, in that it holds out the best chance
of keeping it cold – or anyway tepid (no one could describe Korea as
exactly cold war). It is, as Mr Churchill has repeatedly said, the major
deterrent, the counter-threat to the vast armies and tactical air forces
of our potential enemies. Moreover, it gives us some degree, and an
increasing degree, of initiative in the cold war, instead of always
dancing to the enemy's tune. Imagine what the world would be like
if we in the West had no military answer to the Russian menace but
to match it man by man, tank by tank, and gun by gun!' (*The Great
Deterrent*, Cassell, 1957, p. 121).
Nuclear arms became virtually an article of faith. Anyone who

tinkered with nuclear strategic doctrine, or questioned its assumptions, was looked upon as a simpleton – or even as a traitor in the United States in the 1950s. If the Russians, or their fellow-travellers, objected to these arms, then that in itself showed that these were the best arms for Western strategy. The Establishment point of view is put in another quotation from Sir John Slessor. 'I wish the kindly, well-meaning people who advocate the abolition of atomic weapons would realize what a disservice they do to the cause of peace. Why do they suppose the communists constantly bang the drum of atomic disarmament? Of course they do: it would suit them down to the ground, with their hordes of expendable man-power and their thousands of excellent tanks. If atomic bombs really were abolished, the Red Army, the instrument through which they have enslaved the nations of Eastern Europe, would come into its own again and get on with the good work in the rest of Europe. It never has been and never will be any good trying to abolish any particular weapon of war; what we have to abolish is war. So I am afraid it seems to me to be the climax of absurdity to clamour for the outlawry of the instrument through which war has abolished itself' (ibid., p. 150–51).

Despite Slessor's vastly over-optimistic and untrue assertion that war has abolished itself, it should be emphasized that, in the case of the deterrent, Western leaders, military and political, are prepared and willing to use it *as an instrument of war*. Many people are under the mistaken impression that the West – that is, in particular NATO – would not use nuclear arms unless the Russians used them first. Western leaders have not gone out of their way to correct this misconception in the minds of the public, partly, no doubt, because it pacifies the fears of people in the West, especially in Europe where the destruction would be enormous. Western leaders are naturally evasive on the matter as to when and under what conditions nuclear arms would be used; this ambiguity has also to be maintained for tactical reasons, so that opponents are left uncertain and unable to make plans on adequate knowledge of Western intentions. The official strategic view in the West is that the West might be obliged to use nuclear arms first. Of course, this is a threat which has become increasingly unrealistic, though the development of a continuous gradation in the size of nuclear weapons from 'tactical' arms to thermonuclear ICBMs has kept it alive as an apparent option; if the threat of first use lacked all credibility, the idea of the deterrent itself would lose much of its force. The fact is that if there were a first use of nuclear arms, it would be by definition without precedent, and no one at the present time can know what would be the context of that unprecedented situation. It certainly is not enough to rely on the assurance of Sir John Slessor and other exponents of the deterrent that such a situation will not arise while nuclear arms exist. The possibility of their first use (in addition to Hiroshima and Nagasaki) exists.

3. Sprout, Harold and Margaret, *Foundations of International Politics*, Van Nostrand, New York, 1966, p. 338. They go on to state: 'Naval forces can refuel and carry out even major repairs at sea. Nuclear-powered submarines can remain at sea for months at a time. These developments have reduced the military value of permanent oversea bases, which figured so importantly in Mahan's geopolitical universe. Submarines, bombing planes, and ballistic missiles have eroded the former defensive strength of islands, peninsulas, promontories, and remote ports on coasts protected by mountains, deserts or jungles. Pipelines, motor vehicles, railways, and still expanding highways grids have enormously increased the mobility and capacity of overland movement. Airplanes have shrunk the widest oceans and continents and have surmounted refractory barriers of terrain and distance. These and other changes in weapons and communications have profoundly altered the relative military value of heartlands, marginal lands, rimlands, and islands.'

4. Mackinder, H. J., 'The Geographical Pivot of History', *Geographical Journal*, Vol. 23, 1904. In 1942 Professor Isaiah Bowman, a geographer who was President of the John Hopkins University and an adviser to President Roosevelt and the State Department, wrote that, 'Neither Mackinder nor Haushofer had theories that could stand up to the facts of air power and its relation to industrial strength' (*Geographical Review*, 1942).

5. Bloch, I. S., *Is War Impossible?*, Grant Richards, London, 1899, p. lxi. Bloch is one of the select few who was able to predict the evolving nature of warfare which brought about the deadlock on the Western front. 'Your soldiers may fight as they please, the ultimate decision is in the hands of famine,' he wrote. This is largely what happened in the First World War. The following is an extract from the work quoted: 'At first there will be increased slaughter – increased slaughter on so terrible a scale as to render it impossible to get troops to push the battle to a decisive issue. They will try to, thinking that they are fighting under old conditions, and they will learn such a lesson that they will abandon the attempt forever. Then, instead of a war fought out to the bitter end in a series of decisive battles, we shall have as a substitute a long period of continually increasing strain upon the resources of the combatants. The war, instead of being a hand-to-hand contest in which the combatants measure their physical and

moral superiority, will become a kind of stalemate, in which neither army being able to get at the other, both armies will be maintained in opposition to each other, threatening each other, but never being able to deliver a final and decisive attack. That is the future of war – not fighting, but famine, not the slaying of men, but the bankruptcy of nations and the breakup of the whole social organization . . . It will be a great war of entrenchments. The spade will be as indispensable to a soldier as his rifle . . . All war will of necessity partake of the character of siege operations' (pp. xvi–lvi).

Lloyd George also later made the analogy between the First World War and siege warfare. It was different from all previous wars in that manpower enabled countries to form a continuous front; 50,000,000 males were mobilized. On all previous battlefields, the warring nations only had enough troops on the field to cover at most several miles of front. Now there were no flanks round which an army could turn, and the machine gun also greatly increased the power of the defence. Mobilization on such a scale would have been impossible without the development of modern communications. There had never before been total war of this nature, in both a civil and military sense, in Europe. The emphasis in fighting was upon destruction and attrition.

6. Terraine, John, *Haig: The Educated Soldier*, Hutchinson, 1963, p. 135.

7. Mr Terraine, nevertheless, points his finger at the crucial element – 'The key to the whole matter was communications' (ibid., p. 135). He adds that it was not possible to obtain swift and overwhelming victories elsewhere. This is begging the question: it was not possible because the decision had been accepted, at the dictation of the Germans, to make the Western front the decisive arena. Essentially Terraine accepts the idea that land communications were superior to sea communications. This is an odd position for an Englishman to take, since the British Empire was a sea empire; it is admitting that sea transport had lost its historic advantage.

8. Fuller, J. F. C., *The Conduct of War*, Eyre & Spottiswoode, 1961, p. 240.

9. Dr Noble Frankland, another defender of the strategy of Westernism in the First World War, was also an advocate of strategic bombing in the Second World War; this stresses the point that there is a connection between the two. Frankland wrote: 'Haig's military judgement was proven by events to be absolutely correct. Whatever else might have happened, there cannot be a doubt that the result of the First World War was determined from the trenches, that the decisive factor was the military break-through and the subsequent defeat of the

German Army in the field' (*The Bombing Offensive against Germany*, Faber, 1965, p. 37). Historically, however, the first 'defeat' of the will of the German general staff resulted from the collapse of the Macedonian front, not the Western front. The blows struck at the Balkan front were a threat to the German rear and a primary threat to Austria–Hungary. A decisive factor in war is when the will of the enemy is upset. Sea power, by its very nature, is able to apply such indirect blows to the will of an opponent. On p. 16 Frankland wrote, 'Strategic bombing is, after all, the heart of air power.' On the First World War, Frankland wrote: 'The only way to win the war was to pour more and more men, material and support, including air support, into the effort to overrun the German trenches so as to achieve a break-through' (p. 37).

10. Fuller, J. F. C., *Dragon's Teeth*, Constable, London, 1932, p. 230. 'Turning to the recorded history of war, it will show that there have been two grand military cycles in Europe – the Classical and the Christian. The first began about 1100 B.C., endured in all approximately 1500 years, and ended in the Pax Romana. It was followed by two and a half centuries of chaos and anarchy, out of which the second grand cycle began to emerge. Each of these grand cycles passed through three tactical cycles, namely, the shock cycle, the shock and projectile cycle, and the projectile cycle. Thus, we have the constant tactical factor at work' (p. 227). The constant tactical factor is, according to Fuller, essentially the shifting balance between hatred and fear – the desire to close with an enemy in order to destroy him and the fear that one may be destroyed oneself. Thus, 'Every improvement in weapon-power (unconsciously though it may be) has aimed at lessening terror and danger on one side by increasing them on the other . . .' (p. 203). Naturally more advanced civilizations are reluctant to close with an enemy in shock tactics; they become more sedentary and tend to rely upon fire power. 'This astonishing progress from push of pikes to long-distance fighting, the urge of the constant tactical factor, undoubtedly led to a deterioration of Greek and Roman morale; not because increased weapon-power necessarily decreases the offensive spirit, but because the difficulty in moving the war engines reduced mobility, and "movement" has rightly been called the "soul of war". A still more potent influence was, and more especially so among the Greeks, that generalship did not keep pace with tactical inventions. Decadence can be traced to this cause, for the generalship which took no notice of inventions, and which used men against machines in the same way as they were used before their adoption, destroyed valour through stupidity' (p. 234).

11. ibid., pp. 229–30, 299.

12. I. F. Stone wrote: 'When machines begin to think and make war on men, their biggest error will be their inability to grasp the wayward irrationality of human beings, the defect in their clockwork which leads them to persist in struggle – and therefore to upset calculation and and sometimes surprisingly to win – against such unfavorable odds that to give in would be the clearly correct, the computer-directed course.

'Our war in Vietnam bears a strong resemblance to that war of the future. An invading machine civilization has stubbornly persisted in the machine's oversimplified strategy based on the best it could muster – the bomber, the bulldozer, and the computer. Now the machine's last gasp of hope is that somehow victory can still be won via a smashed or blockaded Haiphong by denying the other, the human, side – *hardware*. It is as if determination, will, spirit were invisible to the machine, too spectral to be quantified by its computers, existing in some fifth dimension for which they had never been programmed' (*New York Review of Books*, 1 June 1972).

13. In guerrilla warfare, it is especially important that purely military considerations do not displace political ones, and that strategy and tactics are clearly formulated to serve policy. The guerrilla soldier is consciously a politician turned soldier. T. E. Lawrence wrote in *The Seven Pillars of Wisdom* (Penguin, 1962, p. 202) that 'A province would be won when we had taught the civilians in it to die for our ideal of freedom. The presence of the enemy was secondary.' In other words, political action was the base from which to operate. In this world, the orthodox soldier is often completely lost. So in many ways the battle in Vietnam was lost even before it had begun through ignorance.

14. Though Allied generalship in the Second World War was competent, it lacked imagination or brilliance. The Allied generals were quite inferior over all to their German opponents, who were more aware of the need for mobility in order to ward off the static situations produced by the projectile cycle. John D'Arcy-Dawson, a British war correspondent, noted how Allied forces in 1944 and 1945 were slower-moving than the Germans. 'Give the enemy credit, he managed his side of the affair with considerable skill. He was short of transport and short of guns, but he managed to move his artillery screen from one threatened point to another with amazing speed. The German was much more quick moving than we were . . . "You have tremendous firepower," said one High German officer, "but you have no movement." He had put his finger unerringly on our weakness –

inability to take advantage of our overpowering fire superiority by speedy movement. The weakness does not come from the troops, who merely carry out orders, but must be attributed to the higher command . . .' (*European Victory*, Macdonald, 1945, p. 113). This slow-motion approach to tactics is directly traceable to the great emphasis placed upon projectile warfare with its insistence on destruction. It is true that there were a number of Allied leaders who were quite capable in thinking and dealing with mobile warfare, but they were seldom viewed with favour by either the military or the political establishment. According to Fuller: 'The point to note here is, and we do not see it again clearly until after the Industrial Revolution, that directly projectile weapons become superior to shock weapons, more and more is the power to wage war economically influenced by the civilian inventor, by science and by industry, in place of by the soldier and his professional tactics. The result of this is . . . that generalship is apt to fall behind inventiveness . . .' (*Dragon's Teeth*, p. 233).

15. Childe, Marquis W., from the 'Evaluation' in Adams, Brooks, *America's Economic Supremacy*, Harper's, New York, 1947, p. 42.

16. The evidence indicates that strategic bombing was largely a waste of effort. When bombing was directed towards truly vital areas such as transportation centres and oil refineries, then it could, and did, achieve remarkable results. But when it was applied indiscriminately to the industrial and economic power of Germany, the results were hardly worth the effort. The plea that any destruction was of value since it meant that the Germans had to divert energy from other areas to defeat these attacks seems invalid. German war production increased throughout the war – even in the last months. Moreover, Allied war production, while vastly greater, was by no means infinite, so that war production spent upon efforts which did not bring optimum results had to be diverted from those endeavours which would have been more rewarding. The decision to devote most of the energy to the Air Force and to bomber production was one of the most significant steps ever taken by a British government. As R. W. Thompson wrote, 'This decision, dominating British industrial capacity, starved the navy of landing craft, and the army of armour. It deprived them also of the support aircraft vital to the full performance of their roles' (*The Montgomery Legend*, Allen & Unwin, 1967, p. 24).

This decision had enormous importance upon the conduct of the war. Vice Admiral Sir Herbert Richmond, writing of the loss of Crete, stated: 'The loss of Crete in June 1941, after a seven months' occupation, was attributed to the lack of airfields on the island, of aircraft, and of anti-aircraft artillery, and to the difficulties and delays due to the long sea transport round the Cape. If in its strategic doctrine the Cabinet had assigned primacy at this time to the command of the sea, with the bombing of Germany in second place, the needs of the defence of Crete in at least three of these matters could have been met. The value of that island was well recognized. The intention to hold it to the last had been expressed. What was lacking was the means, which were allocated to other purposes (*Statesmen and Sea Power*, Oxford University Press, 1946, p. 319).

The lesson is that it was a mistake in strategy to divert so many resources into what was simply bombardment – wars are not won by this means alone. The crucial tactical calculation is the economy of force. Even the Allied Powers had not the resources to be equally strong in every area. Air power's ability to destroy mesmerized the exponents of the new type of weapon. Movement, in order to be properly decisive, must entail the ability to capture objects as well as effect their destruction.

It is interesting to note the way in which the use of the term 'blitz', referring to heavy bombardment, has followed on from the term 'blitzkrieg', which properly means 'lightning war'. The two concepts are poles apart, but the tendency has been to emphasize destruction rather than mobility in thinking of warfare. Missiles fired from underground siloes or from undersea ships would not represent any real element of mobility in war.

17. Senate Hearings, quoted in Chomsky, Noam, *At War with Asia*, Fontana, 1971, p. 162.

18. ibid., p. 61. The 'smart' bombs – bombs which 'lock onto' the target, guided by laser beams or by television equipment – were developed and were in extensive use in 1972. They transformed the ratio of direct hits to the number of sorties made on sitting targets like bridges. But they did not upset the balance in favour of the attack to the extent which the U.S. air force had believed. The laser bomb exposes the aircraft to enemy missiles for a few critical extra seconds, and the sophisticated equipment has a significant failure rate. Aircraft are inevitably vulnerable to the development of more sophisticated counter-measures. And against underdeveloped areas like Indo-china, the number of suitable targets to attack by 'pin-point' bombing is so limited that the cost in the air is disproportionate to the damage on the ground.

19. The eleven days of bombing of the Hanoi and Haiphong area in late December 1972 were estimated to have cost the United States 250 million dollars (Stone, I. F., *New York Review of Books*, 25 January 1973). The loss per raid in the planes participating was stated at

the time by the US Air Force to be between 2 and 3 per cent. In the most conservative figures, the United States lost 20 per cent of the B-52s used or 10 per cent of its entire B-52 fleet in the Far East. This rate of loss could obviously not be sustained. Ninety-three pilots were also lost; these must have cost about half a million dollars per head to train.

A telling sidelight on this bombing offensive was reported in *The Times* of 13 January 1973. The severe shortage of fuel oil in the United States made it impossible to be assured of a supply sufficient to maintain the air war at that level. 'The strain that the Vietnam war has thrown on fuel reserves in the United States has been one of the less appreciated side-effects of the conflict.'

I. F. Stone summed up the air war: 'With us Americans aerial bombardment is more than tactical or strategic: it has become a disease' (ibid.).

Michael Getler, Pentagon correspondent of the *Washington Post*, reported the South Vietnamese Senator Tran Quang Thuan as saying: 'Americans value their soldiers' lives very much, and you have a lot of materials available like airplanes and bombs. So why not use them? Why engage your troops and be killed? Better to destroy the whole thing and rush in afterwards. We South Vietnamese have followed the same example.' Thuan was not commending the example set. He was pointing out what 'air support' meant: destroying a large village to clear it of half a dozen enemy soldiers. 'You can change things only if you have well trained troops with enough daring ... and good leadership ... to do the job. But if their leaders can't instil that, why should the soldiers risk their lives?' (*Guardian*, 16 January 1973).

20. Even in the Second World War the demise of the long-range bomber was in sight. Air Chief Marshal Lord Dowding, who commanded the British fighters in the Battle of Britain, stated: 'The fact is, of course, that the defence has a basic advantage which increases with the distance between the attacker and the targets, and it seems not unreasonable to suppose that exclusively long-range warfare between two remote and self-supporting opponents would result in an innocuous stalemate' (*Sunday Chronicle*, 20 September 1942). In other words, it would lead to the same sort of attrition warfare as exemplified in the stalemate on the Western front in the First World War. Lord Dowding's words were pure heresy in terms of the official air dogma and one suspects that his views were behind the decision to remove him from his post. Alastair Buchan supports this view of the role of aircraft. He wrote: 'Had nuclear weapons not been developed as a part of the intensive deployment of scientific skill in the Second World

War by Britain and the United States, it is probable that anti-aircraft devices, radar, the proximity fuse, new fire-control mechanisms, and later, ground-to-air missiles, would have led to the same sort of drawn battle between offensive and defensive measures that has occurred with submarines and would have destroyed any notion of the invincibility of air power' (*War in Modern Society*, Watts, 1966, p. 106).

Bernard Brodie, in his book *Strategy in the Missile Age* (Princeton, 1959), wrote: 'The World War II experience with strategic bombing was the first of its kind in the history of warfare and also, we can be reasonably certain, the last. No campaign on a comparable scale is likely ever again to be carried on between great belligerents with HE or other chemical bombs, not only because of the availability of nuclear weapons but – in the unlikely event that nuclear weapons could be outlawed and stay outlawed in an otherwise total war – also because technological developments have made long-range sorties with bombers or missiles far too costly to be accepted as a means of delivering bombs of such very limited capacity' (pp. 143-4). An article in the *Sunday Times*, 12 March 1972, concerning the start of the development of the Multi-Role Combat Aircraft (MRCA) by Britain, Germany and Italy, stated: 'A military aircraft is nothing more than a machine for killing people and engineers have at last begun to think in terms of the productivity and cost-effectiveness with which it can do this unpleasant job. If we are thinking of fighting in Western Europe against well-organized defence, for example, as opposed to scattering bombs at random over half Vietnam, nothing that flies over 200 feet up has much chance of staying in the air.' Actually in North Vietnam US aircraft have had to fly at such low altitudes. It is hard to continue to believe that military aircraft have much future with such restrictions. Counter-measures at such low heights would be easy and relatively cheap. A defensive development might be the erection of a latticework of plastic tubing filled with lighter-than-air gas, or thin wires suspended by small balloons, upon which are hung aerial 'mines'. These 'spiderwebs' would make it extremely difficult for jet aircraft to be effective. The ability of aircraft to have much influence is therefore rapidly diminishing.

21. Corbett, J. S., *Some Principles of Maritime Strategy*, Longmans, 1911, p. 39.

4. Policy and Strategy

> War is commonly supposed to be a matter for
> generals or admirals, in the camp, or at sea. It
> would be as reasonable to say that a duel is a
> matter for pistols and swords. Generals with
> their armies and admirals with their fleets are
> mere weapons wielded by the hand of the
> statesman. It is for him to decide when to strike,
> where to strike, and how to strike; and to enable
> him to strike truly and effectively he must first
> know definitely and exactly what object he
> wishes to attain by striking. It is not enough to
> aim random blows with the vague hope of
> inflicting some injury somewhere.
> Sir John Fortescue (*Ford Lectures, 1911*)

The idea that warfare must have some political objective, some
rational aim, is so obvious that it hardly needs explaining. Indeed,
perhaps because it is so elementary, it is often forgotten. This has
been the case in the twentieth century with the great confusion
between the terms 'policy' and 'strategy'.

Three reasons have contributed to this confusion. First, liberal
democratic countries look upon war with such horror that whenever they do wage war, it can only be fought, and justified, in
terms of highly idealistic aims which are so sweeping as to be
largely meaningless. Second, the present projectile cycle of tactics
has helped to obscure the intrinsic relationship between force and
policy. Third, the fact that war involving modern industrial
nations has become so complex has forced the soldier to become
largely a technician or scientist. In this situation he has become
completely lost in the 'nuts and bolts' of his profession and the
meaning of war as an instrument of policy has been lost.

Thus the strategy of the deterrent is often called the 'policy' of
the deterrent. Is it a policy or a strategy? Or can these terms be
used interchangeably? Policy comes from the same root as
'politics' and, in the context of international affairs, means the
course of action or direction for a particular state. The term

'strategy', on the other hand, refers to the means of action whereby a policy or set of policies may be carried out. War is, of course, the ultimate means of carrying out policy – it is the final argument. Since states are theoretical equals, with no visible higher authority, there is bound to be friction and opposition in carrying out certain policies. None the less, there are hundreds of disagreements between nations which do not lead to war, since countries can have friendly, or more or less restrained, differences of opinion. Moreover, there are some policies which may seem highly desirable from the point of view of a government, yet are not worth the risk of war. And for many states certain policies are beyond their means of fulfilment and so must remain dreams until the international scene changes in their favour. War is the last means of carrying out policy – and perhaps the crudest method. Policy can be furthered through diplomatic, financial, economic, and other means, or a combination of these means.[1]

There is no better place to start than with Clausewitz, in order to emphasize this elementary point that war and the weapons of war should be controlled by reason. He was quite clear on the matter of the relationship between policy and strategy. He wrote:

> That the political point of view should end completely when war begins would only be conceivable if wars were struggles of life or death, from pure hatred. As wars are in reality, they are . . . only the manifestations of policy itself. The subordination of the political point of view to the military would be unreasonable, for policy has created war; policy is the intelligent faculty, war only the instrument, and not the reverse. The subordination of the military point of view to the political is, therefore, the only thing which is possible.[2]

Modern soldiers pay at least lip-service to the ideas of Clausewitz and in theory his writings are their chief guide. There exists, however, an insuperable credibility gap between precept and practice. Whatever the reasons for the confusion between policy and strategy, it goes back at least to the First World War. Mackinder claimed that one of the central issues involved was a struggle to determine whether Eastern Europe should be controlled by Slavs or Germans. It was a matter of great concern for Russia and France if Germany attained dominance in Europe; it was also of great importance for Great Britain, particularly when the Germans began to build a large fleet. However, as Mackinder pointed out, 'Berlin had not decided between the political objectives – Hamburg and overseas dominion, or Bagdad and the Heartland – and therefore her strategical aim was also uncertain.'[3]

Even if the Germans had not decided to build a large fleet at that time, the expansion of Germany and Austria–Hungary would have been of vast importance in terms of the traditional British policy towards Europe: to try to maintain a balance of power on the continent. Harold Nicolson briefly outlined this policy in a speech in the House of Commons on 5 October 1938: 'For 250 years at least the great foundation of our foreign policy, what Sir Eyre Crowe called "a law of Nature", has been to prevent by every means in our power the domination of Europe by any Single Power or group of Powers. The principle necessarily had the corollary that we shall support the Small Powers against the strong.'[4] Sir Eyre Crowe's 'law of Nature' was in reality the geopolitical position of Britain, which implied this policy.

It was also of vast importance to Britain, and indeed to humanity, that the defeated nation, or nations, should not be completely destroyed whenever the resulting war was successful. Since Britain had a unique geopolitical position, and was not obliged to send in huge armies, she was able to supply a stabilizing influence upon the making of the peace. If the defeated nation had been dismembered or disabled in some manner, then, of course, the balance would have been upset in a different way, with the continental victors taking the place of the vanquished.[5]

Unfortunately, in the First World War Britain abandoned her traditional strategy of reliance on sea power; this entailed the gradual abandonment of the balance of power policy, since geopolitically the two went together. The continental-minded people in Britain had their way and Britain was trapped into fighting on the Germans' own terms and, indeed, even on the Germans' own chosen ground. Forcing an opponent to fight on your conditions is half the battle.

The Allies won the war, but it greatly weakened Britain and France, besides helping to set the pattern for the next war. The fact that the British were willing to sacrifice a great many lives in Europe helped to obscure the basic relationship between policy and strategy. If the British had resisted this course of action, then the French military would not have been so wasteful of human lives, nor would the French politicians have allowed them to be so. The British would have been little loved for this, and perhaps even scorned, but a great many lives would have been saved and, equally important, the ground would have been prepared for a more rational approach to the objectives of the war. But Britain allowed herself to be unwittingly drawn into the continental land battle on a scale out of all proportion to her resources and to her interests. One of the major difficulties was that the casualties were allowed to escalate with no regard to the political aims of the war. If the means escalate, then the aims are also bound to escalate – as indeed they did. The killing and disabling of large numbers of soldiers was bound to have an important influence upon the nature of the peace. The strategy of attrition meant that the means dictated the ends.

This disregard of political aims should have been obvious, but only a few public figures such as Hans Delbrück in Germany and Lord Lansdowne in Britain seemed aware of this vital point. The business of fighting seemed to have a life and will of its own. Bernard Brodie summed up the matter by writing:

True, the Allies disregarded the point as much, and they nominally won. Yet what they won and what they lost, prove Delbrück was in fact putting his finger on the most ominous lesson of World War I. It is that the vast technology of war which distinguishes the twentieth century from the nineteenth has been attended by the *suppression of rational concern with the political aims of the war.* During World War I the 'national interest' seemed to require that no one should question where that interest lay or what it was. Thus a war that was clearly not being fought for total objectives, such as the political extirpation of the enemy state, was allowed to become total in its methods and intensity.[6]

This important lesson from the First World War was not fully appreciated or understood in the inter-war years. Many people in Britain thought that the old conditions had changed with the development of new technology. In November 1932, for example, Stanley Baldwin, the leader of the Conservative Party, gave a speech in the House of Commons which has often been referred to – it contained the famous phrase: 'The bomber will always get through.' He stated: 'I think it is well also for the man in the street to realize that there is no power on earth that can protect him from being bombed. Whatever people may tell him, the bomber will always get through . . . The only defence is in offence, which means that you have to kill more women and children more quickly than the enemy if you want to save yourselves . . .'[7] Here was a former and future British Prime Minister telling the Commons, and the country, that the British Isles were at long last vulnerable to attack from the continent and that no power on earth could prevent it. The implication was that sea power, as the chief means of defence for Britain, was dead.

If the vital instrument of British foreign policy was no longer available, then the policy itself was no longer possible; there was a striking rejection of the balance of power policy. A. L. Rowse, the Oxford historian, recorded an extraordinary conversation which he had with Geoffrey Dawson, the editor of *The Times* in the late 1930s, on this matter. He wrote:

On all this I had the most pointed, not heated, discussion with Dawson that I ever had . . . I said, 'Look, can't you let up on your campaign against the Italians? It isn't *they* who are the danger. It is the Germans who are so powerful as to threaten all the rest of us together.' Dawson replied with something that utterly staggered me: 'To take your argument on its valuation – mind you, I'm not saying that I agree with it – but if the Germans are so powerful as you say, *oughtn't we to go in* with them?'

I was so astonished I could hardly believe my ears. There was no conception here of the agelong principle of the Grand Alliance that had governed British policy through the centuries and with such success; no idea that we had always made ourselves the linchpin of every coalition against the aggressor who was powerful enough to threaten everybody else's existence – Philip II of Spain, the France of Louis XIV and Napoleon, the Germany of the Kaiser and now Hitler's; no notion that in keeping the balance on our side was our only hope of safety. The sheer ignorance of it! – but then Dawson, unlike Steed, had never read any European history, or English history either; he knew precious little about Bismarck or, for that matter, about Pitt, and evidently nothing about what the policy of the Grand Alliance had done for this country.[8]

In both world wars the theme of fighting for the rights of the weaker countries was widely used for its emotional appeal. Nicolson claimed that this was a natural corollary of the balance of power policy, but gradually it became the major premise. Ostensibly the reason for Britain's and France's declaration of war against Germany in September 1939 was to aid Poland. There is some irony in this; if the Allies had gone to war earlier in order to defend Czechoslovakia, they might well have been obliged to declare war on Poland, since when Czechoslovakia was cut up, Poland and Hungary joined in the dismemberment. The fall of Czechoslovakia shifted the balance of power dramatically; although it was a small country, Hitler reaped a rich industrial harvest with the capture of the Skoda armament works. Moreover, the Czechs had a remarkably strong defensive force.[9]

The Polish Guarantee was a complete change of current British policy and also a reversal of Britain's traditional position. It gave a blank cheque for Poland and, in any case, it was impossible to aid Poland without an alliance with Russia. As Saul Rose noted, 'At one blow the two cardinal principles of British foreign policy – the doctrine of the free hand and limitations of commitments in Europe – had been knocked away.'[10]

The Second World War from the standpoint of the Western Allies came to be viewed largely as a crusade against evil, a struggle of light over darkness. This was quite true in that Nazism represented a great evil for Germany and for Europe; but the impression which the Allies gave to the world was that they intended to destroy Germany completely, without discrimination. This was, of course, the reversal of previous British policy regarding the Continent.

The circumstances in which Britain found herself in 1940 after the fall of France seemed to mean that the only weapon which could be used against Hitler's Germany was air power. This was a weapon, or so it was thought at the time, of unlimited destruction; as the means escalated, then the aims had to escalate, for in order to justify the use of such arms, the idea had to be accepted of a righteous war against evil and tyranny. Churchill himself had said that Britain should never use such weapons against women and children, yet he was now depending upon these arms. On 3

September 1940 he wrote: 'The Navy can lose us the war, but only the Air Force can win it.'[11]

It was indeed fortunate for the West that these instruments of destruction did not live up to expectation. For had they actually performed as expected by the air advocates, had German economic power been destroyed to such an extent that her armies were powerless, then there would have been a great vacuum of power in Europe. Air forces cannot conquer; they can only destroy. The only army ready and able to fill the vacuum of power would have been the Red Army. So if these weapons had been as successful as imagined, then the Russians might well have reached the English Channel and established control over the whole of Europe.

During the war little attention was given to the possible post-war structure of the world, except for the vague notion that everybody would live happily ever after. In the eleventh hour, however, the alarm was raised in the Western camp by Churchill. By that time Britain's power to influence the direction of the Allied war effort was limited. The fear that Russia might invade deeply into Europe and thus become a new menace to replace Germany presented itself. The geopolitical balance could be upset in a different manner.[12]

In the end, of course, Russia did succeed in obtaining control over half of Germany, and the Western Allies soon realized that a strong Germany was essential to try to offset this new situation. The fact that the Russians had suffered heavily in the war was justification enough in Russian eyes for seizing control over as much German territory as possible. In view of the circumstances it was impossible to deny Russia control over Eastern Europe. A new imbalance was created. In spite of this fact, many in the West seemed to pride themselves on their non-political or non-Clausewitzian approach to war. Professor Joseph Jones, a Yale professor who had served with the State Department, wrote in 1964: 'As the Russians had rolled the Germans westward from Stalingrad, they had consistently subordinated military objectives to long-range political goals, whereas the United States and Great Britain had usually done the opposite.'[13]

Suddenly the thought struck the Western Allies that the era of universal peace was not at hand. Undaunted, however, they put forward the hope that if this new evil of communism, manifested by Russia, were defeated, then the world could live in peace. The instruments to attain this modern millennium would be air power and the new terror weapons, nuclear arms! The Utopians, as George E. Lowe called them, saw these weapons as the true means for the salvation of mankind. 'Utopians of all political persuasions fervently believe in victory through air power achieved by air bombardment once command of the air is attained ... The Utopians offered the quick, easy 100 per cent American solution to our problems and American commitments: Utilize the atom bomb ("the ultimate weapon") carried to the Asiatic heartland by the epitome of American industry – the long range bomber.'[14]

It is not surprising, with the emphasis upon destruction in the projectile cycle and the confusion between the terms 'policy' and 'strategy', that the Pentagon should have come to play an increasingly dominant role in the formation of policy for the United States. There was no reaction when an American admiral claimed that policy should not guide strategy in war-time for the United States. This is the opinion of an educated naval officer, Rear Admiral J. C. Wylie, Jr, who has lectured at the US Naval War College. 'Is war in fact a continuation of policy?' Wylie asked, and came up with the surprising answer, 'For us, I think not.' He elaborated on this by writing:

War for a nonaggressor is actually nearly a complete collapse of policy. Once war comes, then nearly all prewar policy is utterly invalid because the setting in which it was designed to function no longer corresponds with the facts of reality. When war comes, we at once move into a radically different world. Even looking past a war, a postwar world has very little resemblance to any prewar situation; and the more comprehensive the war, the more valid this assertion. It is a fairly safe bet that no participant, even Russia, in World War II had any clear idea before war started what the world would really look like after it was over.[15]

This is quite different from the Clausewitzian view of war, in which policy for both sides must be the guiding or intelligent factor. It is a conflict of policies which has created the war. Whether or not it is possible to forecast the future is beside the point; the object of the struggle is still the political structure, and the aims of war include the post-war settlement. Policies of a nation can be, and indeed often are, founded upon mistaken assumptions concerning one's ability to wage war. Nevertheless, as Clausewitz stated, 'That the political point of view should end completely when war begins would only be conceivable if wars were struggles of life or death, from pure hatred.' Wars are a matter of life or death for the individual soldier or sailor, but not necessarily for a nation as a whole. To assume that all wars are life or death struggles for a country implies that all wars are, or should be, all-out total wars. However, most wars throughout history have been limited simply because the political objectives of wars have been limited. The idea has arisen in the twentieth century that limited wars are something of an anomaly and that total wars are natural, or the norm. The very term 'total war' implies a struggle in which the relationship between policy and strategy has been completely eroded.

If nuclear weapons have performed any real service, then it has been to wake people up to the stark realization that war must be an instrument of policy. Use of the term 'limited war', albeit in some curious contexts, is a step towards this aim; but it still seems an idea which is difficult for modern soldiers and statesmen to understand. Undoubtedly the reason for the delay is the contradiction, as noted in the first chapter, that although Clausewitzian war assumes no nuclear arms, Mackinder's Heartland theory demands, or seems to demand, such arms.

In the United States, and to some extent throughout the West, Herman Kahn has been looked upon as the leading cerebral soldier. His book *On Thermonuclear War* was widely regarded as a classic when it first appeared in 1960. The very title suggested an attempt to emulate Clausewitz's famous work entitled *On War*. Indeed, many writers have called Kahn a neo-Clausewitzian strategist. This seems a loose interpretation of Clausewitz. In truth Kahn's work and his thesis indicates that he is the opposite – the complete non-Clausewitzian cerebral soldier.

In a subsequent book entitled *Thinking about the Unthinkable*, Kahn consistently used the terms 'policy' and 'strategy' interchangeably. This fact alone would be enough to make Clausewitz roll over in his grave. In one section of the book, Kahn listed 'Fourteen Alternative National Policies', but in the very first sentence he wrote: 'In order to give some orientation to the range of strategies which a nation like the United States might choose to follow, I will describe fourteen different possibilities here.'[16] But are they strategies or are they policies? This is left in doubt. He lists them as follows:

1. Act of Renunciation
2. Unilateral Initiatives
3. Minimum Deterrence
4. Rule of Law
5. Fortress America
6. Accept the Arms Race Reluctantly
7. Follow Technology
8. Not Incredible First Strike
9. Concert of Powers
10. The Aggressive Democrat
11. Credible First Strike
12. Protracted Conflict
13. Win
14. Preventive war.[17]

Even from simply reading this list of categories, and without further explanation, it should be fairly obvious that some of these are policies and some are strategies. Indeed, some of the strategies might well be the means to attain certain of the political aims implied in the list, but in the lexicon of Kahn, and of many other academic strategists, they are the same. This is ridiculous; they cannot be both aims and means.

One can easily understand, in view of this confusion, how the United States became trapped in the Vietnam War. Force was escalated without regard to the political objectives. Hugh Hanning wrote of the Vietnam War: 'Above all, the Americans never got around to defining their aims. As a result, it was not clear who was in charge, the ambassador or the commanding general.'[18] The reason remains to this day a great puzzle. The irony of the situation is that, as Senator William Fulbright pointed out, 'It simply does not matter very much for the US, in cold, unadorned strategic terms, who rules the states of Indo-China.'[19]

This concern with policy and strategy is not just a matter of pedantry – rather it is a point of real importance. It was precisely this lack of clarity which enabled the West to become so obsessed with nuclear arms and to accept them so naïvely as legitimate instruments of policy. The literature dealing with defence doctrine since the Second World War has grown voluminous and one constantly sees the confusion between the terms 'policy' and 'strategy'. One also reads of 'defence policy' and of 'military policy'. What exactly is meant by 'defence policy'? Is this supposed to mean the same as a military objective? Or does it mean foreign policy pursued by military leaders? And how does one define 'military policy'? One also finds something called 'political policy'. What can this mean?

The view that nuclear arms cannot be eliminated unless war itself is first abolished is mistaken. If the relationship between force and policy is clearly understood, then nuclear arms will eliminate themselves for the simple reason that they are of no real use in warfare. This may seem surprising. The idea that a weapon might not be powerful enough is quite obvious; stones can be used as lethal weapons, but no modern country would dream of sending its soldiers into combat armed only with stones. But the idea, at the other end of the scale, that a weapon may be so powerful as to be incompatible with any realistic political objective is more difficult to grasp. Yet it is true.

If Clausewitzian war cannot admit the use of nuclear arms, and the Heartland theory demands the view that these weapons are 'needed', then we must return to a re-examination of the ideas of the Heartland theory. The illumination that this will provide will show us a way out of the central difficulty of Western strategic doctrine. Mackinder made a number of assumptions which appeared correct in 1904 and 1919, when he wrote his theory, but which today are no longer valid. These assumptions are:

(1) The Heartland theory tacitly assumed that an increase in the efficiency of land mobility would automatically award an advantage to the attack in warfare.

(2) It was assumed that the Middle East – the crossroads of Western civilization – would always remain a key strategic area.

(3) It was assumed that the submarine ship would only be developed to the extent that it would mean the denial of sea power to seafaring nations. The idea that a nuclear-powered undersea ship might be developed which could mean a new form of sea power for the future was not visualized in 1919.

(4) It was assumed that the Arctic Ocean would for ever remain a barrier to ocean-going ships. Although Mackinder was aware that ships, with the aid of ice-breakers, used the Arctic Ocean in the summer months, free navigation was not possible and he assumed this would remain so indefinitely. Thus, sea power would always be refused access to the Heartland.

(5) It was also assumed that sea transport had reached a plateau in development. The steel, steam-driven ship seemed to be the ultimate stage in ship development with perhaps a few minor improvements.

These five assumptions will be taken up in this order in the following five chapters.

Notes to Chapter 4

1. Whether or not it is possible that at some time in the future all differences between nations can be settled in a non-lethal manner is another matter. At this time, the first step towards more control over the causes and consequences of war must involve a better intellectual understanding of war. A lot has been written in recent years on the connection between war and aggression in individual and collective man, but, though the connection appears quite convincing in relation to many forms of violence, it is by no means clear that it is a key element in war between nations, and if it is, it is a matter which is too inaccessible to control to promise amity in international society. On the face of it, there appears more truth in Arthur Koestler's observation that sociologists who see war as a manifestation of man's aggressive urges make one feel that they have no experience of actual modern warfare (see *The Ghost in the Machine*, Hutchinson, 1967).

A better intellectual understanding of war should begin with a clarification of the relationship between means and aims, which implies an understanding of strategy and policy. Wars between nations

82

are calculated acts, even when the calculations are immoral or mis-calculated, or arise from arbitrary reasons of greed or power or fear. They are fought for a political purpose. The carrying out of policy must involve some assessment of the two factors of gain and of cost.

As long as nations are armed and differences between them can lead to fighting, the West must be concerned with the rational place of force in policy. A great danger is that this is distorted by misplaced idealism. There has been a strong tendency to look on wars as some sort of moral crusade.

2. Clausewitz, Karl von, *On War*, Random House, New York, 1943, p. 598. It is interesting to read J. S. Corbett (*Some Principles of Maritime Strategy*, Longmans, 1911) on this matter. 'Hence, says Clausewitz, the first, the greatest and most critical decision upon which the Statesman and the General have to exercise their judgement is to determine the nature of the war, to be sure they do not mistake it for something nor seek to make of it something which from its inherent conditions it can never be. "This," he declares, "is the first and the most far-reaching of all strategical questions"' (p. 25). Corbett also noted how this has a direct bearing upon strategy. 'When a Chief of Staff is asked for a war plan he must not say we will make war in such and such a way because it was Napoleon's or Moltke's way. He will ask what is the political object of the war, what are the political conditions, and how much does the question at issue mean respectively to us and to our adversary. It is these considerations which determine the nature of the war' (pp. 24–5).

3. Mackinder, H. J., *Democratic Ideals and Reality*, Norton, New York, 1962, p. 154.

4. Nicolson, Harold, *Hansard*, 5 October 1938.

5. Professor Herbert Butterfield wrote in 1949 of the danger of looking upon wars as moral crusades: 'There is a very good historical precedent for a thesis which belongs to the cream of diplomatic tradition in better times . . . It is the thesis that if two rival giants are offering an alternative threat to the existing order of things on the Continent, and if you are unwilling to let the rascals fight it out by themselves, choose carefully the time of your intervention in their struggle and see that you intervene only in order to save whichever of the two it may be from being destroyed by the other. For so long as there are two of these giants on the Continent the whole world can breathe; but if you devote a war of righteousness to the purpose of destroying one of them you are using your blood and treasure to build up the other one into a greater monster than ever, and you will infallibly have to face it at the next stage of the story. In other words the

policy of ridding the world of aggression by the method of total war – of the war of righteousness – is like using the devil to cast out the devil; it does not even have the merit of being practical politics' (*Christianity and History*, Bell 1949). Professor Butterfield is quite perceptive in noting that the strategy of total war implies a certain policy just as today the projected use of nuclear arms involves a definite political goal. Of course, it should be the reverse – the political aims should determine the force used or the nature of the war.

6. Brodie, Bernard, *Strategy in the Missile Age*, Princeton University Press, 1959, p. 67.

7. Baldwin, Rt Hon. Stanley, *Hansard*, November 1932.

8. Rowse, A. L., *All Souls and Appeasement*, Norton, New York, 1968, pp. 28–9. There is a remarkably common failure to appreciate the British balance of power policy and the strategy which went with it. Correlli Barnett, for example, in an interview in the *Guardian* (8 October 1969), maintained that throughout British history there had been a succession of theories about back doors to victory. 'It is a perennial British delusion . . . to always think there is some way to victory other than by smashing the main enemy army in the field. Going outside and kicking his dog, which is what the Mediterranean campaigns in the Second World War were, is no substitute . . .' Had this strategy been adopted by, say, Pitt there would undoubtedly never have been a British Empire, and it proved to be a sure way of losing it. Barnett added: 'The British are supposed to be a moral people, but basing your policy for European war on the availability of mugs is not moral, and it hasn't worked very well. Sometimes the mugs haven't been strong enough, and sometimes there hasn't been a mug.' 'Mugs' here means European allies. It hardly seems necessary to point out that Britain's European policy was successful for centuries because it was in the interests of the European allies, or 'mugs' as Barnett disparagingly refers to them, as well as Britain herself. It was impossible for Britain to go it alone because it was impossible to maintain a great land army and be a first-rate sea power at the same time.

9. Albert Speer recorded: 'The Czech border fortifications caused general astonishment. To the surprise of experts a test bombardment showed that our weapons would not have prevailed against them. Hitler himself went to the former frontier to inspect the arrangements and returned impressed. The fortifications were amazingly massive, he said, laid out with extraordinary skill and echeloned, making prime use of terrain' (*Inside the Third Reich*, Macmillan, New York, 1970, p. 111).

10. Rose, Saul, 'Britain', *in Foreign Policies in a World of Change*,

ed. Black, J. R., and Thompson, K., Harper & Row, New York, 1963, p. 37. Both France and Britain feared Germany, but because of communism they also had an antagonistic attitude towards Russia. If it had not been for the bogeyman of communism, they would automatically have allied with Russia in the middle thirties. As L. B. Namier wrote, 'The tragic core of diplomatic history during the half-year preceding the outbreak of war is in Anglo-Russian negotiations. It is difficult to write about them without the painful consciousness that here was perhaps the one chance of preventing the Second World War, or of ensuring Hitler's early defeat' (*Diplomatic Prelude*, Macmillan, 1948).

11. Churchill, Winston S., Memorandum, 3 September 1940.

12. It is interesting to note that the Spanish seemed more aware of the traditional British policy than the British themselves. Efforts were made on the part of the British Foreign Office to win the cooperation of Franco. Sir Samuel Hoare, the British Ambassador to Spain, pointed out to Count Jordana, the Spanish Foreign Minister, in the latter part of 1942 that '. . . it was not the future policy of Russia to interfere in the international affairs of other countries'. Jordana replied, seeing the situation in a more geopolitical context, by writing: 'If the events develop in the future as they have done up to now, it would be Russia which will penetrate deeply into German territory. And we ask the question: if this should occur, which is the greater danger not only for the Continent, but for England herself, a Germany not totally defeated and with sufficient strength to serve as a rampart against communism or a Sovietized Germany which would certainly furnish Russia with added strength of her war preparations . . . which would enable Russia to extend herself with an empire without precedent from the Atlantic to the Pacific? . . . And we ask a second question: is there anybody in the centre of Europe, in that mosaic of countries without consistency or unity, bled moreover by war and foreign domination, who could contain the ambitions of Stalin? . . . For this reason we consider the situation as extremely grave and think that the people in England should reflect calmly on the matter, since should Russia succeed in conquering Germany, there will be no one who can contain her . . . If Germany did not exist, Europeans would have to invent her . . .' (Hoare, Samuel, *Ambassador on Special Mission*, Collins, 1946, pp. 189–91). The picture which Jordana presented would have been essentially the same regardless of his emotional attitude towards communism.

13. Jones, Joseph M., *The Fifteen Weeks*, Harcourt, Brace & World, New York, 1964, p. 41.

14. Lowe, George E., *Age of Deterrence*, Little, Brown, Boston, 1964, pp. 23–4. Lowe maintains that in modern defence thinking, at least as far as the United States is concerned, there are two schools of thought – the Traditionalists and the Utopians. In a curious twist of language, the Utopians are politically classified as conservatives. 'The basic disagreement between the Traditionalist and Utopians revolves around the use of force as an instrument of American foreign policy' (p. 5). The Utopians look upon nuclear arms as the best weapons for the United States and postulate a belief in the technical superiority of the West. 'Thus a few brave highly skilled knights can be substituted for the millions of farmers' sons and city poor slugging out the war on the ground. The country with the most mechanics and strongest industry will win future wars, not the nation with the largest land armies' (pp. 6–7). But Lowe does not get to the intellectual heart of the matter by examining the geopolitical foundation. He does state: 'The Anglo-American bomber fleet would do for the twentieth century what the British battle-fleet had done for the nineteenth' (p. 7). The sea power theory, as Mahan pointed out, rested upon a geopolitical view of the world, as does the current air theory. The question is: what is this foundation and is it valid today?

15. Wylie, J. C., Jr, *Military Strategy: A General Theory of Power Control*, Rutgers University Press, New Brunswick, N.J., 1967, p. 79. In the Korean War, the cry was produced by the neo-conservative elements in the United States that military objectives should supersede political aims. Roger Leonard, in the excellent introduction to his edition of *A Short Guide to Clausewitz* (Weidenfeld & Nicolson, 1967), has written: 'Certainly there should never be a point where policy ends and disappears from the stage, and military action takes over. The notion that at some stage the military establishment takes over from those who formulate and direct policy – a notion championed by General Douglas MacArthur during the Korean War – was declared "irrational" by Clausewitz' (p. 13).

The distinction between policy and strategy *must* be emphasized. If there is confusion between the two, the military are liable to have a dominant hand in the formation of the direction of force, that is, in policy. One significant aspect about the *Pentagon Papers* was that they were compiled by the Defense Department, yet they dealt with matters of policy and policy-making. These documents were classified and it was an act of civil disobedience upon the part of the Press to publish them; but the central issue is whether the government of a democratic state has any right to classify matters which pertain to the making of policy. In fact, there were no clear ideas on policy for Vietnam, but it is vital if force is being used that the political aims are clear, the motives and reasons debated and made apparent, for the sake both of the process of making the policy at home and of having the policy understood abroad.

The military mind tends to be insensitive to political factors. The inclination of the soldier is 'to get the job done' – but the job is ultimately a political one and military commanders need instructing on what it is. 'The political object of any war determines the kind of war that is to be waged, the form that it should take, and the intensity with which it should be fought,' writes Roger Leonard (ibid., p. 13). Unfortunately modern cerebral soldiers have not been of much help in solving this difficulty of the relationship between policy and strategy. The fact that the Pentagon is contributor of substantial funds towards academic research in universities has not aided the situation; the power of the purse is very important and the Pentagon has a very fat purse.

There is no clear view of the relationship between military and civilian leaders in the United States. As has been noted, the ability of the military leader has become of much less consequence because of the nature of modern warfare but, on the same account, his role in military affairs has not diminished and, in the United States, has actually assumed more importance beyond the military sphere. He manages the largest business concern in the country; as Richard Barnet has observed, the Pentagon 'by having $40 billion a year to spend in the economy has become the principal planner in American society'. The direction of the military machine, as it has grown in size, has come increasingly under the control of the military leaders themselves; this in turn means that they tend to dominate policy. The cart is put before the horse. This evolution is very subtle and is implicit in the escalation of force. This is an extremely important aspect of the dilemma of modern Western doctrine inasmuch as the United States is the acknowledged leader of the Western bloc of nations.

Michael Howard in *The Continental Commitment* (Temple Smith, 1972) provides a particularly tasty illustration of how the military planners can assume a life of their own regardless of policy considerations. It is a quotation from the Imperial Defence Paper of 22 June 1926. 'The size of the forces of the Crown maintained by Great Britain is governed by various conditions peculiar to each service, and is not arrived at by any calculations of the requirements of foreign policy, nor is it possible that they should ever be so calculated' (p. 94).

But this looks like a mere eccentricity when compared to the influence which the military establishment in the United States has been able to exercise not only over the armed services but over American civil life. It was pointed out in a review of a book on the Oppenheimer case in *The Times Literary Supplement* on 19 November 1971: 'Oppenheimer, in short, was an early victim of the forces which have since done so much damage to his country. He has sometimes been presented as a disdainful elitist, justly punished for his undemocratic attitude. In fact he was the victim of the grossly undemocratic power of the USAF. The rise of that power has been almost unmitigated disaster for the United States. The empire-builders of the three services have competed for an ever larger share of the ever larger national budget. With a cunning unlike anything displayed in their professional capacity, they have crushed all critics and resisted all attempts to cut them down to size. They have warped American foreign policy, distorted the American economy, and poisoned the American democracy. Finally they have failed to evolve a military doctrine, whether strategic or tactical, capable of protecting or even identifying America's true interests.'

It is natural that military leaders should be advocates of their own particular field of action. But this is especially dangerous when it comes from the Air Force, as the nature of their weapons, i.e. air power, determines to a considerable extent political objectives. The success of American policy is likely to have some correlation with keeping the US Air Force employed; the obverse of this is that Air Force leaders are particularly keen to shape foreign policy. In the Korean war, when the US ground forces were succeeding very well in holding the Chinese and inflicting a great defeat on them, the US Air Force was seeking to extend the battlefield and get the United States involved in a far larger war with communist China. This illustrates how force tends to shape the task and the task for which it is suited to shape policy. No one asks, 'What is the nature of the projected war? What would be the political goals?' Instead the advice is, 'Here is the level of force we *must* use, cut the political objectives to this.' Air Force leaders are like Procrustes shaping the person to the bed.

According to the US Air Force Association, speaking out on US *foreign policy* in September 1971: 'Freedom must bury communism or be buried by communism. Complete eradication of the Soviet system must be our national goal, our obligation to all free people, our promise of hope to all who are not free . . . We are determined to back our words with action even at the risk of war. We seek not merely to preserve our freedoms but to extend them . . . Soviet aims are both evil and implacable. The people are willing to work toward, and fight for if necessary, the elimination of communism from the world scene.

Let the issue be joined' (Lowe, George E., *The Age of Deterrence*, Little, Brown, Boston, 1964, p. 231). This objective is little removed from that given by the fictional General Jack D. Ripper in *Dr Strangelove*: 'I can no longer sit back and allow the international communist conspiracy to sap and impurify our bodily juices.'

16. Kahn, Herman, *Thinking about the Unthinkable*, Weidenfeld & Nicolson, 1962, p. 283.

17. ibid., p. 234.

18. *Guardian*, 19 May 1969.

19. U.S. Senate, 2 April 1970. Louis Heren, in his book *No Hail, No Farewell* (Weidenfeld & Nicolson, 1971) – a book describing the Johnson Administration in somewhat sympathetic tones – noted that a number of people involved in the Administration's policy-making gave an interesting answer to the question of why the country had become so deeply committed in Vietnam. The answer was simply that they thought the United States could win. Since the United States was the most powerful state in the world, it seemed almost axiomatic that with enough effort victory could be attained. What this meant was that the means were justifying the ends.

5. The Blitzkrieg and the Counter-Blitzkrieg

> Until the mechanical arts have advanced far
> enough to cause the attack in war to predominate
> over the defence, centralization cannot begin . . .
> Brook Adams
> (*The Law of Civilization and Decay*)
> Now it is generally recognized that defence is the
> stronger of the two forms of fighting.
> Field-Marshal Erich von Manstein
> (*Lost Victories*)

At the end of the Second World War Russia stood as a colossus on the World Island: she possessed Eastern Europe as well as an immense land area stretching from Europe to the Pacific Ocean, and she had administered the first defeat to the once invincible Wehrmacht. There seemed no country in Europe, Asia or Africa which could match the power of this giant. The economies of the European nations, including Great Britain, were severely disrupted and people themselves were exhausted in the aftermath of the war. The economic miracle of recovery was still to come, and it was by no means certain that European countries could regain their pre-war economic status. It appeared almost beyond question that there was no nation in Europe capable at that time or in the foreseeable future of containing the ambitions of Russia.

However, on the other side of the hill, behind the Iron Curtain, the Russians were not as powerful at that time as the West believed them to be. Stalin had always been an extremely cautious politician in using force in international affairs. While the odds appeared to be in his favour from the standpoint of the West, the same view could not be held from the Kremlin. The Russians had suffered enormous losses in the war both in manpower and industrial equipment. The United States, on the other hand, had suffered only minor losses in dead and wounded and no damage to the country itself. The population of Russia was only a little larger than that of the United States. None the less, a fear of Russia which bordered on public paranoia slowly developed. In Western – and especially American – eyes Russia took on the image of an overpowering giant.

The fact that Russia was controlled by communists seemed to confirm her evil intention of aggressive adventures in pursuit of territory and 'Bolshevik' rule. The Atlantic powers took little account in their reasoning of the possibility that the Russians might have good reasons for neutralizing and controlling as much of Germany as possible after their terrible losses in the war. In the belief that the millennium had somehow arrived, the United States put forward the Baruch Plan in June 1946. The Soviet Union rejected the idea of inspection to assure the elimination on control of nuclear arms. In theory, if the Soviet Union believed that she was in a position strategically superior to the West's, then it would have been to her advantage to have accepted the Baruch Plan. However, Russia even under the Tsars had used secrecy to conceal her deficiencies, and the Iron Curtain served more to hide weaknesses than to cloak strength. The evidence from the Cold War is that the Russians felt themselves to be in their traditional vulnerable position and never accepted the Heartland theory. Russia had also been exposed throughout her history to invasion across the North European Plain. She had vast borders to protect, and remembered that the Western Allies had put troops on to Russian soil after the First World War.[1] We are not concerned here with an attempt to assign historical responsibility for the Cold War; it is obvious that on both sides there were legitimate and imagined fears. What is most pertinent to our argument is that the Atlantic powers quite misread the situation in relation to strategy, and this error afflicted Western strategic thinking even after the policy of so-called 'peaceful coexistence' was promulgated; a conspicuous example to this day is NATO's attachment to tactical nuclear arms.

It was generally accepted in the West that the Russians had enough land strength easily to sweep over Western Europe. The possibility of a Russian blitzkrieg was strong in people's minds, vividly supported by the fact that in 1940 the Germans had driven through France and the Low Countries in less than a month. It was clearly noted that the Russians had kept ahead of the Germans in tank development during the war. The centre of the European war had been the Eastern front, and the West knew it: more German soldiers had been lost in the Russian campaign by the time the first Allied soldier set foot on the Normandy beach than the entire Allied force committed to the invasion. The impression grew that the West could not possibly match the Red Army in strength; this seemed to involve an arms race that the Atlantic powers had to avoid.[2]

Even in 1971 an American academic writer, Professor Edgar A. Bottome, maintained that the Russians could easily overrun Western Europe and be in Antwerp in ten days. He wrote:

While fighting a minimal hold-action on other fronts, the Soviets could easily muster a 4–1 division advantage on the North German Plain. A conservative estimate of the time that it would take a determined Soviet effort to break through the northern front would be less than a week. This would place Soviet forces at the rear of the United Seventh Army in about eight days or less and in Antwerp in about ten days. There could be no Bastogne this time; the American forces would be flanked and would be lucky to make it to the Pyrenees safely before they were destroyed by a Soviet 'wheeling action' at the base of the Swiss and French Alps.[3]

This is all very reminiscent of the German blitzkrieg which swept over France to the English Channel in about ten days in 1940 and astounded the world. While Bottome is clearly talking about a Russian blitzkrieg, he is reluctant to employ this particular term, and one wonders why. Professor Bottome admits that not everyone agrees with this analysis. He states: 'That the United States and its allies did not have a conventional capability during the 1950s and early 1960s is admitted by most, but certainly not by all observers.' At this point the reader is given a footnote referring him to Sir Basil Liddell Hart's book, *Deterrent or Defence*, published in 1940.[4]

NATO was formed primarily to prevent a Soviet blitzkrieg from over-running Western Europe. The classic example of the blitzkrieg is the Battle of France in 1940. Probably no other event, apart from the dropping of the first atomic bomb on Hiroshima, had such a widespread and dramatic impact; indeed, there has long been a great intrinsic connection between these two events. In a war filled with spectacular happenings, these two stand out. Both contain elements of science-fiction, a surrealistic aspect which even now makes one wonder whether or not they did indeed take place. But equally important is the fact that there is a subtle psychological and intellectual connection between the two. In Western eyes the use of nuclear arms came to be regarded as the inevitable answer to the apparent invincibility of the blitzkrieg attack.

Contrary to popular opinion, the Germans in 1940 did not have an overwhelming superiority of force – only superiority of military ideas. As General J. F. C. Fuller, who was one of the theorists of the blitzkrieg, stated: 'It was not that the French were altogether unprepared, they were not. It was that their preparations did not coincide with the type of war the Age of Velocity demanded'.[5] One of the best guides to the events behind the disaster is a book entitled *The Battle of France: 1940*, by a French officer, Colonel Adolphe Goutard. The analysis which Goutard made tallies very well with the impression given by Fuller. The Allies and the Germans were, in fact, fairly evenly matched, although the Germans had an advantage in aircraft. On the whole the Anglo–French armies were better equipped than the German army, including superiority in one decisive weapon, oddly enough, tanks. However, the French and British still clung to the outdated notion that tanks were to support infantry and, accordingly, designed their tanks for this role. The Germans, on the other hand, reversed this thinking and constructed their tanks with the idea in mind of a mobile long-range striking force – the blitzkrieg.

The author of the plan which resulted in the defeat of France was General (later Field Marshal) Erich von Manstein, who in 1940 was on the staff of von Rundstedt's army. The original plan was a warmed-up version of the Schlieffen Plan from the First World War, and again called for the main effort to be on the German right wing – this time through both Holland and Belgium, as well as Luxembourg. The armies would push around Paris and away from the Channel ports. Far from being reluctant to attack, as was thought at the time, Hitler had issued orders for attack on eleven different occasions, starting in the autumn of 1939, but each time they were cancelled. Manstein reasoned that this new version of the Schlieffen Plan was much too obvious and would be expected by the Allies. This was an accurate observation, since the French High Command counted on such a move and planned for no other. Manstein thought that a better idea would be to use the right wing move into the Low Countries as a feint, drawing the best French and British troops into a trap, and then to strike the main blow at the loosely held Ardennes Forest region with the bulk of the German Panzers. General Heinz Guderian, the Commander of the Panzers, gave his assurance that the plan was technically possible.

Liddell Hart, who was the foremost theorist of the blitzkrieg, had written before the war that, contrary to popular opinion, the Ardennes Forest region was not as formidable an obstacle as was imagined. Seven years before the event he had predicted that a tank thrust could be made through the Ardennes, but the French and British General Staff discounted his view. Manstein, in trying to convince Hitler and the German General Staff, cited Liddell Hart as an authority on the matter.

A number of war-gaming conferences were held by the Germans in considering the new Manstein Plan. The last was attended by Hitler. Guderian, who had a leading, indeed, vital, part in the attack, described the high point of the meeting. He told of his projected role in the attack, which was to break through to the Meuse River by the fourth day. He wrote:

. . . On the fourth day I would arrive at the Meuse; on the fifth day I would cross it. By the evening of the fifth day I hoped to have established bridgeheads on the far bank. Hitler asked: 'And then what are you going to do?' He was the first person to have thought to ask this vital question. I replied: 'Unless I receive orders to the contrary, I intend on the next day to continue my advance westwards. The supreme leadership must decide whether my objective is to be Amiens or Paris. In my opinion the correct course is to drive past Amiens to the English Channel.' Hitler nodded and said nothing more. Only General Busch, who commanded the Sixteenth Army on my left, cried out: 'Well, I don't think you'll cross the river in the first place!' Hitler, the tension visible in his face, looked at me to see what I would reply.

I said: 'There's no need for you to do so, in any case.' Hitler made no comment.[6]

The distance from the Meuse River to the Channel at the point where Guderian intended to cross was approximately 160 miles – a fantastic objective for an advancing army. Goutard noted of the actual attack: 'In four days, May 16–20, the Panzer divisions had covered 156 miles in a corridor which narrowed to a width of 35 miles between Arras and Péronne. And after May 20 this corridor was lengthened by some sixty miles to Calais.'[7] This meant that the Panzer divisions were moving at the rate of about forty miles per day. Nothing quite like it had ever happened before in military history – it seemed impossible. General Fuller, commenting on Guderian's account of the war game, wrote:

The English Channel as Guderian's next objective! – as the crow flies 160 miles west of the Meuse at Sedan. No wonder General Busch was astonished, because no conventional general would have placed it more than a dozen miles west of that river. So distant an objective discloses the secret of Guderian's Blitzkrieg. It was to employ mobility as a psychological weapon; not to kill but to move; not to move to kill but to move to terrify, to bewilder, to perplex, to cause consternation, doubt and confusion in the rear of the enemy, which rumour would magnify until panic became monstrous.[8]

And this is precisely what happened. Interestingly enough, the fall of France amazed Berlin as much, or even more, than it did the rest of the world. Guderian's initial orders were merely to seize bridgeheads on the far bank of the Meuse, but he exceeded his orders by 160 miles. The subsequent fear of carefully laid plans for an invasion of England was unfounded since victory was completely unexpected.[9]

While the speed of Guderian's advance undermined the confidence and morale of the Allies, the atmosphere in the German Supreme HQ was anything but calm and collected. For after the German Panzers had broken through and were racing to the Channel, huge gaps were created between these forces and the slower-moving infantry needed to hold the flanks of the corridor. Goutard wrote of this amazing development: 'It was obvious that the infantry could not follow the Panzers going at this speed and over such distances. It is also obvious that the few motorized divisions, which were following in the tracks of the armour, but were two or three days behind, would become stretched out more and more and would provide a very inadequate flank protection.'[10] There must have been gaps – that is, open country with no German forces – of between thirty and sixty miles at times, and perhaps even more. On the German side they were only too aware of this dangerous and precarious situation. Hitler was especially alarmed and even frantic about it. Halder recorded in his diary on 18 May: 'The Fuehrer torments himself to an extraordinary extent over the southern flank. He is furious and shouts that we are doing our best to jeopardize the whole campaign, and leading Germany to defeat. He wants no part in extending operations further west!'[11]

Even when Guderian reached the Channel on 20 and 21 May, there were still gaps between the Panzers and the following German infantry. It was a tense situation for both sides at that point since the French generals, like sleepwalkers, began to realize that an opportunity was presented which had to be exploited with the utmost speed. A complete and devastating reversal of the battle was possible – but time was crucial. Goutard analysed this remarkable opportunity for the Allies: 'The situation of the Panzers in their corridors between May 20 and 24 gave us a chance of bringing about a miraculous reversal of positions; all the more so, as Hitler's nervousness and anxiety had created the right moral conditions in his generals, in that *they already had believed themselves beaten.*'[12] This brilliant German victory might well have gone the other way at the last minute and become a tremendous Allied victory, for had the Allied forces been able quickly to step in between the Panzers and the infantry, then the former – the élite troops of the Wehrmacht – could have been cut off and destroyed at leisure. It would have produced a Dunkirk in reverse, but with no possibility of escape for Guderian and his Panzers. Like von Paulus at Stalingrad, later in the war, he would have been forced to surrender or be destroyed. It is possible that the Allies could have won the war in 1940.

Goutard went on to explain how time was the key factor. 'Nevertheless, it was still necessary for our Command not only to see the possibility of turning the tables but to carry out its plan with vigour. For on the battlefield there is never a change of fortune which does not first exist in one person's mind and will.'[13] Gamelin, the French Commander-in-Chief, issued orders to take advantage of the situation. Unfortunately he was replaced by Weygand who cancelled these orders but re-issued them later. But too much time had been lost; since these vital orders were never carried out, the British Expeditionary Force (BEF) and remnants of the French and Belgium forces were forced to make a hasty exit from the Continent.

Thus a great German victory, which stunned the world and still has great impact upon our thinking, could well have gone the other way and been an Allied victory. Since the blitzkrieg did result in the fall of France in 1940, entirely incorrect military lessons were drawn from this campaign. It was tacitly assumed that in land warfare the attack would usually be able to overwhelm the defence, everything else being equal. General Foch had stated years before that any improvement in weaponry was bound to aid offence, and here seemed solid proof of that assertion. Liddell Hart, however, drew exactly the opposite conclusions. Writing a year after the fall of France, he stated: 'Superficially this year's campaign may look like a vindication of the orthodox military doctrine as to the superiority of attack over defence. Actually, its evidence leads to a very different deduction. The French army paved the way for its own defeat because it failed to adopt or develop a defensive technique suited to modern conditions.'[14]

The blitzkrieg had been Part One, or Lesson One, of Liddell Hart's theory, and Part Two, or Lesson Two, was the antidote to the blitzkrieg. Lesson Two was that, all things being more or less equal, the defence would be stronger than the attack by a ratio of at least three to one. Lesson One had been demonstrated to the world in a dramatic manner with the astounding German defeat of France, but Lesson Two was never shown in the same forcible way. First impressions have a way of creating lasting images. If the Allies had turned the tables in 1940, as was possible, then it would have been an entirely different story. None the less, the truth of Lesson Two was amply demonstrated in the latter stages of the Second World War and the Korean War. Liddell Hart had presented both parts of his theory before the Second World War, but it was rejected by the military and political establishment in Britain and France. Indeed, there was a general inability to distinguish clearly between the two ideas and it was not until 1960 that the essence of Lesson Two began to make a small impact upon Western thinking. In the aftermath of the fall of France, Liddell Hart's theory was severely criticized and the charge was made that the acceptance of his ideas was largely the cause of the Allied defeat. It was true that his ideas were chiefly responsible for the defeat of France, but not in the way the critics meant. The Germans had accepted Liddell Hart's ideas – at least a few key people had – and the Allies had not. Hanson Baldwin, the military editor of the *New York Times*, in a book entitled *United We Stand,* attacked Liddell Hart's '. . . mistaken theory of "limited liability"' as one of the major causes for the fall of France.[15]

The same theme was presented in an article entitled 'Maginot and Liddell Hart' by Irving M. Gibson (a pseudonym) in the volume *Makers of Modern Strategy.* Gibson made it quite clear in this piece that he thought it was the influence of Liddell Hart upon the Allies which paved the way for the disaster of Dunkirk. It was not the quality of the BEF which was the major error, according to Gibson, but its size. He wrote:

> On October 25, 26 and 27, 1937, Liddell Hart, as military correspondent of *The Times*, published three articles which suggested that Britain should definitely accept the theory of limited liability in her military obligations and return to her traditional policy of blockade and economic warfare, for which she was eminently suited by her mighty navy and the unlimited resources of her empire. With respect to the Continent, he favoured a strictly defensive strategy because it was more suitable to the British temperament, and because in view of the great superiority of defence over attack, it would bring better results in the long run. Only a small expeditionary force should be sent to France and, since the Maginot Line with its French garrison would hold the enemy, the British force should be kept in the rear as a strategic reserve of high mobility.[16]

The key clause in this quotation is the last. Gibson claimed that a huge BEF should have been sent to France, and that the failure to do so was the real error. How mistaken! If Gamelin had had a strategic reserve of high mobility, as Liddell Hart suggested, then it could quickly have moved into the gap between the German Panzers and their slower infantry. Slow-moving Allied infantry divisions could not have done this and the French had an abundance of these divisions. They proved useless; speed, not size, was the essential element.

There is no doubt that the idea that mobility could have made the defence stronger than the attack was hard for the soldier to comprehend. The theory behind the idea was that the increasing technical developments over the past two or three hundred years were providing military forces with more and more power which was an overall advantage to the defence. It meant that progressively fewer and fewer troops were needed to hold a line or a position. Light-weight weapons together with increased fire-power had made it exceedingly difficult for an attack to succeed. Machine guns had made the frontal attack almost suicide. Heavy artillery with tremendous fire-power could wipe out such hornets' nests, but an enemy had time to prepare defensive positions further back. Moreover, this artillery fire tore up the ground to such an extent that it was difficult for the attack to move forward quickly. The tank, together with the aeroplane, emerged as a solution for the attack. They formed a potential team of mobile artillery immune to the withering fire of machine guns and stationary artillery. None the less, even this had its Achilles' heel, since once these forces were committed to a drive they were dependent upon 'soft troops' for support on the flanks. An enemy could strike at the flanks of the blitzkrieg with a counter-blitzkrieg of his own and pinch off the attack. This happened repeatedly in the later stages of the war. Mobility based upon the internal combustion engine meant that an attacking force could quickly mount an assault, but conversely the defending troops could swiftly move forces so as to threaten the attackers.

One major obstacle in accepting Liddell Hart's theory of the superiority of defence over attack was that such an idea went against the prejudices of the military mind. Wars could only be won by an attack. To go into battle or war on the assumption that the defence was stronger than the attack seemed very much akin to admitting a defeatist or lethargic attitude. The basis for Liddell Hart's accent on defence, at that time, according to his own writings, was that, after the Germans had obtained control over the Skoda armament works in Czechoslovakia, the balance of power had shifted to Germany. He stated that the war preparations of the Allies were so far behind those of Germany 'that there was not a ghost of a chance of being capable of carrying out an effective offence if war came early . . .'[17] There was, however, the possibility of creating an effective mobile defence. The course of the war illustrated quite clearly the power of the defence over the attack and it was used later on when an opponent would be deliberately induced into attacking first.

On the Eastern front during the Second World War both sides used the defence–offence gambit. A classic example is the Battle of Stalingrad. Hitler had put in the bulk of his reserves in a desperate frontal struggle for that city under the mistaken impression that Stalin would be forced to do the same. However, Stalin was busy building a reserve army to strike at the flank of the German position held by the Italian, Rumanian and Hungarian troops. Many of the German generals thought that such a blow was inevitable, but they were unable to convince Hitler. Meanwhile Stalin '. . . was building a strategic reserve, and utterly insensitive to the desperate cries for reinforcements that came from the hard-pressed commanders in the field. "No matter how they cry and complain," he instructed his Chief of Staff, "don't promise them any reserves. Don't give them a single battalion from the Moscow front."'[18]

In the aftermath of this battle the Germans quickly turned the tables in a similar manner, by a riposte made by Manstein in the wake of the Russian drive after cutting off Stalingrad, which had overextended itself in the same manner that the Germans had done. Thus the Russians fell into the same trap. Using an indirect approach Manstein was able to defeat a much larger force. The success of this attack led him to suggest its use on a broader scale and in a more calculated way. The idea was to use an elastic defence, allowing the Russians to attack while preparing for a counter-attack to be delivered at the opportune moment. Manstein wrote about this idea:

Even in 1943 there was good reason to reckon a favourable prospect from a change-over to defence in a mobile form. Experience had shown that, on the defensive, the Germans could count on inflicting losses on the attacking Russians out of all proportions to their own casualties. The consensus of opinion among German strategists was that, by carrying out a well-designed plan of elastic defence, they could wear down Russia's strength and her will to continue the war. It might even be possible to gain an opportunity for a counterstroke that would radically change the situation.[19]

This was a realistic approach, considering the growing disparity between the strengths of Russia and Germany. As Russia recovered from the initial blows, the balance of force was shifting from the Germans. They had failed to knock out Russia with their offensive strength, and the changing balance demanded a more calculated plan. However, Hitler refused to give up the idea of the immediate attack. The Manstein approach was exactly the course which Liddell Hart had suggested for the Allies in the pre-war period.

In the post-war era, Liddell Hart interviewed a number of the German generals and wrote:

... it should have been clear to any thoughtful analyst by 1943 that modern defence was stronger than the attack *pari passu* wherever there was 'no room for manoeuvre' ... Before the war I suggested that an attacker needed a superiority of 3 to 1 for success against a front where manoeuvre was cramped. General Heinrici – who commanded the German 4th Army in Russia, and later conducted the Battles of the Oder and Berlin – has expressed the conclusion that a 3 to 1 ratio underestimates the superiority of the defence over attack on such fronts, rather than overestimates it. In the light of experience in the Russian campaign he said that an attacker needs odds of at least 6 to 1 against any well-knit defence that has a reasonable front to cover. He cited examples where the defence held out against odds more than double that figure.[20]

It should be obvious that these lessons of the Second World War are very relevant for the present and future. The Western Allies could have taken some comfort in the knowledge that the defence in modern warfare is superior to the attack. Professor Bottome, as previously noted, entirely dismissed the evidence and authority of Liddell Hart's analyses, but he cites no evidence or authority in support of his own belief in the efficacy of a Russian blitzkrieg.[21] Bottome is representative of others who think not only that the West is inferior in conventional strength to the Russians in Europe, but that Western armies could never hold their own against the Red Army. He wrote: 'Officially, NATO was formed in 1949, and its initial military goals were the establishment of 20–22 divisions. But no amount of *feasible* rearmament could have protected Western Europe against a conventional attack if the Soviet Union had launched one'.[22] This is an *idée fixe* – an unshakable belief that 'the Castle always has the advantage'. It is a mental outlook on the world shaped in the Cold War.

If Liddell Hart's Lesson Two on the strength of the defence over the attack is valid, then it has great significance for NATO, and it also undermines one of the central points of the Heartland theory. It means that it would be extremely difficult for the Russians to overrun Western Europe, provided the West had the force and the will to fight. Nor would it be easy for any World Island power to conquer a large portion of the central land mass. The emergence of China as a power independent of Russia underlines this basic fact, for it would be very difficult for the Russians to defeat the Chinese. Moreover, the success of guerrilla warfare in Vietnam against a great power has illustrated that small countries can hope to hold their own against larger states. The bipolar world of the 1950s has given way to a much more complex system of nations; it has been realized that nuclear arms have little political meaning and the defensive power of land armies has repeatedly been demonstrated. This provides a measure of reassurance for the future.

Notes to Chapter 5

1. The extent and significance of the Allied intervention against the Bolsheviks has become apparent now that the British records are publicly available. On this matter, see Peter Sedgwick's introduction

to Serge, Victor, *Year One of the Revolution*, Allen Lane, The Penguin Press, 1972.

2. The ideas of Mackinder, which had been of great interest in the United States in the 1940s, brought out the analogy between the blitzkrieg – the mobile striking force of tanks and aircraft – and the Mongol horsemen of Genghis Khan who had swept to the gates of Europe in the twelfth century. The hoary fear of the 'yellow peril' emerged in a new form. It was believed that the Russians had fantastic reserves of manpower (frequently described as 'hordes' even in serious journals) despite their enormous losses – 20 million dead in the struggle with Germany. The American newspaper magnate William Randolph Hearst had for years been conditioning the public to fear of the 'Asiatic hordes', and to many the Russians seemed to be Oriental or Mongolian.

The belief that the Russians, after the defeat of Nazi Germany, could easily have penetrated much further into Europe ignores the military realities. Marshal Zhukov admitted the difficulty, and in fact the impossibility, of this action. Chester Wilmot wrote: 'In its summer offensive the Red Army had suffered such losses that by October Zhukov at any rate feared he had reached the limit of his westward advance. After the war Zhukov admitted: "When we reached Warsaw, we could not see how we could get beyond the Vistula unless the German forces on our front were considerably weakened."' (*The Struggle for Europe*, Collins, 1965, p. 630).

Isaac Deutscher commented on the West's fear of Russia: 'And this nation which had lost 20 million men dead alone – and only think how many of the 31 million that were left alive were the cripples and invalids and the wounded of the world war and how many were the old-aged – this nation with so tremendous, so huge a deficit in its population, this nation, of which a whole generation was lost, this nation was supposed to threaten Europe with an invasion!' *Containment and Revolution*, Edited by David Horowitz, Beacon Press, Boston, 1967, p. 14.

'Not since the seventeenth century had a war in Europe been fought so ferociously and caused so much destruction,' writes Walter Laqueur (*Europe since Hitler*, Weidenfeld & Nicolson, 1970, p. 166). It is worth noting the scale of destruction suffered by the peoples of Eastern Europe during the Second World War; according to Laqueur, Poland had lost twenty per cent of its total population, and Yugoslavia ten per cent. Britain and France suffered less in loss of lives than during the previous world war, but the total ravages in Europe were far greater.

3. Bottome, Edgar A., *The Balance of Terror*, Beacon Press, Boston, 1971, pp. 101–2.

4. ibid., p. 99.

5. Fuller, J. F. C., *The Second World War*, Eyre & Spottiswoode, 1948, p. 83. De Gaulle said of Gamelin, the Allied CIC, 'There he was, in a setting which suggested a convent, attended by a few officers, working and meditating without mixing in day-to-day affairs. He left General Georges to command the North-Eastern Front – an arrangement which might work as long as nothing was happening, but which would certainly become untenable if battle were joined . . . In his ivory tower at Vincennes, General Gamelin gave me the impression of a savant, testing the chemical reactions of his strategy in a laboratory' (*War Memoirs*, Vol. 1, *The Call to Honour 1940–1942*, Collins, 1955, pp. 39–40).

Regarding the relative strength of French and German land forces at the outbreak of war, General Heinz Guderian wrote: 'France possessed the strongest land army in Western Europe. France possessed the numerically strongest tank force in Western Europe.

'The combined Anglo-French forces in the West in May 1940 disposed of some 4,000 armoured vehicles; the German Army at that time had 2,800, including armoured reconnaissance cars, and when the attack was launched only 2,200 of these were available for the operation. We thus faced superiority in numbers, to which was added the fact that the French tanks were superior to the German ones in armour and in gun-calibre, though admittedly inferior in control facilities and in speed. Despite possessing the strongest forces for mobile warfare the French had also built the strongest line of fortifications in the world, the Maginot Line. Why was the money spent on the construction of those fortifications not used for the modernization and strengthening of France's mobile forces?' (*Panzer Leader*, Michael Joseph, 1952, p. 94).

6. Guderian, Heinz, op. cit., p. 92. Guderian noted: 'Now I had the opportunity to prepare them for their hard task ahead, in whose successful outcome nobody at that time actually believed, with the exception of Hitler, Manstein and myself. The struggle to get our ideas accepted had proved exhausting in the extreme' (p. 91). The orthodox procedure when meeting a river barrier was to halt and wait for a build-up of force before attempting a crossing. Therefore, the French High Command, still thinking in terms of the 1914 time-schedule, thought they had ample time to bring up reinforcements. This was a reaction made by Churchill as recorded in his writings. He excused himself by stating, 'Not having had access to official information for so many years, I did not comprehend the violence of the revolution effected by the incursion of a mass of fast-moving heavy armour.'

Fuller's acid comment on this was that State Papers were the last place to look for such knowledge. Nevertheless, Churchill admitted, 'I knew about it, but it had not altered my inward convictions as it should have done' (*The Second World War*, Vol. 2, *Their Finest Hour*, Cassell, 1949, p. 39). He knew about it from talks with both Fuller and Liddell Hart.

Guderian was also aware that the French would not move as long as the German positions were fluid; safety was therefore in movement. 'Also we were aware of the existence of a French reserve army, some eight infantry divisions strong, which was being set up in the Paris area. We did not imagine that General Frère would advance against us so long as we kept on moving ourselves. According to basic French formula, he would wait until he had exact information about his enemy's position before doing anything. So we had to keep him guessing: this could best be done by continuing to push on' (op. cit., p. 111).

7. Goutard, Adolphe, *Battle of France: 1940*, Washburn, New York, 1960, p. 200.

8. Fuller, J. F. C., *The Conduct of War 1789–1961*, Eyre & Spottiswoode, 1961, p. 256. Liddell Hart has called this the strategy of the indirect approach which strikes at the nerves of an enemy. In an interview in 1960, Liddell Hart stated: 'Some 35 years ago I made an analysis of all the wars of history when I was military editor of the *Encyclopedia Britannica*. During that investigation the impression became increasingly strong that throughout all history, effective results in war have rarely been attained unless the approach has such indirectness as to assure that the opponent is unready to meet it. Now that indirectness of approach has usually been physical – but it's always psychological. In strategy the longest way around is often the shortest way home. More and more clearly does the lesson emerge that a direct approach to one's objective tends to produce negative results because it's the line of natural expectation for the enemy. You've got to throw him off balance. That is the objective of indirect approach' (Walters, Robert, 'Interview with Captain Liddell Hart', *Marine Corps Gazette*, November 1961). In an answer to another question he provided this insight into the blitzkrieg. 'The secret, as I defined it years ago, lies partly in the tactical combination of tanks and aircraft, partly in the unexpectedness of the stroke in direction and time, but above all in the follow-through – the exploitation of a tactical breakthrough into a deep strategic penetration carried out by armoured forces operating ahead of the main army. The pace of such forces, as I always emphasized, promised a decisively deep penetration so long as it could be kept up. It's that persistent pace, coupled with the variability

of the thrust point, that paralyses the opponent. In every stage after the original break-through, the flexible drive of armoured forces carries simultaneous alternative threats. The threat that actually develops into a thrust takes place too quickly for the enemy reserves to reach the spot in time to stiffen the resistance before it collapses. In effect, both strategic and tactical surprise are maintained from start to finish.'

An anonymous British staff officer's diary was found later and published after the war. It recorded on 19 May: 'News that the Panzers are in Amiens. This is like some ridiculous nightmare ... The Germans have taken every risk – criminally foolish risks – and they have got away with it ... The French General Staff have been paralysed by this unorthodox war of movement. The fluid conditions prevailing are not dealt with in the textbooks and the 1914 brains of the French Generals responsible for formulating the plans are incapable of functioning in this new and astonishing lay-out' (*The Diary of a Staff Officer*, Methuen, 1941, pp. 26–7).

9. Guderian wrote: 'I never received any further orders as to what I was to do once the bridgehead over the Meuse was captured. All my decisions, until I reached the Atlantic seaboard at Abbeville, were taken by me and me alone. The Supreme Command's influence on my actions was merely restrictive throughout' (op. cit., p. 92).

10. Goutard, op. cit., p. 200.

11. ibid., p. 202.

12. ibid., p. 206. This statement is particularly striking since the German defeat of France gave the Wehrmacht an illusion of invincibility which it did not lose until the Russian campaign. Guderian wrote of the Battle of France and of the forthcoming invasion of Russia: 'As one of the uninitiated, I could only now hope that Hitler was not planning an attack on the Soviet Union, and that these preparations were a bluff. The winter and spring of 1941 passed as in a nightmare ... it also became increasingly plain to see how inadequate were our preparations for so enormous an undertaking. Our success to date, however, and in particular the surprising speed of our victory in the West, had so befuddled the minds of our supreme commanders that they had eliminated the word "impossible" from their vocabulary. All the men of the OKW and OKH with whom I spoke evinced an unshakable optimism and were quite impervious to criticism or objection' (op. cit., pp. 142–3). Guderian was one of the very few people outside Russia who foresaw that the Russians would have not only a great numerical superiority in tanks, but also a technical superiority in tank designs.

13. Goutard, op. cit., p. 206. An unfortunate and curious set of

circumstances brought ruin to the French efforts to save the day. General Weygand, who had replaced Gamelin, thought it possible to close the gap between the Panzers and the German infantry. He flew to Belgium to tell the various commanders their precise roles and, in particular, to see Lord Gort, the British commander, who was understandably beginning to have doubts about the French High Command. The message to Gort was delayed and Weygand, after first deciding to spend the night there in order to see Gort, reversed his decision at the last moment and boarded a French destroyer which landed him at Cherbourg the next morning. Weygand left at 6 p.m. and Gort arrived at 8 p.m. to find that the French CIC had abruptly left by ship. Gort was left in the air with the impression that events were beyond hope since Weygand had departed so quickly. To make matters worse, the French commander whom Weygand had told to give the message to Gort was immediately involved in a fatal road accident. He had no papers with him to tell what Weygand had in mind, so Gort's only recourse was to try to save his army, which miraculously he did at Dunkirk.

14. Liddell Hart, B. H., *Dynamic Defence*, Faber, 1940, pp. 16–17. Liddell Hart observed later: 'As Guderian stated, in his war memoirs and elsewhere, that he owed his success largely to applying my ideas of tank strategy and tactics – describing himself as my "disciple and pupil" – I have particularly good reason to gauge how this fatal thrust could have been checked. Having thought out the new method of attack in the nineteen-twenties, it did not require any great effort to discover the antidote well before 1940. It was hard, however, to get it understood by generals who were still thinking in terms of 1918. By 1942 all armies had learned how to check a *Blitzkrieg* attack – but a lot would have been saved if Hitler's opponents had learned before the war' (*The Liddell Hart Memoirs*, Cassell, 1965, Vol. II, p. 281).

In the November 1961 issue of the *Marine Corps Gazette*, he said that the German drive through France could easily have been stopped, 'If the defence had been conducted by anyone who understood the new technique of attack . . . Unfortunately the defence was conducted in 1940 by the French but with leaders who didn't understand this technique at all, who were always moving 24 hours too late or more. Winston Churchill, as well as the French military chiefs, was still living in the past . . . Now, during those pre-war years, Churchill had a number of talks with Fuller and myself, so there's no reason he should not have understood it, except he was so governed by tradition and the traditionalists.'

15. Baldwin, Hanson W., *Defence of the Western World*, Hutchinson,

1941, p. 11. Before the actual attack on France much was written on the supposed superiority of the Allied armies, in amazing contrast to what followed. After the fall of France the illusion grew that the Allied forces were somehow unprepared or did not have proper equipment. John F. Kennedy wrote his famous book *Why England Slept* (Hutchinson, 1940) in the aftermath and stated: 'Why was England so poorly prepared for the war? This question has been asked again and again in America as we watched Hitler's mechanized juggernaut churn into Holland and Belgium, and on towards Paris. Always the emphasis, in the accounts of German victory, has been on the tremendous superiority of the German in armoured equipment' (p. xxvii). This is, of course, all nonsense. It was not lack of equipment but lack of modern ideas that weighted the balance against the Allies.

16. Gibson, Irving M., 'Maginot and Liddell Hart', in *Makers of Modern Strategy*, ed. Earle, Edward, Princeton University Press, 1943, p. 381.

17. Letter from Liddell Hart to Professor John Kovac (Irving Gibson). Liddell Hart wrote: 'So much of the controversy about attack and defence is superficial. There is a very common failure to realize that the choice between offensive and defensive is essentially determined by conditions of relative national strength. Defence is always inevitable where conditions do not afford a chance of winning a war, but only frustrating the enemy's success. But while it is obvious that defence *may* lead to sluggishness, it is untrue to argue it *must*.

'When the Greeks fought the Persians they were bound to be on the defensive, but that did not make them inactive or irresolute. When Elizabethan England faced the great power of Spain she was also bound to be on the defensive, that did not make her "drift into a lethargic attitude of passive defence". Could anything have been less lethargic than Drake?' (ibid.).

18. Deutscher, Isaac, *Stalin*, Oxford University Press, 1949, p. 483.

19. Manstein, Erich von, *Lost Victories*, Methuen, 1958, p. 443.

20. Liddell Hart, B. H., *The Other Side of the Hill*, Cassell, 1948, p. 324.

21. The Korean War had also demonstrated the validity of Liddell Hart's thesis. In the early stages of the war, North Korean forces almost overran the whole of Southern Korea, but a masterful defensive action by scratch British and American troops prevented this from happening. David Rees, in his book *Korea: The Limited War* (Macmillan, 1964), wrote: 'By then it had become apparent that Walker had won the perimeter battles; the performance of this master of the defensive strategy is an excellent contemporary illustration of the thesis

... advanced by B. H. Liddell Hart in *Deterrent or Defence* that the power of the defence in modern war is increasing. The four US divisions which had defended the Naktong had at different times held fantastic frontages varying from between twenty to forty miles, while the British Brigade south of Waegwam with under 2000 men, were holding an "immense" front of 18,000 yards, over 10 miles' (p. 53). However, just the opposite conclusion was drawn from this war by Western military and political leaders. It was thought that tactical nuclear arms would be necessary to prevent repetitions of the Korean type wars. Unfortunately this has been a belief which has persisted.

22. Bottome, op. cit., p. 26. It is a view which has made tactical nuclear arms necessary for NATO. Despite the evidence that it would be possible to maintain in Europe conventional forces sufficient to deter any aggressive Russian move, the initial impressions of the Soviet Union's strategic superiority on account of its geopolitical position and of its greater land forces has stuck in the minds of Western military planners. A leading article in the *Guardian* of 23 February 1972 stated: 'It is true that the Warsaw Pact forces could tomorrow invade Europe and cross the Rhine at the drop of a hat,' though it did add that nobody in the Kremlin is likely to drop his hat. The wargames conducted by NATO are often based on the most adverse assumptions. What constitutes an adequate and realistic level and disposition of NATO forces, relative to Warsaw Pact forces, is a detailed consideration (and at least the question has now been opened out into a matter of current controversy among military authorities); the essential point to be recognized is that it comes within the capability NATO could plan to deploy in conventional forces. NATO thinking has been distorted by an unfounded pessimism regarding Europe, and it has neglected the vulnerability of the Soviet Union in other respects. It has also not related the theoretical military capability of the Soviet Union to any realistic political intentions of the Soviet leadership. Nor has it understood that conventional forces could both provide defence and, in some circumstances, be used flexibly as an instrument of policy; whereas the role of tactical nuclear weapons must be more that of deterrence than of defence, and is of no use as an instrument of policy except in a situation of large-scale and devastating war. (Even a year later, the *Guardian* (17 January 1973) was still discussing the question of a nuclear deterrent for NATO in a leading article, saying that the question for Western Europe of creating or not creating one of its own will become urgent as the Americans lower their commitments in Europe. 'The American nuclear guarantee underpins the whole of NATO's strategy.')

6. The Crossroads of the World

> The importance, absolute and relative, of
> portions of the earth's surface, and their
> consequent interest to mankind vary from time
> to time.
>
> Captain A. T. Mahan

The World Island, according to Mackinder, consists of the three joint continents of Europe, Asia and Africa. The distinction between Europe and Asia is not clearly demarcated by a natural boundary. Geographically, Africa is easily distinguished; it is separated from Europe by the Mediterranean Sea and from Asia by the Red Sea, but the narrow strip of land between Egypt and the Sinai Peninsula joins it to the Middle East. It is in the Middle East that the three continents effectively meet. It is from this centre that the expanses of the World Island radiate.

Historically the importance of the Middle East is difficult to overstate. Western civilization grew up around the shores of the Mediterranean Sea and it was through the Middle East that East and West met. It was the passageway between the three continents. The great overland trade routes passed through this region to provide tenuous commercial and cultural contact. It became the global crossroads, and it was natural that it should be looked upon as the centre of the world. This is how Mackinder saw the Middle East:

In a monkish map, contemporary with the Crusades, which still hangs in Hereford Cathedral, Jerusalem is marked as at the geometrical centre, the navel of the world, and on the floor of the Church of the Holy Sepulchre at Jerusalem they will show you to this day the precise spot which is the centre. If our study of the geographical realities, as we know them in their completeness, is leading us to right conclusions, the medieval ecclesiastics were not far wrong. If the World-Island be inevitably the principal seat of humanity on the Globe, and if Arabia, as the passage-land from Europe to the Indies and from the Northern Heartland to the Southern Heartland, be central in the World-Island, then the hill citadel of Jerusalem has a strategic position with reference to world-realities not differing essentially from its ideal position in the perspective of the Middle Ages, or its strategic position between ancient Babylon and Egypt.[1]

Mackinder looked upon the Middle East as the strategic axis of the World Island. 'As the War has shown,' he wrote, 'the Suez Canal carries the rich traffic between the Indies and Europe to within striking distance of an army based upon Palestine . . . It cannot be wholly a coincidence that in the self-same region should be the starting point of History and the crossing point of the most vital of modern highways.'[2] At the turn of the century and for many years afterwards the Mediterranean Sea and the Suez Canal represented the vital lifeline upon which Britain depended. It was assumed that if this could be cut the British Isles could be starved into submission. Moreover, there was historical evidence which seemed to support the importance of the Middle East. The idea has recurred throughout Western civilization, in ancient and modern times, that for any great empire to succeed it must conquer Egypt. It was therefore tempting to make sweeping generalizations about the importance of the Middle East.[3]

The Middle East is the only land passageway between Europe and Africa or between Asia and Africa. Man since time immemorial had been landbound, or when in ships forced to hug the coastline. This changed when the galley ship was succeeded by the sailing ship, which could range out far from land. Historical analogy can be a deceptive snare. The real significance of the Middle East is linked with the dominant mode of transport of an age. Sir John Glubb wrote of the transition which took place in the late Middle Ages:

In 1492 Columbus discovered America and five years later, in 1497, Vasco da Gama sailed around the Cape of Good Hope. All of a sudden, within five years, Europe which had been blockaded for 600 years found the oceans of the world open to her. Not only so, but the Europeans quickly nipped around the Cape of Good Hope and obtained naval command of the Indian Ocean – first the Portuguese, then the Dutch and afterwards the English. And from the Indian Ocean they sailed back up the Red Sea, and whereas the holders of

Egypt had always enjoyed all the free commerce with the East, Egypt and the Muslim countries found themselves in turn blockaded so that they couldn't trade, and this put the whole situation into reverse. The Dark Ages of Europe came to an end, and the Dark Ages of the Middle East began.[4]

So when the sailing ship came into use, the Middle East declined in relative importance. It was no longer the crossroads of the world. Although the Muslim countries had built a rich and varied culture, they became the backwater of the world.

In the latter part of the nineteenth century technical events occurred which gave the Middle East more importance than it had had in the preceding centuries. There were two major developments. The first of these was the coming of the steam ship, which unlike the sailing vessels had a limited range. The sailing ship had almost no limitations, depending only on the winds for motive power and on the endurance of the seamen themselves. The steam ship, however, needed a chain of fuelling stations and the corresponding need for shorter routes was evident. It was this new type of limited-endurance ships which gave the impetus for building the Suez Canal and later the Panama Canal; engineering skills had also advanced to a point when such enterprises were possible. This made the Middle East once again a vital route on the world map.

A second development was the discovery of large amounts of oil in the Middle East. At the time when Mackinder wrote, the internal combustion engine had just been developed. Oil was gradually to replace coal as the method of propulsion for ships in the coming years. This created an economic interest in the Middle East for Western industrialized countries, which has grown enormously and is still increasing.

But it was the supposed strategic importance of the Middle East because of inherent geopolitical factors which prompted Mackinder to give so much attention to this region. He wrote: 'In short, a great military power in possession of the Heartland and of Arabia could take easy possession of the crossroads of the world at Suez. Sea-power would have found it very difficult to hold the Canal if a fleet of submarines had from the beginning of the war been based on the Black Sea'.[5] This view of the importance of the Middle East was based upon the situation in 1919, but technological developments made it invalid for a later period. None the less, the strategic significance of this region was accepted as a fact until as recently as 1967, when the Suez Canal was closed.

In the course of the Arab–Israeli War of 1967, the Israelis overran the Sinai Peninsula and the Suez Canal became the front line separating the Egyptians and the Israelis. The Suez Canal was naturally closed. The route through the Mediterranean Sea and the Suez Canal had been looked upon as a vital Western communication line, especially with regard to oil – the most important energy source for modern industrial society. Just as the war machines in the Second World War depended upon a constant supply of oil, so the industrial machine needs this fuel in huge quantities. Until the time that the Suez Canal was closed it was thought that this waterway was crucial for the Western economies; however, the experts were surprised, for the closure had very little adverse effect upon the West. (Quite possibly the Egyptians also thought that the closing of the Suez Canal would be disadvantageous to the West, in which case they would have had an ideal means of putting pressure upon the Western countries to force them into a more neutral position regarding the Arab–Israeli conflict. If this was the Egyptian hope, then it was badly in error. The Canal has been closed for six years with no great harm to the Western economies; on the other hand it has had a great effect upon the more fragile Egyptian economy and forced them to become more dependent upon the Russians.)

By another twist, the introduction of oil for modern steam ships has made them less dependent upon using the Suez Canal. Oil-fired ships operate more economically than coal-fired ships and this has increased their range; moreover, super-tankers have been developed which when loaded cannot even pass through the canal. The tolls for using the canal itself had been rising because of maintenance costs and the enlargement of the locks for larger ships. The progressive increases of tolls seemed to be fighting a losing battle in trying to maintain the canal's commerce. The closing of the canal has telescoped into a few years what would have happened anyway over a longer period; the economic trends in shipping have led to the building of super-container ships as well as super-tankers. Several pipelines have been built which by-pass the Suez Canal. There have been discoveries of oil in other regions of the world. The importance of the Suez Canal as a great sea crossroads has been diminishing, and even if it were soon to be reopened, its place would continue to decline. The importance of the Middle East is not absolute, but is dependent upon the technology of any particular era.

However, there are certain more limited reasons which have given the Middle East a genuine importance today – especially for the United States and Russia. The first is, of course, the vast oil reserves of this region. Another is the Arab–Israeli conflict, which has involved Russian and American interests. A third substantial reason for the importance of the Middle East today is that historically the Russians have always had an interest in finding open access to the oceans of the world. As can readily be noted, there are conflicting interests.

The Middle East is an essential source of oil for modern industrial states; Japan and Europe, in particular, are dependent upon it for the greatest part of their energy supply, and will be for some years to come. Enormous strikes of oil have occurred in the North Sea; other sources of oil are being opened up, notably in the Arctic, and nuclear reactors are an increasingly important means of power. The Western countries are aware of the need to forestall the threat of being held to ransom by Arab oil-producing states. But, on the other side of the equation, the consumption of oil is rising at a critical rate; the United States is now importing larger quantities each year, and on present predictions imports will rise to about half of its annual requirements by the early 1980s. By then, the Soviet Union too may be short of oil; though it is currently increasing output by about 30 million tons a year, there are also increasing production costs, and it is estimated that there will still be a substantial deficit in supply within the decade. The additional needs of both powers will have to be met mainly from the Middle East, unless there are some new developments which transform the present state of the world's energy supplies. In the short and medium term, the Middle East is likely to continue to have considerable economic importance on account of its oil.

Since this oil is so important to the Western powers, it is a potentially vulnerable point; if the supply were to be stopped, the wheels of Western industry would run down. In the immediate future, control of Middle Eastern oil supplies will be politically significant, and obviously the play of power and influence will be much more fluid and complex than it was in the past when the West had a virtual monopoly of these assets. The oil-producing nations of the Middle East have now joined together to bargain over the price of oil and for more control over the operations; in some instances Western-owned enterprises have been nationalized in a way which amounts to simple seizure of the oil companies' assets. The Arab nations themselves naturally do not want to halt the flow of oil, since they receive a substantial income from its sale. But the emotional consideration of the Arab–Israeli struggle could have more influence in the future. Egypt has in the past favoured the use of some form of economic warfare against the Western nations in order to put pressure on them (chiefly the United States) to withhold aid from Israel. Since Egypt had no oil to sell she could afford to suggest such a course. The Arab oil-producing states, such as Saudi Arabia, help Egypt financially in the conflict with Israel. These oil-producing countries have in the past been more pro-American than pro-Russian, but this position could change. Iraq was the first Middle Eastern country in which the Russians took over some of the operating functions in the oil industry which were previously performed by Western companies, and there are indications that it will not be the last. The policy of the United States has moved towards more open support of Israel, and this has alienated Arab opinion; in fact, the Americans have in general lost ground in the Middle East through their own ham-handedness. Now that it is apparent that the United States could face an energy crisis within the decade, American relations with the Arab countries are of growing importance to safeguard Middle East fuel supplies, and a settlement of the Arab–Israeli conflict is the most pressing issue for America in this region.

In the longer term, the economic importance of the Middle East seems bound to diminish. As oil resources are depleted, industrialized nations must make themselves no longer economically dependent upon oil. At the present rate of consumption, oil resources may be exhausted around the turn of the century, and the change to other technology for energy supplies must gain momentum from now on.[6] Frank McFadzean, the Chairman of Shell Transport and Trading, has remarked significantly that if he were running the British Government, he would go all out for nuclear power. While nuclear power provides a fairly straightforward alternative for generating electricity to be fed into a country's national grid, it offers no such ready conversion for the engine power of mobile vehicles. The implication of this is that radical changes in the whole transportation system are inevitable. One field of transportation for which nuclear power is certainly suited is shipping, and as the cost of oil mounts with diminishing supplies the nuclear-powered ship will become a dominant vehicle of commerce. Its strategic importance will be considered in the next chapter; the point to be noted here is that it looks as though the Middle East will again, sooner or later, become a backwater in the current of the world's affairs, without its former significance either as a crossroads or as owner of a key natural resource.[7]

The Arab–Israeli conflict has been a windfall for the Russians since it has allowed them to step into the Middle East with little difficulty.[8] In less than twenty years they have established a powerful influence in the region. Egypt was, of course, the main recipient of Russian aid and attention during most of this period, until Sadat's government reacted against what the Egyptians had begun to feel as a humiliating over-dependence upon the Russians. But the treaty of 1972 between the Soviet Union and Iraq seems to deliver to the Russians more than the relationship with Egypt could offer, including a prestigious entry into the Arab oil business and naval facilities in the Persian Gulf. Russian aid projects have multiplied impressively in the Arab world, which is a good indication of the importance they attach to gaining a strong position.

One of the principal long-term objectives of the Soviet Union in the Middle East is to obtain an outlet to the sea; this was an aim even in the days of the Tsars and it has remained unchanged. Undoubtedly the Russians would like to see the Suez Canal reopened. While it was open they made considerable use of it as a sea-link for shipping between the Black Sea ports and Asiatic Russia; the canal is also a valuable pathway for the Russian navy from the Black Sea into the Indian Ocean. It would be of great value to the Russians to have shore establishments for their naval and merchant fleets in the Indian Ocean, the Persian Gulf, and the Mediterranean, and they have already met with reasonable success in obtaining berthing facilities at several places from Arab host countries and base facilities in the Persian Gulf.

In recent years, the Russians have increased their naval presence in the Indian Ocean, and it is likely that there will be a substantial extension of Russian naval influence around the shores of the Arabian Sea. This might lead to some novel situations, such as the Russians being called upon by the oil-producing states to police an economic quarrel which might erupt, or in some circumstances even to the harassment of Western shipping.[9] Above all, in general terms, it is clear that a new outlet to the oceans of the world from the Middle East would be a great asset for the Soviet Union both strategically and commercially, and it is the more important as she is vigorously extending her maritime interests in every field.

Russia has been able to obtain increasing influence in the Middle East while the United States was bogged down and preoccupied with Vietnam. The Western powers, like Russia, have real interests in the Middle East, which they have mishandled in the short run, and the importance of which will decline in the long run. But the overall importance of the Middle East has been exaggerated by the Heartland theory; its present importance depends upon transient technological and political factors which are quite distinct from the inherent strategic importance which Mackinder attached to it because of its location.

The West has tacitly assumed that it is put on the defensive by the superior strategic position of the Soviet Union. The United States has felt obliged to counter constant threats or possible threats from the Heartland. It was outside their range of imagination that Russian threats in the Middle East might be neutralized by posing counter-threats to Russia at other points. It could be done by normalization of relations with China; this need not pose any direct threat, but the very existence of Chinese–Western accord could easily move into a further stage, if Russia became more aggressive. Previously this course was not thought possible because of the assumption that the Castle always had the advantage. As long as this was felt to be the case, the Heartland could act in a role which was far beyond its actual strength. The defensive strength of Russia was magnified out of all proportion through the lens of the Heartland theory. In fact, the Western powers, if they had been more perceptive, had a future which was in many ways more favourable than that of the Russians in maintaining relationships with the Arab countries. What has been needed in the West is a more subtle and more flexible approach, more realistic and therefore more effective. The crude assumptions made by the Western powers have lost them more ground than necessary in a situation in the Middle East that was neither as crucial or as permanent as they supposed.

Notes to Chapter 6

1. Mackinder, H. J., *Democratic Ideals and Reality*, Norton, New York, 1962, p. 89.
2. ibid., p. 89.
3. Napoleon made the remark, 'The great thing to remember is that Egypt is the most important country in the world.' His Egyptian campaign was intended to secure control of that country. The idea was to use Egypt as a base for sea power so that he could drive the British fleet and merchant ships out of the Indian Ocean. The theory was based upon sheer nonsense, as Nelson demonstrated in the Battle of the Nile. In order for Napoleon to hold Egypt he needed a superior fleet to control the Mediterranean – which would have been the lifeline from France to the Middle East. A navy must be concentrated in order to be strong enough to win a decision. Dividing the fleet between the Red Sea and the Mediterranean would merely have compounded the existing problem whereby France, because of her geographical position, had a fleet divided by the Atlantic and the Mediterranean.
4. Glubb, Sir John Bagot, 'The Middle East Situation', from *The Arab-Israeli Impasse*, ed. Khadduri, Majidia D., Robert B. Luce, Washington, D.C., 1968.
5. Mackinder, op. cit., p. 111.

6. If some of the gloomier forebodings of the conservation prophets come about, and the technological structure of modern society outruns all practicable sources of energy required to support it, then it will dramatically hasten the arrival of a shock period in warfare. Without accepting the assumptions of the more pessimistic of the informed predictions, it is still likely that we will reach a time when no country can afford the type of projectile warfare which the US waged in Vietnam.

7. The whole question of energy supplies is obviously going to be one of the crucial geopolitical considerations for the future. It has, of course, played a fundamental part in economic power since the time of the Industrial Revolution. But there has been a major shift in the economics of energy in relation to transportation and manufacturing industry in this century; formerly, industry necessarily grew around the location of fuel supplies, but now it is generally more advantageous to transport fuel supplies to the location of industry. Another basic transformation is now in prospect: whereas hitherto energy supplies have been easily able to meet the requirements of industrial growth, it is now possible a gap will develop between energy supply and demand. It is by no means certain how this gap will be bridged. Though there will be a great expansion in nuclear power, this may not take place fast enough to meet industrial requirements before oil supplies have run into a situation of acute shortage.

In the short run the fossil fuels, i.e. oil, natural gas and coal, will become very much more expensive; in the long run, they will be exhausted. Industry will be dependent upon other sources of power; nuclear fission power is likely to be superseded by nuclear fusion power, and other new energy technologies will eventually be developed, of which the most likely candidate at present is probably solar power (which would carry striking geopolitical corollaries).

The crucial period for the Middle East is the transitional phase, which we are just entering. For a time oil production will increase, but the price of oil will increase much faster; there will follow a period when oil production is diminishing and, of course, the price will increase further. During this transitional phase, the interests of the super-powers in the Middle East will be at their height. There are substantial grounds here for conflict. But, as the continuity and reliability of energy supplies is of concern to all, there are also grounds for accommodation and trying to ensure some stability in this oil-producing region. The Chinese, for political reasons, have moved into southern Arabia by means of economic and military aid, in competition with the Russians. It seems most unlikely that any super-power will be able to exercise a controlling influence throughout the Middle East and the Arab world. The Middle East states must attract a great deal of diplomatic attention from the competing super-powers. However, these powers are likely to have to do a good deal of bargaining among themselves in pursuance of their economic interests, and economic self-interest may lead to a balance of understanding, as it were, in Middle East affairs. The United States, relieved of the great diversion of Vietnam and having made some rapprochement with China, should be in a more favourable position to carry out a policy in the Middle East which will protect Western interests without conflicting with the intensely nationalistic interests of the states in the region.

8. The Arab forces, spearheaded by the Egyptians, have been defeated on three separate occasions by the efficient Israeli Army. The superficial analysis in the West is that Russia has lost ground in her support of the defeated side. Sir John Glubb has suggested another theory. 'After the destruction of the Egyptian army in Sinai, the British press expressed jubilation at the rebuff suffered by Russia, who had "backed the wrong horse". Unfortunately, the Soviet government are not quite so simple-minded as that. On the contrary, Russia may have been fully aware that the Egyptians would be disastrously defeated and wanted it that way.

'None of the Arab countries wished to become a Soviet satellite. They are, in some cases, willing to accept Russian subsidies, armament or technical assistance, but only up to a point. They will not go so far as to sacrifice any of their sovereignty.

'If Egypt had, by some wild chance, defeated Israel, her strength and prestige would have been so enhanced that she would have been less prepared than ever to be subservient to Russia. If, on the other hand, she were humiliated, she and her friends would realize that they were utterly incapable of standing up to Israel. In these circumstances, they would have no alternative but to beg for Russian help. It was, therefore, essential, under the Russian plan, that the Arabs should be defeated in as humiliating a fashion as possible' (*The Middle East Crisis*, Hodder & Stoughton, 1967, p. 12). Despite the fact that the Egyptians had outlawed the Communist Party, the Russians were not deterred in obtaining influence in that country. If Russian motives are guided by *realpolitik*, then obviously a strong, independent-minded Egypt is desirable. A number of US political writers, notably Joseph Alsop, have observed that the Russians want to destroy Israel. This is a crude analysis, and Glubb seems nearer to the truth. The very existence of Israel provides the rationale for Soviet entry into the Middle East without the use of overt force.

9. In an article attributed to a high Soviet official, published in July 1967 in *Le Nouvel Observateur*, it was stated: 'As for the Americans, we shall exploit to the utmost the blackmailing of their oil interests and navigations through the Suez Canal.' Russian naval ships and aircraft have in the past harassed the warships of Western navies, and it would be possible for them to do the same to merchant ships.

Admiral Elmo R. Zumwalt, Chief of Naval Operations for the United States Fleet, has been quoted as saying that one thousand tankers will be transporting oil to the United States by the mid eighties, and Victor Zorza has set beside this a broadcast by Moscow Radio referring to the large proportion of this oil which will be carried from the Middle East, and which pointedly commented: 'but the scale of the national liberation movement of the peoples of Asia and the Middle East is inflicting blows on the predatory plans of the American monopolists' (*Guardian*, 8 June 1972). The Russians might be in a position to cause some serious disruption by proxy, by encouraging appropriate subversion among the unstable régimes around the Persian Gulf. They would no doubt like a direct say in the control of the oil operations themselves, even as far as sharing in the profits. At the same time there are other factors, including Arab nationalism itself, the Muslim religion, and the volatility of Arab internal politics, which will make the fruits of Russian tactics in the Middle East uncertain.

Western shipping could be in a vulnerable position in other ways. Arab guerrillas have hi-jacked Western commercial aircraft. In the future this might also happen with Western shipping. Modern supertankers, in their trend towards automation, have very small crews and it would not be difficult for a small, well-armed boarding party to obtain control. One of the aspects of shock warfare, as opposed to projectile tactics, is that in the past it has led to capture of the enemy and property rather than mere destruction. One sees this trend beginning once again. The Arab world at one time abounded with pirates and the new guerrilla soldier is half a pirate.

7. The Undersea Ship

> The man who goes into action in a wooden ship
> is a fool, and the man who sends him there is a
> villain.
>
> Sir John Hay

It was Earl St Vincent who in 1804, as First Sea Lord, presented
the attitude of Britain towards the idea of a submarine. It is a
view which has persisted until the present day. The American
inventor Robert Fulton had journeyed to Europe in an attempt to
sell his version of a submarine ship. Lord St Vincent remarked,
'Pitt is the greatest fool that ever existed to encourage a mode of
war which those who command the sea do not want and which if
successful will deprive them of it.'

The idea of a submarine was not really practicable for many
years to come, until after the introduction of steel ships and the
internal combustion engine. When operable submarines were
eventually developed Britain, as the leading sea power, did
everything she could to outlaw or discourage their use. The submarine was considered as a denial of sea power or a means of
undermining control of the seas. The extreme dislike of the
submarine by seafaring countries was due to the fact that such
vessels were primarily suited to one role in warfare – commerce
raiding. It became the view of naval strategists that commerce
raiding would not be an effective form of warfare. This was a view
which was pragmatically more or less accepted by British seamen
throughout the rise of the Royal Navy. As the power of Britain
grew, so did her merchant fleet. Her ships dominated the trade
routes of the world and it was this commercial strength which
formed the backbone of her sea power. In the eyes of potential
enemies, this large merchant fleet was a tempting target, and
commerce raiding seemed the ideal way to defeat England. This
was in fact quite mistaken.[1]

Commerce raiding has always been a method favoured by the
weaker naval power. It was a very attractive form of warfare,

especially in the days of sailing ships when the object was not so much to destroy enemy ships as to capture them. The capture of these ships, which were called prizes, enabled seamen of all ranks to reap a handsome profit from naval actions. All hands shared in the profits from selling the cargo and the ship itself, with the higher-ranking officers getting the lion's share. It was tempting to be deluded into believing that this could be a major means of defeating an enemy, for it meant attacking unarmed or easily defeated ships, and also meant that cruising would be of short duration so that the seamen could enjoy the fruits of their victory ashore.

The object of the major sea power, on the other hand, was to seek out and destroy the opposing fleet. In contrast to land warfare, it was impossible to take advantage of terrain. One spot on the ocean was much like any other, although it was advantageous to fight nearer to one's home base. There were no mountains, rivers, woods or other features which a navy could use to fight defensive battles like an army. The only purpose in having a fleet was in having a superior one and it was necessary to concentrate this fleet, or ensure that it could easily be brought together, in order to destroy the opposing navy. This, according to Mahan and others, was the chief aim of a fleet. Other action, such as commerce raiding, detracted from this concentration of effort.

The conventional submarine was a very unsatisfactory ship, on account of its means of propulsion. It had two separate power systems – one for the surface and the other for underwater movement. On the surface, petrol engines were first used, but the danger of accidents caused them to be replaced by diesel engines. For the underseas, storage batteries were used and the undersea performance was far inferior to that achieved on the surface. In the latter stages of the Second World War the Germans made many improvements to overcome these liabilities, but these developments came too late to have any influence upon the war. They were soon overshadowed by the development of nuclear propulsion in the 1950s.

The fact that the submarine had two power plants meant that it could carry very little cargo. Every inch was taken up with equipment and necessary machinery. In the early submarines crews had to sleep on the machinery itself. The underwater speed of these submarines was very low – about 7 to 10 knots – and even so a submarine could only maintain these 'top' speeds for a few hours. On the surface, they could reach speeds of between 14 and 24 knots. The conventional ship was really a surface ship which had the ability to go below the surface to relatively shallow depths and only for short periods of time. Nevertheless, such ships proved to be very dangerous weapons in capable hands.

The development of nuclear power for the submarine ship is such an advance as to suggest an entirely new classification for that type of ship. This idea has been vaguely suggested in the recent past by naval writers who have said that the nuclear-powered ship is the first true submarine. The choice of the name 'submarine' for the conventional ship was unfortunate; a much more apt term would have been 'the submersible ship'. Nuclear power has solved all the past problems of the submarine.

Nuclear energy has cured, or greatly alleviated, not one but two of the submarine's greatest weaknesses as compared to surface craft. Until now it not only has been limited by its energy supply but also had the unenviable distinction of being the most inefficient load carrier at sea. The pressure hull, tanks, engines, and various appurtenances weigh so much it has carried a ridiculously small payload.[2]

Now, quite suddenly, all that has changed.

In 1899 the British naval writer Sir Julian Corbett made a classification of ships in terms of their historical importance.

The first period is that of the galley, beginning in prehistoric times and culminating in the year 1571, at the battle of Lepanto; the second is that of the 'greatship', or 'ship-of-the-line', which was established in 1588 with the campaign of the Grand Armada, and reached its highest development at Trafalgar; the third is that in which we now live, the period of the 'battleship'. Or, to state the classification in terms of its real basis, there is a period of oars, a period of sails, and a period of steam.[3]

Now we have a period of nuclear propulsion.

Corbett goes on to state that this classification of ships is not artificial but natural.

The classification, it will be seen, is no arbitrary device invented for clearer exposition of naval history, but one that is natural and inevitable. Not only do the divisions lie between well defined chronological limits, but they are rooted in the essentials of the art. The essence of naval strategy is sea endurance by which is meant the degree of fleets' capability of keeping the sea. The essence of naval tactics is the nature of the motive power; that is to say, tactics primarily depend upon how far the movements of the fleet or ship are under human control, and how far dependent upon conditions that lie beyond it, or, in other words, whether the units of the fleet are free or of subservient movement.[4]

The galley, using oars as motive power, had great manoeuvrability, but little sea endurance. It was suitable for closed waters such as the Mediterranean, but the fact that it could not keep at sea for long periods meant that it was of little use in the open seas. The sailing ship had almost unlimited sea endurance, but its tactical movement was restricted since it was dependent on the wind. Voyages of two or three years in sailing ships could be made, although a ship would need to touch land at times to replenish its water and food supplies. The development of the steam ship restored to ships their tactical mobility, but reduced their sea endurance. A ship dependent upon either coal or oil was forced to refuel, and stations were needed for this purpose. In the Second World War, the US Navy developed a method of replenishment at sea so that fleets could be kept on station for longer periods. The development of nuclear propulsion has solved these past difficulties: it enables a ship to maintain almost unlimited sea endurance and retain its tactical movement. It is the seaman's dream ship since, as Corbett summed up the matter, '. . . the main problem which lies at the root of all naval history [is] the problem of reconciling sea endurance with free movement . . .'[5]

One might recall that the chief difference between the views of Mahan and Mackinder concerned the modes of transportation, and furthermore, that mobility is a vital aspect of warfare. Nuclear engines for land or air movement have not been developed, yet the nuclear engine is the most modern form of propulsion in the world today. This fact has not been understood or even considered. Nuclear power introduces a new type of ship.

The nuclear-powered 'submarine' is truly a ship of the under-seas. Previously, the underwater performance of ships was inferior to surface performance; this situation has now been reversed, and the inherent physical advantages of movement in the underwater medium can be fully extended. Its underwater speed is potentially faster than that of any other ship. The hull of the conventional submarine is shaped like that of a surface ship, since it spends most of its time on the surface. Nuclear-powered ships are more whale-shaped, as befits a ship intended to spend most of its time beneath the surface of the seas. They have crossed the Arctic Ocean and sailed around the world submerged. They could remain submerged during their entire lifetime, using underwater naval bases. This is technically possible now; submerged platforms are also bound to be developed for commercial reasons, as the West exploits more and more the continental shelf areas for oil and other resources.

If the nuclear-powered ship is classified as a new type, then obviously it should be given a different name. There is a connection between the submarine and the nuclear-powered ship, but the gap between them constitutes a fundamental division in technological evolution. The term 'undersea ship' will be used to denote the nuclear-powered ship to emphasize that this is a new type of ship. Perhaps someone can come up with a better term, but the essential point is to understand that it represents a distinction which marks a new era in sea power. Its potential power is such that the undersea ship is destined to be the capital ship of the modern navy. 'It may well be that the nuclear sub-marine, like the battleship of the past, will prove to be the only answer to its own kind.'[6]

The power of navies began to decline in the twentieth century because of difficulties in moving about freely. Fear of mines and torpedoes demanded a fleet of auxiliary escort ships. In the age of the ship-of-the-line such ships could go almost anywhere unescorted, and the submarine ship eventually went a long way towards restoring much of this former versatility. In the Second World War, conventional submarines were the only type of war-fare ship which could make regular cruises into enemy-infested waters. They were also used for reconnaissance patrols, cloak-

and-dagger operations, acting as guides for invading fleets, picking up downed airmen, carrying essential cargoes which could not be carried by surface ships, shelling enemy installations and other missions. With the development of undersea ships this will no doubt increase.[7]

The surface ship, nuclear-powered or conventional, cannot compete in warfare with the nuclear-powered undersea ship. The development of reconnaissance satellites makes the surface of the sea an open book. Detection under water by sonar has lagged far behind the development of the undersea ship; the range of detection is still measured in terms of thousands of yards. A major breakthrough has been predicted yearly by Western naval leaders, but none has come despite the huge sums of money devoted to the problem.

No such breakthrough has occurred and there is now less anticipation that it will. The sea is a variable medium, and the literature on ASW [anti-submarine warfare] is replete with vivid explanations of how changes in salinity, presence of marine life, configuration of the bottom and, above all, layers of water of varying temperature that refract sound not only reduce ranges of detection, but make the performance of detection systems erratic and unreliable. Moreover, the modern submarine is capable of perceiving and exploiting these anomalies so as to make the hunter's task as difficult as possible.[8]

The evidence now seems to be that the best anti-submarine ship is the submarine itself. The undersea ship also has the advantage in combat with the surface ship; the former roles will undoubtedly be reversed and the hunted will become the hunter. In NATO naval exercises in Arctic waters in 1967, the British aircraft carrier *Eagle* was 'sunk' three times by undersea ships.

Besides surface ships, the other major enemy of the conventional submarine has been the aeroplane. Since the conventional ship was forced to spend most of its time on the surface, radar could be used to detect submarines from aircraft. But now this is less feasible, since most of the cruising time of undersea ships will be spent below the surface. There was a wild idea that satellites could be used to detect undersea ships, but this has been dismissed. 'Those who claim that reconnaissance and surveillance satellites, infra-red detection systems and so on have eroded if not entirely obviated the submarine's classic advantage of invisibility are talking nonsense. There is nothing except sonar which can penetrate to the depths at which nuclear submarines are likely to operate.'[9]

The roles of aircraft and ship might now be reversed.

The power of aircraft over the submarine in the past has progressively been reduced as it developed into the 'true' submarine. It is now only a matter of time before surface-to-air guided weapons are adapted for submarines and they acquire the power to shoot aircraft down . . . The slow anti-submarine aircraft and helicopter would be very vulnerable to a simple short-range missile launched from a submerged submarine . . . In the future, far from the submarine living in fear of aircraft, it is likely to be the other way round, and aircraft flying over the sea will never be sure that a guided weapon is not about to be launched at them from an undetected submarine.[10]

It would also be possible for undersea ships to carry VTOL aircraft.

There are difficulties in using undersea ships together in fleet operations. 'The single most serious remaining handicap of the nuclear submarine is perhaps that, while its acoustic detection capabilities are higher than those of any other vehicle, its other senses are correspondingly blunted by the surrounding sea. As a result, its capacity for precise or long-range perception of the scene around it is limited, which makes it difficult to communicate with for tactical purposes.'[11] This problem has been exaggerated, however, because Western navies, surface-minded, see the problem of communication as of that between undersea and surface ships, while the primary consideration is communication among undersea ships themselves.

The West took a giant step forward with the development of the undersea ship, but the accompanying tactical tools have been neglected. The torpedo seems obsolete and doubtless the future undersea ship will rely upon missiles fired from any depth. Moreover, the undersea ship moves in a medium much like an aircraft – both are vehicles of three-dimensional movement. It would seem that in the future undersea ships must have the ability to move in the same manner as aircraft – with loops, rolls, and other manoeuvres for tactical purposes. Depth for the undersea ship is equivalent to altitude for an aeroplane. A deeper-diving undersea ship would have the advantage over others. It is thought that US undersea ships can dive to 2,000 feet. If the Russians were able to develop undersea ships capable of cruising at 3,000 feet or more, they would gain a tremendous advantage.[12]

While the West has accepted the Heartland view of the world, there is no evidence that the Russians themselves have ever accepted these ideas. What is evident is that the Russians are moving into the sea and have been doing so for some time. In theory, at least, the Russian Navy should not be able to challenge the West – chiefly the United States Navy. The gross national product of the United States is roughly twice that of Russia. Moreover, the Russians are in a position much like that historically occupied by Germany, with strong land powers who are potential enemies on both borders, so that they cannot afford to relax their guard. The position of the United States is similar to that of Great Britain, with no strong enemies on her borders. But this geopolitical vantage will be wasted while Western strategic doctrine, including naval strategy, is in a state of disarray.[13]

While Western naval leaders recognize a Russian maritime threat today, they tend to look down their noses at its quality. It seems to be assumed that the West, by virtue of the mystical attributes of tradition, has a privileged proprietorship in naval wisdom. The moribund state of Western naval doctrine is overlooked. But the fact is that in the past new blood has often revived sea power from a state of decay: for example, Cromwell's generals of the sea helped to restore life to the British Navy after the Civil War.

The Russian leaders have previously demonstrated to the world that they have the ability to concentrate upon the decisive weapon of the moment. Before the Second World War they placed great importance upon tank development and production; the result was that Russian tanks were far superior to those produced by the Germans. Guderian was in Russia in the 1920s and saw what progress was being made. He predicted before the war that the Russians must have had about 10,000 tanks. Everyone thought that Guderian was mad, since the Germans themselves had only about 5,000. And, of course, everyone 'knew' that the Germans were far superior in the wisdom of land warfare to the primitive Russians. As it turned out Guderian's estimate was under the mark rather than over it. Later in the war Hitler told Guderian that if he had thought that the figure which Guderian gave was correct, then he would never have started the war. In more recent years the Russians made an early decision to concentrate upon long-range missiles. The stage could be set for another major surprise.

The Russians moved much of their submarine production to the Arctic shores during the Second World War to protect it from the Germans. On the Arctic coast it was necessary to put these shipyards in sheds for protection from the severe weather in this region. Today, this covering could also serve another purpose in preventing proper aerial or satellite reconnaissance. Western military leaders have paid relatively little attention to what the Russians might do in the way of undersea ship development and production; the great obsession in the West has been with nuclear arms.[14]

The advantage of the Germans over Britain and France in the opening stages of the war lay not so much in weapons themselves, although they were important, but in their advanced military thinking. Today the Russians could conceivably forge ahead in philosophy – in modern ideas related to naval strategy. One British academic strategist and military writer, Neville Brown, has observed the state of Western naval doctrine and commented:

Various exotic methods of waging naval war have been officially contemplated in recent years. The Navy Department in Washington has a long range study under way on the merits of changing the paths of cyclones to destroy enemy fleets. Investigations have been carried out also into the possibility of drowning enemy bases beneath tidal waves. When naval communities pay attention to ideas as quaint as this, it is a sign that they are lacking something. That something is good contemporary naval doctrine. Our seafarers have yet to complete their intellectual adjustment to the disappearance of the battleship and the approach of thermonuclear sufficiency.[15]

One reason for the parlous state of naval doctrine in the West is that Western strategists, including naval leaders themselves, have lost any clear idea of the place of sea power. Its importance seemed to be undermined by the tacit acceptance of the Heartland theory, and by belief in the myth of air power, which appears to be the dominant arm in a projectile cycle of warfare. The whole subject of naval strategy makes little impact on the public, and items concerning naval developments are consigned to the least conspicuous columns of newspapers. In addition seamen, commercial shipping interests and naval circles have tended to be conservative and even reactionary in their professional outlook, so that there has not been the dynamic drive towards new ideas which has characterized some other enterprises.

Official naval doctrine has clung to the cliché of a 'balanced fleet', but in modern conditions this is nonsense. It should mean the absence of a capital ship, but while all are equal, some are more equal than others. The term sometimes seems like a euphemism for the pre-eminence of aircraft carriers in naval thinking. (Although three of the four top commands in the US Navy during the Second World War were held by submariners, the High Command of the US Navy, as well as the Royal Navy, has been dominated by naval aviators since that time.)

The possible functions for a navy remain extremely varied, and there will be a place for some mixture of vessels in a fleet. But the real versatility of a navy finally depends upon its strength, and its strength today lies underseas. Surface ships can easily be identified by satellite; no other ship, nor indeed any other realistic vehicle of war, can attain the invulnerability, the performance, the mobility, the flexibility of choice or the command of force which the undersea ship can have. A naval power of consequence must concentrate on the development of undersea ships and of undersea techniques and tactics. The essential step towards a revival of naval theory is to recognize the revival of naval power in the underseas. There are subsidiary roles for the navy, but it is a belief in the reach and primacy of sea power itself which must be at the heart of naval doctrine.

The confusion of doctrine in the West is illustrated by the confusion of terminology touched on previously: the term 'submarine' is used ambiguously for conventional submarines and undersea ships. Furthermore, the term 'nuclear submarine' is sometimes used to mean a Polaris-type ship rather than a nuclear-powered ship. The West is obsessed with nuclear arms, and mobility takes second place to destruction in its thinking.

The Polaris ships themselves are a curious element in Western navies. Clearly they have no naval function in terms of classical naval theory. The object of a fleet is to meet and destroy the opposing fleet of the enemy. The Polaris ships have no part in this: they are fighting another war – a war based upon the Heartland view of the world. The Western powers have in effect two separate navies; one is ostensibly based upon the thinking of Mahan and the other upon Mackinder's Heartland theory. When the Polaris missile ships were first developed, the US Air Force claimed the right to control them. This thinking was largely correct. If there is a need for a nuclear deterrent, then obviously it must be concentrated. When Robert McNamara took office, he noted this dilemma. Naval and air forces were both aiming at the enemy with no coordination. As a result some targets would be hit twice, since they were fighting separate battles. McNamara combined them together, at least administratively, into the Strategic Strike Force. But there is no reason why navies should control the Polaris missile ships, since they have no naval function. If there were a nuclear war, then the best place to be would be in the sea. Going into the ocean is analagous to digging into the earth. Moreover, it enables dispersion over a wider area, which is helpful in frustrating an attack. The oceans cover most of the earth's surface and it is easier to go into the sea than to dig holes in the earth; also, one can easily change position in the sea. If human life were to survive a nuclear attack, then it would most likely be in the seas – in undersea ships and underwater bases. Mairin Mitchell noted this in 1948. She wrote:

That we live in the dawn of the atomic age is commonly accepted; that we have arrived at the oceanic age is no less true, but rarely stated . . . For reasons arising from the technique of warfare, as well as for reasons geographical, we may expect to see nations looking to the oceans for the conservation of their main sources of strength. The Bikini tests showed that the defences against atomic attack are dispersal and distance; the seas and the oceans which cover three-fourths of the globe offer the better prospects than land does for such defences. And the safest place of all may be under water, for the coming of the futuristically armoured super-submarine, and the deep-level atomic-propelled submersible ship, may provide anti-aircraft shelters, as well as mobile operational bases.[16]

Immunity from attack could also be of consequence for merchant ships; there are security reasons why a nation might want part of its merchant fleet underseas. But the most compelling reason for building merchant undersea ships in the immediate future is to open up certain trade routes. It is clearly technically feasible to build undersea merchant ships, and there is no doubt that this will be done in the foreseeable future, for they will soon approach the point of becoming economically viable. Sir Barnes Wallis and Vice Admiral B. B. Schofield are advocates of the building of such ships for the British merchant fleet. Admiral Schofield has written: 'Apart from the initial cost which need not be as great as is often supposed, since great strides have been made recently with the building and operation of nuclear reactors for marine purposes, the advantages to be gained from the commercial operation of such ships are great, and include a quicker turn-around, faster and shorter passages and an independence of surface weather conditions which often cause delay and damage to surface ships.'[17]

It should be observed at this point that there is a relationship between economic interests and relevant military force to protect and further them. The emphasis on the word 'relevant' means that the force available must be of a kind which can be effectively brought to bear in some particular dispute; this is another way of expressing the principle that the means of implementing policy should be related to the aims. This will always be the case until the hypothetical and desirable time in the future when a recognized body of international law will cover all matters over which major disputes might arise between nations; even such law would itself have to be policed and therefore supported by some form of international force.

As we move into a new oceanic age, in which not only maritime commerce but the resources of the seas themselves are vital interests of the major powers, rivalry at sea will increase and the occasions for a clash of policy are likely to become more frequent. It is pertinent to note that not only are the Russians greatly extending their naval sea power, but now they have a merchant fleet which is as large as that of the United States, a fishing fleet which is three times as large as that of the nearest contender (Japan), and an oceanic research fleet which is larger than those of all the other maritime countries put together.

The undersea ship will supersede the submarine and all surface ships as the most modern ship afloat on the oceans of the world. The fact that such a ship might be developed was outside the imagination of almost everyone when Mackinder wrote. A few people had thought in rather vague terms that it might be possible for science to develop something like an atomic bomb. No one seemed to have suggested that this same energy might be used as a source of engine power.

Mackinder had stressed the role of the submarine and aircraft as instruments of war. They were in the early stages of development when he wrote, and by 1919 the submarine seemed useful mainly as a commerce raider or as a means of thwarting control of the seas. The Heartland theory assumed that submarines would continue to develop and would be weapons of land power aimed at sea power; the development of the nuclear-powered undersea ship is still seen by modern Western strategists as essentially an arm of land power. But its potential range of roles is incomparably far-reaching. The undersea ship signifies a fundamental break with the past; the message is clear: if you can't beat them, join them.

The undersea ship destroys two of the basic premises of Mackinder's theory. The day of the supremacy of the surface naval ship is almost over, and the conventional submarine, which was viewed as a denial of sea power, has been relegated to a minor place. This new classification of ships introduces a new era of maritime enterprise. Rather than seeing the end of sea power, we are moving into a period which will bring a vast expansion of sea power.

The second premise of the Heartland theory invalidated by the undersea ship is the idea that the Heartland is inaccessible to the influence of sea power. The undersea ship makes the Arctic Ocean navigable, which means that the World Island can be circumnavigated freely. It is an island. The prospect of the navigation of the Arctic Ocean is of immense significance for the future, and the next chapter will be devoted to this subject.

The undersea ship represents the indirect use of nuclear energy. The point has repeatedly been made that if war is considered as an instrument of policy, then movement is of far greater importance than mere destruction. The nuclear engine offers the greatest potential for mobility, and the nuclear-powered undersea ship is now the capital ship of the modern navy. If this is accepted, then he who rules the underseas will control the surface. Although it is not obvious, the undersea ship offers an alternative strategic doctrine to that of the nuclear deterrent. Critics of the deterrent have railed in the past because they have been unable to offer a satisfactory alternative.

If we accept the idea that war is a lethal argument, then the first step in limiting the extent of violence is to understand this and then proceed from a rational standpoint. Undoubtedly there are deep psychological factors in the propensity for violence of individuals, which have meaning in terms of policy for a state. But rationally considering the relationship between the aims and means of policy goes some way towards understanding and controlling violence on the international scene. Therefore, while it might seem strange, the primary objective should be to make the world safe for war, which means making the world safe for settling arguments between nations without destroying the entire world. At first this may seem cynical, but it is a necessary step in controlling war. Thus, if we are to cherish any instrument of war, then rather than love the bomb we should regard with special favour the undersea ship – especially those of us in the West.

Notes to Chapter 7

1. Mahan wrote: 'There was such an impression held by French officers of that day, and yet more widely spread in the United States now, of the efficacy of commerce-destroying as a main reliance in war, especially when directed against a commercial country like Great Britain. "The surest means in my opinion," wrote a distinguished

officer, Lamotte-Picquet, "to conquer the English is to attack them in their commerce." The harassment and distress caused to a country by serious interference with its commerce will be conceded by all. It is doubtless a most important secondary operation of naval war, and it is not likely to be abandoned until war itself shall cease; but regarded as a primary and fundamental measure, sufficient in itself to crush an enemy, it is probably a delusion, and a most dangerous delusion, when presented in the fascinating garb of cheapness to the representatives of a people' (*The Influence of Sea Power upon History*, Methuen, 1965, p. 539).

2. Cohen, Paul, 'The Future of the Submarine', *Foreign Affairs*, October 1959.

3. Corbett, J. S., *Drake and The TudorNavy*, Longmans, 1899, Vol. I, p. 2.

4. ibid., p. 2.

5. ibid., p. 3. This historical analysis is not new. Vice Admiral Sir Arthur Hezlet, in his book *The Submarine and Sea Power* (Peter Davies, 1967), wrote: 'The historical study of the turning-point of naval warfare and the reasons why the galley was replaced by the galleon, the ship of the line by the steam ironclad and the battleship by the carrier-borne aircraft is very relevant. It is difficult to escape the conclusion that another such turning-point has been reached' (p. 262).

6. ibid., p. 260. Hezlet is a distinguished British submariner, and other naval officers have made this point. Captain S. W. Roskill, the official historian of the Royal Navy and a Fellow of Churchill College, Cambridge, has supported the idea that the nuclear-powered undersea ship represents a new era in sea power. He wrote: 'Nevertheless, the submarine had firmly established itself as the capital ship of the nuclear era. Moreover, the scope for employment of submarines on duties hitherto performed by surface ships or aircraft appeared to be limited only by the cost of submarine production. Indeed, the command of the surface sea, whereby a maritime power seeks to secure the uninterrupted passage of mercantile or military cargoes, seemed likely to depend increasingly on control of the waters beneath' (*Encyclopaedia Britannica*, 1970, Vol. 21, p. 343). However, the general prejudice against the idea of an underseas navy is still so strong that the subject seldom gets openly aired. Admiral Hezlet was forced out of the Royal Navy because of his views on the value of these ships. The submarine started out as just a commerce raider. When undersea ships are developed to the point where they carry commerce themselves – as undoubtedly will happen – then it will be a different story.

7. Naval theory maintained that conventional submarines were basically inferior ships; when ASW vessels approached they were forced to take evasive action. However, in the Pacific in the Second World War, US submarines began to fight back with devastating results for their opponents. They devised what were called 'down the throat' shots. When an ASW ship charged, this new tactic was to fire a spread of torpedoes instead of, as before, hastily submerging. The oncoming ship was a small target but growing in size, and with a spread of shots it was difficult to avoid the torpedoes. In the end, Japanese ASW vessels were extremely cautious in approaching US submarines.

8. Martin, L. W., *The Sea in Modern Strategy*, Chatto & Windus, 1967, p. 99. Anti-submarine warfare is the biggest worry in Western navies. It has been quite successful in terms of defeating submarines; however, undersea ships are a very different matter, and it is increasingly apparent that the best answer to them lies in better undersea ships. Martin also noted: 'With its power of indefinite submersion the nuclear submarine is virtually a wholly new weapon and as such cannot be usefully compared in cost with any direct equivalent' (p. 71).

9. French, John, 'The Submarine Service', *Navy*, London, September 1971.

10. Hezlet, op. cit., p. 261. Such weapons have already been developed by the Soviet Union and the United States for use against ships. In December 1972 the decision was taken to develop a rocket torpedo for the Royal Navy to replace the conventional torpedo. This was long overdue. This Under-Surface Guided Weapon (as it is known) would be launched from a submerged ship like a torpedo, take to the air like a rocket, and home in on an enemy surface ship. The undersea ship is in a favourable tactical position in relation to the surface ship, as it is a better detecting platform and has knowledge of the approximate location of surface shipping. In relation to aircraft, the undersea ship of the future will be able to use external surface detection devices which are released and retrieved while the ship stays submerged.

11. Martin, op. cit., p. 93.

12. The power of the undersea ship has become so great that naval tactics are increasingly likely to favour the capture of ships at sea rather than their destruction. Vice Admiral Hezlet wrote: 'If the old-fashioned U-boats' overall performance is represented by m then type XXI would be $10m$, the Walther boat $40m$ and the nuclear submarine $5,000m$' (op. cit., p. 245). There are a number of reasons for this and some precedents are already established. The dangers of

nuclear war have made countries cautious about the use of force. Seizing a ship rather than sinking her has a definite propaganda advantage, besides the fact that the ship together with its cargo will be of some value. If it is a warship, as was the case with the electronic spy-ship, the *Pueblo*, capturing her could provide additional bonuses in matters such as intelligence.

The undersea ship can easily capture any merchant surface ship. It might seem strange for an undersea ship to capture a surface ship, but there would be very little that a surface navy could do to prevent it. The knowledge that the undersea ship could destroy the merchant ship would be enough to halt it. Although there would be a problem in putting on a prize crew and taking off the original crew, this could be easily done with a helicopter. Undersea ships are now large enough, and crews of modern merchant ships small enough, for this to be done very quickly. It would be no problem for an undersea ship to carry one or more helicopters, or even VTOL aircraft. If support for the merchant ship were sent in the form of aircraft or a surface warship, it could destroy the captured ship; however, it might easily be destroyed by a missile from the undersea ship. The only answer would be to send another undersea warship.

13. As far back as Peter the Great the Russians have expressed a desire to reach the open sea and to use the sea to build an empire. Fred T. Jane, writing in 1899, stated: 'Every Russian feels himself a member of the empire that will be the world-empire of the future. And that empire will be a great sea-empire, since the sea is now what land once was in the matter of communications. At some future date that great struggle between the British Empire and the Russians, between Anglo-Saxon and the Slav, that so many prophesy, may come off' (*The Russian Imperial Navy*, W. Thacker, 1904, p. 605).

14. Mairin Mitchell noted the special importance of the nuclear-powered ship for the Russians. This was seven years before the launching of the *Nautilus*, the first undersea ship, which she accurately assumed would take place. 'The position of the world's fleets in the future will depend on their strength underseas; a new chapter in naval history opens with the Age of the Super-Submarine' (*The Maritime History of Russia*, Sidgewick & Jackson, 1948, p. 366).

15. Brown, Neville, *Nuclear War: The Impending Strategic Deadlock*, Pall Mall, 1964, p. 107.

16. Mitchell, op. cit., p. 365.

17. Schofield, B. B., *British Sea Power*, Batsford, 1967, pp. 234-5. There is another significant factor. According to Mahan and other naval authorities, the source of naval power is merchant shipping. It

is desirable that there should be a common bond between naval and civilian shipping. In the era of sailing ships, there existed a unity of maritime interests. The age of specialization had not yet begun and so the seamen of the merchant ships could easily be pressed into service in warships. 'For many centuries from, say, the Peloponnesian War until well after Trafalgar, while sailing ships held sway, it was often difficult to differentiate strictly between the nature of warships and that of other vessels; and between the nature of those who manned the one and those who manned the other, since all were of one common fraternity of mariners whose ships, if not already owned by the state, could most effectively be impressed into the service of the government if needed for war. Sea power was total and indivisible' (Candlin, A. H. Stanton, 'The Return of Total Sea Power', *Naval Review*, U.S. Naval Institute, 1964).

It would appear that the gap between merchant ships and warships need not be so great with undersea ships, at least in some stages. The tendency at the moment is for the crews of civilian merchant ships to become smaller, with automation replacing human control. With an undersea ship, the need for this will be even greater. The old-style mariner whose identification with his profession has waned will be replaced by an enthusiastic generation of generals of the sea. Like their pilot compatriots in the air, these new mariners will command high rates of pay.

8. The Arctic Mediterranean: The Sea of Destiny

> The polar regions, then, cannot fail to become
> more important. And of the two regions, the
> Arctic is bound to play the greater part . . .
> **T. E.** Armstrong (*The Russians in the Arctic*)

The potential importance of the Arctic Ocean to Europeans was recognized almost as soon as the Columbian era had begun. The Cape route was one way of reaching the Orient and the Indies. The discovery of America was the result of an expedition to reach the Orient. The Americas simply got in the way until their potential value was realized. It was natural and inevitable that English seamen especially should attempt to find a northern route around North America or Siberia to the Pacific. One of the early suggestions for such a venture was put forward to Henry VIII by Roger Barlow of Bristol. In a document entitled *A Brief Summe of Geographie*, Barlow wrote of the importance of such a route:

And for such an enterprise no man shuld thinke upon the cost in comparison to the grete profyt that maye therby succede, nor thinke the labour grete where so moche profyt honor and glory maye folow unto this our naturall realme and king . . . And if thei will saylle, in passing the pole, toward occident thei shal go on the backside of all the new found land that is discouered by your graces subiectes, till thei come into the southe see on the backside of the indies occidentales . . .[1]

For Elizabethan seamen the Arctic Ocean was important simply because of its position – its strategic location as the shortest pathway to the Orient. Using globes rather than charts, the North-West and North-East Passages represented the quickest and most logical routes to the Pacific Ocean. A friend of Barlow, Robert Thorne, maintained that Divine Providence had reserved this route especially for England and the appeal was quite effective at the time. The other more southerly routes were dominated by Spain and Portugal. who were then at the height of their power. In the end, English sea power was forced to challenge the might of Spanish sea power, but the northern routes at first appeared an attractive alternative.

However, the northern routes were never technically possible in the era of sailing ships. Although wooden ships later ventured into the Arctic Ocean, it was not until the age of steel-hulled, steam-driven ships that it was reasonable to attempt such a passage. Even these ships need the aid of icebreakers and can only operate in the short summer months. While it is technically possible to use the Arctic Ocean, it is not commercially realistic.

Since Russia's longest coastline is on the Arctic Ocean, the navigation of this sea would be of vast importance to her. One of the largest organizations in Russia outside the armed forces is the one charged with maintaining the navigation of the northern sea route. It operates a large fleet of icebreakers, weather stations, patrol aircraft and scientific stations in order to facilitate the passage of ships in the summer months. However, the route is not thought to be truly viable in purely economic terms. Despite later development by the Russians, this was the situation in the Arctic when Mackinder wrote in 1904 and 1919. He was quite aware that surface ships could use the Arctic coastline only in a restricted manner. 'The northern edge of Asia is the Inaccessible Coast, beset with ice except for a narrow water lane which opens here and there along the shore in the brief summer owing to the melting of local ice formed in the winter between the grounded floes and the land.'[2]

The Arctic Ocean has been called by Vilhjalmur Stefansson, the Arctic expert and explorer, a 'mediterranean sea'. The word 'mediterranean' comes from the Latin words *medius*, for 'middle', and *terra*, for 'land', so it means 'middle land' or 'centre of the world'. It seems strange that this frozen, uninhabited region should be so termed, but it is apt. Most of the land area of the world lies in the northern hemisphere wrapped around the Arctic Ocean. As Stefansson noted:

A map giving one view of the northern half of the world shows that the so-called Arctic Ocean is a Mediterranean Sea like those which separate Europe from Africa or North America from South America.

Because of its smallness, we would do well to go back to an Elizabethan custom and call it not the Arctic Ocean but the Polar Sea or Polar Mediterranean. The map shows that most of the land in the world is in the Northern Hemisphere, that the Polar Sea is like a hub from which the continents radiate like spokes of a wheel. The white patch shows that part of the Polar Sea never yet navigated by ships is small compared to the surrounding land masses. In the coming air age the Arctic will be like an open park in the centre of the uninhabited city of the world, and air voyages will cross it like taxi riders a park. Then will the Arctic islands become valuable, first as way stations, and later because of their intrinsic value . . .[3]

This was written in 1922 and it is a remarkably accurate prediction. Today commercial aircraft do use the Great Circle route between Europe and the Far East as well as to points in the Western part of North America. And, of course, this route was looked upon as America's access path to the Heartland for air power. It is interesting that in this article, Stefansson had also included the idea of using submarines as transport in the Arctic Ocean. However, the *National Geographic* journal thought the idea too futuristic and cut out all reference to it.

Curiously, the idea had been suggested and published years before – in 1648. In a volume entitled *Mathematicall Magick* Bishop John Wilkins of Chester included a chapter called 'Concerning the Possibility of Framing an Ark for Submarine Navigation'. He wrote:

1. Tis private: a man may thus go to any coast of the world invisibly, without discovery or prevented in his journey.
2. Tis safe, from the uncertainty of Tides, and the violence of Tempests, which do never move the sea above five or six paces deep. From Pirates and Robbers which do so infest other voyages; from ice and great frost, which do so much endanger the passages toward the Poles.
3. It may be of great advantage against a Navy of enemies, who by this may be undermined in the water and blown up.
4. It may be of special use for the relief of any place besieged by water, to convey unto them invisible supplies; and so likewise for the surprisal of any place that is accessible by water.
5. It may be of unspeakable benefit for submarine experiments . . .[4]

A descendant of Bishop Wilkins, Sir Hubert Wilkins, resuggested the same idea in 1919. Nine years later plans were made to attempt the navigation of the Arctic Ocean with a decommissioned First World War submarine. An attempt was made in 1931, but, unfortunately, it proved to be too ambitious for the technical developments of that period. It was not until 3 August 1958 that the first nuclear-powered undersea ship, the USS *Nautilus*, commanded by Commander William R. Anderson, reached the North Pole. The idea of building cargo undersea ships immediately suggested itself. (Conventional submarines had been pressed into service to carry needed supplies to besieged outposts in both world wars, as Bishop Wilkins had suggested, but they were not well suited for the role because of the small quantity of cargo which they could carry.)

If the undersea ship can be developed into a viable commercial ship, the Arctic Ocean will be of vast importance for the future. Sea power has always had a strong commercial basis in the past. The undersea cargo ship has the potential to make the Arctic Mediterranean the narrow waters of the future. There are three main reasons why the use of the Arctic Ocean by undersea ships would be of great significance. Firstly, there is the obvious fact that this sea offers the shortest route between the most industrialized nations of the world. If it were possible to use the Arctic Mediterranean, then it would be practical to establish trade routes between the West coast of North America and Europe or between the East coast of North America and Asia, as well as between Asia and Europe.

Secondly, there is the importance of the Arctic lands as sources of minerals; it is well known, for example, that great mineral wealth exists in Northern Canada and Alaska. The great obstacle is now the problem of transportation in that forbidding region.

Thirdly, there is the strategic aspect: if the Arctic Ocean were freely navigable, it is obvious that the Heartland would no longer be inaccessible from the influence of sea power. It would be possible to circumnavigate the World Island. As Mackinder stated:

One reason why seamen did not long ago rise to the generalization implied in the expression 'World-Island', is that they could not make the round voyage of it. An ice-cap, two thousand miles across, floats on the Polar Sea, with one edge aground on the shoals of the north of Asia. For the common purpose of navigation, therefore, the continent is not an island. The seamen of the last four centuries have treated it as a vast promontory stretching southward from a vague north, as a mountain peak may rise out of the clouds from hidden foundations.[5]

The central aspect of the Heartland theory is that this pivot region has a secure position because the of its immunity from influence of sea power. If ships could use the Arctic Ocean freely, even undersea ships, then, of course, this would no longer be true. If commercial undersea ships used the Arctic Ocean, then its naval importance would soon be realized. It is quite true that the shores of the Asiatic Arctic are shallow waters, but for both naval and commercial usage it is less and less necessary to approach land closely since great strides have been made in offshore loading and unloading.

At present interest in the Arctic, as far as the West is concerned, concerns the large deposits of oil which have been found in Alaska. This oil was first found in 1968. Despite the fact that drilling for oil in the Arctic is estimated to be six times more expensive than drilling in more temperate climates, the oil companies thought it to be a sound investment. So far, however, this has not been the case, since after five years the oil has yet to be moved. It is the age-old problem of transport in the Arctic. Although air transport largely supports the drilling operation, its expense rules it out for the transport of oil.

There are three possible methods for the movement of Arctic oil to the markets of the world. The first method, which is favoured by the oil companies, is to build a pipeline which would carry the heated oil across the Brooks Mountain Range and the perma-frost regions to Valdez on the Pacific side of Alaska. In hearings before the US Department of Interior, held in Washington and Alaska in the winter of 1970–1, the opposition to the pipeline by conservationists and others was so great that a decision on it was postponed. The environment is extremely sensitive in the Arctic regions and the first idea was to bury at least part of the pipeline. Studies indicated, however, that in spite of insulation the perma-frost soil would be thawed to such an extent that it could not support the pipe. When this happened the line would be ruptured, spilling oil over a vast area. Another solution proposed is to support the pipeline on raised concrete standards which would then be insulated by distance from the ground. It would prevent the heat from penetrating into the soil and allow animals to roam at will.

Even if the pipeline is built, it is not the best solution from the standpoint of the overall development of the Arctic. There are thought to be more oil deposits in the various Canadian islands and in the offshore regions of the Arctic Ocean. The pipeline has the great disadvantage of being relatively inflexible. Moreover, there are also huge deposits of other minerals in the Arctic and these could not be handled by a pipeline. The United States seems to be looking towards the Arctic as a potential reservoir of resources for the future. If this is so, then it would be most advantageous to develop a more general system of transport.

The second method suggested for the transport of oil in the Arctic is the use of super-tankers. This seemed a much more fruitful approach since, if successful, it provided a means for opening up the entire Arctic region for development, besides making it possible to consider a North-West Passage between the Atlantic and Pacific Oceans. The idea was to build specially designed super-tankers which would act as their own icebreakers. The optimistic belief of the designers of the scheme was that the route could be used all year round. This would have been an epoch-making advance, if it could have been achieved. The Russians had been using the Arctic for over forty years but, in spite of their extensive concentration of energy and interest, were only able to use the northern sea route in the short summer months and then only with the aid of icebreakers. Humble Oil thought that the project was possible and, together with several other oil companies, invested $40 million in it. The super-tanker *Manhattan* was taken apart and converted into a partial icebreaker. An experimental voyage was made in the summer of 1969 from the Eastern seaboard of the United States around Northern Canada to Prudhoe Bay in Alaska. Despite the fact that the summer was exceptionally favourable with regard to ice conditions, the *Manhattan* needed the assistance of an icebreaker. Even so a hole was knocked in the side of the giant ship, arousing the concern of conservationists, ecologists and the Canadian public; the Canadian Parliament subsequently passed a law extending territorial waters to a hundred miles. The leader of the *Manhattan* project, Mr Stanley Haas, admitted during the voyage that a fleet of icebreakers would be necessary. The opinion of many Arctic experts before the experiment was that it would be difficult for such a route to be economically viable. They felt that there was little prospect that any giant tanker could be built which could make the journey in the winter months with no risk of accident. The outcome was that, although the US Congress seemed willing to provide the funds for a fleet of icebreakers, the oil companies have abandoned the entire scheme and are pinning their hopes upon the pipeline.

But there is, and has been all along, a third method which is potentially much more useful than the other two: to build cargo-carrying undersea ships. The undersea ship will be the catalyst which will open up the whole Arctic for development. This is a most important factor, since the demand for essential minerals will go on increasing in the future. While the billion-dollar pipeline might well be satisfactory for transport of the North Slope oil, it could not possibly have the same inherent flexibility as an ocean-going ship.

Though the first attraction of the undersea cargo ship lies in its usefulness in opening up the Arctic, this is by no means the only reason for its consideration. The introduction of nuclear power has transformed the position of naval ships and it could have a similar impact on mercantile shipping. It makes possible a kind of undersea ship which is in many ways potentially more efficient and more versatile than its surface counterpart can be. The Arctic Ocean offers a shorter route between the North Pacific and North Atlantic regions of the world, and this factor, together with the greater speeds possible under water, will eventually give the undersea ship a competitive place in commerce.

In the United States, General Dynamics' Electric Boat Division suggested to the oil companies with an interest in

Alaska the idea of building a fleet of super-undersea tankers.
The ships were to be 255,000-ton vessels, far larger than any
existing undersea ship (the largest to date are the Polaris ships
of roughly 8,000 tons). This would, indeed, be a giant step; the
ships would be capable of carrying 1·8 million barrels of oil per
trip at 17 knots. According to Mr Samuel B. Winram, the director of the project, 'The problem in Alaska and in the Arctic
islands is not finding the oil but getting the oil out without damage to the environment, inexpensively and quickly.'[6] The
Electric Boat design represents a vast jump, and it has been
criticized as too ambitious a step to make in one stage. While it
is true that large surface ships have been built, it would be
difficult to extrapolate from this experience into the underseas
without building and operating intermediate-size undersea
ships. The great problem is not necessarily in the building of
such ships, but rather in the intrinsic aspects of undersea operations, such as terminal connections and navigation and the train-
ing of personnel. The risk of major disasters must be avoided.
This more gradual approach is advocated by many experts. Dr
H. E. Sheets, who was Vice President in charge of engineering
and research at the Electric Boat Division and is now Professor
of Ocean Engineering at Rhode Island University, thinks that it
would be far wiser to start with a more modest-sized prototype
ship. It would obviously be much cheaper to construct a smaller
ship, it would take less time to design and build it, and it would
be easier to attract the necessary financial interest. Furthermore,
it could be technically possible to develop a system of container-
type barges which could be towed under water, and this would
have many advantages over the super-ship. With a smaller
prototype one could experiment at this stage and compare it with
the idea of building larger undersea cargo ships.[7]

A number of studies concerning the design and construction
of cargo-carrying undersea ships were made in the 1960s. The
one which was furthest developed was perhaps the British design
study for the *Moby Dick* which was a 50,000-ton ship able to
haul 28,000 tons of cargo from Northern Canada to Great
Britain. The project study was made by Mitchell Engineering;
one version of it was for a tanker, and another was for a bulk

carrier to haul iron ore from Canada to Britain. The overall length was 604 feet, the maximum diameter 72 feet, and the draught 59 feet.

One problem about ventures into new technology is the initial uncertainty about development costs. This is inevitable in the prototype stage, as experience in the aero-space world has vividly shown. The Mitchell Engineering company thought that the *Moby Dick* could be built for approximately £6 million, but some knowledgeable people considered that this figure was too low and that £18 million was more realistic; since that time, of course, costs have risen. Until some prototype ships are built, it will not be possible to make accurate estimates of production costs. But the essential engineering requirements for undersea cargo ships need not make any radical departures from present practice. The hulls of tankers and container ships are now so designed that they could, with very few problems, be converted into undersea hulls. The decks of these ships are usually awash as they sit very low in the sea. Naturally, the integrity of the hull of undersea ships would have to be ensured; but once techniques were standardized, the construction of the hull for an undersea ship would be as cheap as or cheaper than for the hull of a corresponding surface ship. Nuclear power would be expensive, estimated to cost 20 to 40 per cent more than conventional power, but this differential is likely to be considerably reduced over the next few years.

Almost every improvement in transportation in the past has resulted in more expensive vehicles. The sailing ship was far more expensive than the galley, and the steam-driven steel ship much more costly than the wooden sailing ship which it replaced; on land the steam locomotive was vastly more expensive than the horse-drawn coach. As Barlow stated, 'For such an enterprize no man should thinke upon the cost in comparison to the grete profyt that maye therby succede.' The additional cost of the undersea cargo ship could be more than offset by the economies made by increased speed and shorter routes. An official United States study reported: 'Hydrodynamic studies long have shown that a submarine is more efficient at high speeds than a surface vessel. The Maritime Administration believes that a 40-knot submarine tanker is a "possibility". To attain that speed, the sub would require far less power than its surface counterpart.'[8] The speed of an undersea ship could easily be at least twice that of its surface counterpart.

The undersea cargo-container ship would be able to use the trans-polar route. This would shorten many voyages considerably. The distance between London and Tokyo over the polar route is about 6,500 nautical miles compared with about 11,200 nautical miles for a surface ship. Putting these two factors together, it is evident that an undersea ship going between London and Tokyo could make four trips for every one of a surface ship's.

But for some purposes there is not even a comparison, because the undersea ship is the only possible contender. This would be so, for example, not only in the development of the Arctic, but in bulk transportation associated with the economic development of the continental shelf regions. And there may be other economies which a new technology of underseas transportation would produce; the advantages of undersea container barges have been mentioned earlier in this chapter. The next chapter will consider some other ways in which we are moving into the underseas, and obviously undersea transportation facilities will become more sophisticated alongside other developments.

There are some problems concerning navigation and terminal connections for the undersea ship which will need to be resolved. Sonar beacons could be used to establish routes. If considerable traffic did develop, then international rules of the road would have to be formulated in the same manner as they have been for surface ships and aircraft. The deep draught of undersea ships would present a problem in finding suitable harbours. This is a difficulty which has faced the giant tankers, and offshore loading and unloading has provided the answer in their case. There are other alternatives which could be developed for undersea ships. The idea has been suggested of having terminal connections under water for tankers, which would mean that the undersea ship need never surface. There is a case for this, as the undersea ship is most vulnerable on the surface and, if built with a cylindrical hull, is not adapted to surface movement. It might also reduce the problem of pollution if oil tankers had terminal connections on or near the continental shelf and the oil was pumped ashore from underwater pipelines.[9] Another suggestion has been to build undersea cargo ships with a box-shaped rather than circular cross-section, which would allow shallower draughts. With containerized cargo, it would be possible to use undersea barges, which could be towed into quite small ports by surface tugs.

For the Arctic Ocean, there is really no competition for the nuclear-powered undersea ship. As far as Arctic resources are concerned then, without the undersea cargo ship all or most of these minerals will remain buried in the frozen soil. A North-West or North Passage again depends on the undersea cargo ship. There is no alternative.[10] There is an inevitability about the use of the Arctic Ocean in the future by undersea ships. Mahan started his first book on sea power by writing:

> The first and most obvious light in which the sea presents itself from the political and social point of view is that of a great highway; or better, perhaps, of a wide common, over which men may pass in all directions, but on which some well-worn paths show that controlling reasons have led them to choose certain lines of travel rather than others. These lines of travel are called trade routes; and the reasons which have determined them are to be sought in the history of the world.[11]

If the Arctic Ocean were to become a major trade route, there would obviously be profound geopolitical implications for the future. The Arctic Ocean would then be part of the narrow waters of the future in the same way as the English Channel has been the narrow seas in modern times. The World Island is only an island in theory and not in practice, as Mackinder pointed out. If it were possible freely to use the Polar Mediterranean, then the World Island would be an island in the true sense of the word. The navigation of the Polar Sea in 1958 by Commander William Anderson was a historic achievement of monumental geopolitical significance. Though largely ignored at the time, in the perspective of the future it may be seen to be as important as was the rounding of the Cape of Good Hope by Vasco da Gama in 1497.

The navigation of the Arctic Ocean means, in principle, that the Heartland is no longer an inaccessible Heartland. Russia has the longest coastline of any country. Usually a coastline exists as a possible frontier with sea power. A seafaring nation could not be attacked across this border, but sea power itself could attack along an exposed coastline. In the past, the nature of the Arctic provided the defence for this coast. This natural protection is no longer valid with the emergence of undersea ships. Large-scale military operations can be launched and sustained today even in Arctic conditions. While other nations might not actually want the land over which they were fighting, the northern coast of Siberia is connected to more vital regions. In addition, the Russians have a number of important installations on the Arctic coast. At present no great provisions are needed to repel a land movement in this area, although there are naturally defence installations to counter the Western nuclear deterrent. But in the future the Russians may have to face in three directions, which would present tremendous problems for Kremlin strategists.

Difficulties would exist for an invasion based upon undersea ships. The coastal waters are shallow on the Siberian side of the Arctic Ocean. However, with helicopters and other surface-effect vehicles, the landing force could afford to lie offshore at a distance greater than is usual in an invasion.[12] If this were made into a viable option by the West, the Russians would have to contend with the defence of a long coastline. Russia is a vast country, but her very hugeness means that there is a great area to defend. This vastness has in the past been a source of strength in which the sheer size of the country overwhelms the attacker. But it can also overstretch the defence. The population of Russia is not tremendously great in comparison with the United States. The so-called 'Russian hordes' are a figment of the Cold War imagination, and the Russian planners would face a manpower shortage if they had to guard all their borders. However, the navigation of the Arctic Ocean might not have a totally adverse effect upon Russia. It would present her with a means of communication across the top of the world between the Atlantic and Pacific. Today the Russian fleet is separated into four sections –

the Far East, the North at Murmansk, the Baltic, and the Black Sea. The navigation of the Arctic Ocean would make it possible to coordinate the Arctic fleet with the Far Eastern fleet.[13]

None the less, the main advantage would lie with the West in exposing the Heartland to the possible influence of sea power, besides making the Arctic Mediterranean the sea of destiny for the future.

Notes to Chapter 8

1. Barlow, Roger, *A Brief Summe of Geographie*, ed. Taylor, E. G. R., Hakluyt Society, London, 1932, pp. 180–2.
2. Mackinder, H. J., *Democratic Ideals and Reality*, Norton, New York, 1962, p. 62.
3. Stefansson, Vilhjalmur, 'The Arctic as an Air Route of the Future', *National Geographic Magazine*, August 1922. Later, in *Under the North Pole*, ed. Wilkins, Sir Hubert, Brewer, Warren & Putnam, New York, 1931, Stefansson wrote about this article: 'In 1922 I found myself broke one day in Washington. So I went to Gilbert Grosvenor, then, as now, Editor of the *National Geographic Magazine* and also President of the N.G. Society. I told him about my financial difficulties and offered him at $1000 for publication in his journal a plan for Transarctic commerce by air above the ice and by submarine under the ice. Within the half hour he was sold on both ideas; but when he received the draft of the article and consulted various Navy men, he weakened on the submarine part and finally cut it out entirely' (pp. 14–15).
4. Wilkins, Bishop John, *Mathematicall Magick*, London, 1648, pp. 187–8.
5. Mackinder, op. cit., p. 62.
6. 'Submarine Oil Tanker Designed For Polar Run', Associated Press dispatch, San Diego, California, 17 March 1971. Winram also said: 'Subtankers will be the most reliable, economical and flexible means of moving oil from Alaska's North Slope and Canadian Arctic islands to ice-free North Atlantic terminals.'
7. The present trend towards larger and larger vessels has many liabilities, and an alternative to the large-ship theory for the handling of cargo would be of great interest. A Japanese invention has established the fact that container barges can be towed under water. The

mother ship, in this case, would be a surface ship, and the barges would be submerged. Towing on the surface of the sea is a hazardous operation and only practical in relatively calm seas. Undersea towing is a different matter, however, and the next natural stage would be to have the mother ship underwater. (The barges would not actually have to be towed, as the mother ship could supply power from her reactors for propellors in each barge ship.)

With such a scheme, turn-around time would be kept to a minimum; barges could be dropped at the destination ports and others picked up in a matter of hours, rather than days. The handling of container barges at the terminals should be easier and more flexible.

At present, large tankers and container ships have to adopt some roundabout practices in order to have their cargo delivered to ports which have not the deep-water space to handle them. Ports which can handle them are few, as natural deep-water harbours are confined to certain coasts with the appropriate geological formations; the offshore loading facilities at major ports are at present expensive and, even so, generally unable to take a fully laden super-tanker. One expedient now being adopted is to transfer the oil at sea to smaller vessels near the destination, in order to lighten the great ship. Another is to unload at ports a considerable distance from the destination, so that cargo from the industrialized region of the North-Western mainland of Europe may be first unloaded on the West coast of Britain or even of Ireland; if it is containerized cargo, it may then make a land journey to an East-coast port in Britain and another sea journey in a smaller vessel across the North Sea. So great are the benefits of containerization and of super-ships that these practices are economic and large developments to extend their use are being planned.

The possible economies which undersea container barges could bring are obvious. The engine ship itself, much the most costly part of the system with its nuclear reactor and small crew, would never need to be held up by the handling of the cargo or by difficulties at the port of destination, and it could serve a much greater variety of ports than the present super-ships (indeed, it could even deliver to more than one port on its journey, like the old tramp steamers). In addition, the system would go a long way towards avoiding the turbulence of the seas and the delaying effects of weather and tides.

When Mackinder reflected on the most convenient means of movement of freight by land or by sea, in fact only twenty years ago, few foresaw even such a basically simple idea as the so-called 'container revolution'. It has indeed transformed the shipping business; undersea barges may mark another leap forward in the same line of evolution. It should be noted that even inland waterways are much the cheapest means of transportation, and the network of European waterways able to take very large barges is being considerably expanded. Soon it will be possible for ships to journey from the North Sea to the Black Sea through the heart of Europe. Another advantage of barges is that it is easy to handle a mixture of cargo: bulk commodities of oil, iron ore, coal, etc., can be hauled together with container ships of general-purpose cargo with no difficulty. Already some large surface ships on the transatlantic journey carry their cargo in barges, which are lowered off at the sea port and can then be pushed in groups by a tug to the industrial regions of the Rhine.

The container barge scheme may have one other significant advantage, and that concerns the increasingly important matter of pollution. The danger of accidents would, of course, always be present, but having a number of barges should lessen the overall dangers. The engine ship itself would be relatively small and would not normally be exposed to hazards in its operation. While great care would have to be taken with the coupling and uncoupling of the barges with the mother ship, this process would take place in the underwater calm, and in their final docking the barges would probably be split into individual, or at least smaller, units. At worst, it would be most unlikely that total disaster would overtake the transport, as happens when a large tanker breaks up.

Such a system is no doubt some years away, but the very precise manoeuvres necessary for docking in space flights suggest how quickly technological answers can be developed when there is an incentive for it. Once transportation begins to move underseas, such sophistication will probably develop sooner than might be anticipated. The excitement of technological frontiers and of innovation which in recent years has been associated with the air and outer space will be turned to another outlet in the underseas. We are just at the time of reaching this turning-point, when man's next great adventure in technology will be looking to the oceans of the world.

8. *Report of the National Commission on Marine Science, Engineering and Resources*, 1968. An undersea ship requires only half the power of a surface ship. As Sir Barnes Wallis explains, 'It's the waves, 50 per cent of the total resistance of the ship. A submarine when it's more than three diameters down doesn't set up any wave motion at all. It's all pure fiction.' And just as there have been great advances in design in aerodynamics, so there will be in the underwater medium. Sir Barnes Wallis, in an interview in the *Observer* supplement, 3 December 1972, stated the ideal when he said that what was wanted was

something between the conventional ship and an air freighter, with the capacity of one and the speed of the other. He added forcefully, 'Conventional surface ships are out. As a means of transport in the future, they are as dead as a dodo.'

There will of course always be roles for surface ships, but they will to a large extent be displaced in long-distance freight transport. Nuclear power can offer no great advantages for surface ships. The development of hydrofoil craft and hovercraft has local applications, but they cannot serve as large freight carriers, nor could they ever contend with conditions on routes such as the North Atlantic in the winter months, where waves of thirty feet and more can break up even conventional craft if they try to maintain their normal speed. When more energy is put into the military development of undersea ships, they will no doubt acquire greater versatility, even for surface operation. Smaller undersea ships could be fitted with retractable foils for high-speed operations close to the shore, disappearing when not in use. They will be adapted to take the fullest advantage of their inherent characteristics of mobility and surprise, and be equipped for sea-borne raids or landings.

9. Underwater oil storage tanks are also a logical development for undersea oil wells, and these would enable an undersea tanker ship to load at the source of production and transport the oil direct to its destination. This avoids the process of pumping oil ashore, and then loading it onto a tanker which carries it to sea again. If the safeguards against the risks of pollution are satisfactory, there are also conservationist grounds for siting storage tanks at sea, as coastal land by its nature is likely to be a particularly valuable amenity. As oil wells are being sited at greater and greater distances from the shore, the use of underwater fuel caches, in preference to the construction of longer pipelines, is bound to increase.

10. Most Western undersea ships carry auxiliary power sources in case of a breakdown of the reactor or turbines, though in fact nuclear engines have proved extremely reliable. A military writer for the *Guardian* expressed concern about the possibility of a cargo undersea ship getting trapped underneath the Arctic ice. There is little fear of this. Presumably any such cargo ships built in the West, at least, would have the same safety provision of auxiliary power. Moreover, the Arctic ice is not one solid sheet of ice. It is continually moving and numerous holes occur, giving a way to the surface; even conventional submarines would be able to find open spaces.

11. Mahan, A. T., *The Influence of Sea Power upon History*, Methuen, 1965, p. 25.

12. There can be no doubt that, with the development of the undersea ship, it will be possible to carry out amphibious operations on any coast in the world. Obviously, the less well defended the coast, the less difficulty would be encountered in the operation. A glance at a political map of the world will show that in this manner sea power could be brought to bear against nearly every state in the world. The growth of human society has tended to be near the sea, and access to the sea is of great importance even to countries whose main centres are inland. In the case of the Heartland country, the Soviet Union, it happens that it also has the longest 'sea coast of any state in the world. There are a handful of independent countries which are truly insulated from the sea, such as Tibet before its annexation by China; even in such a case, the neighbouring land powers (e.g. China and India) who might quarrel over the landlocked state or threaten it are themselves almost invariably exposed to sea power, and therefore it would in principle be impossible for a sea power alliance to intervene if the issue required it.

One key factor in amphibious assault is surprise, and the undersea ship provides this as never before. Because of its capacity for undersea transport, it can also provide for unloading the means for rapid movement on land in considerable quantities, using between ship and shore helicopters and surface-effect vehicles which travel both on land and sea. With the great versatility possible in the development of undersea ships, a very formidable invasion force could be available.

The idea of a direct invasion of Russia is not necessarily farfetched in military terms, but it may be objected that the political contingency in which it is likely to occur is excessively remote. If it appears an unlikely hypothesis at the present time, it is no more unlikely (in fact, less so) than a direct Russian invasion of Western Europe. From the point of view of Western strategic planning, the important element is that it could be a real possibility, and would force Russia to look in this direction and cover the contingency by keeping troops and conventional arms in this region which would not then be available for other purposes.

It may be thought that any direct invasion of Russian soil would be met with nuclear arms. But this is hardly likely if the aims are kept limited. Undersea operations need only result in the escalation to the use of nuclear arms and to all-out war if we forget the fundamental point that war is an instrument of policy. In the Russo–Chinese border clashes, there has been little possibility of the introduction of nuclear arms. (A more serious military conflict between Russia and China is one of the contingencies in which sea power based beyond the World Island might well wish to assert its influence.) Hezlet answers the

156

question about the introduction of nuclear arms in response to such
operations. 'There are many who think that the consequences of an
all-out nuclear attack are so suicidal that it would never be used, except to retaliate on any enemy who had already launched such an
attack. As the order to bomb Moscow cannot be given without the
order to bomb Washington and vice versa, there is much sense in this
view. If this is accepted, then the all-out nuclear attack cannot be used
to stave off defeat in a conventional campaign, which may have
started as a limited war. Therefore, if a country such as Great Britain
loses command of the sea in such a situation, she cannot regain it by
unleashing Polaris on the enemy. This would be like saying: "If you
continue to starve me, I will commit suicide." The only valid defence
is to regain command of the sea in the conventional manner and herein
lies the justification for other instruments of sea power' (Hezlet, Vice
Admiral Sir Arthur, *The Submarine and Sea Power*, Peter Davies,
1967, p. 258).

Obviously, in any such amphibious operations the objectives would
be limited, and it would be important that the nature of the war
should be understood. One hopes that such an eventuality is indeed
extremely unlikely, but it enables the West to make a favourable and
radical reassessment of its strategy, and if it did come to the point, it
is preferable to the alternatives.

13. The Russians have had a great and long interest in the Arctic,
while the West is now beginning to develop such an interest. The
Arctic is the region where the West and East meet in a frozen no-
man's-land. But these lands are becoming increasingly important for
mineral wealth and for transit between the Pacific and Atlantic regions.
In this there are the seeds for future friction between Russia and the
West.

9. The Oceanic Alliance

> But far beneath this wondrous world upon the
> surface, another and still stranger world met our
> eyes as we gazed over the side.
>
> Herman Melville (*Moby Dick*)

The central issue between Mackinder's Heartland theory and the sea power theory is over the means of transportation. While it is true that both land and sea are important for communication, it is the relative emphasis which makes the salient difference. Western civilization in the modern era was built upon sea power. Britain, by her unique geographical position, represented the epitome of the development of this mode of transport. The ships of the Columbian period enabled Europeans to encircle the globe so that modern political history has been essentially European history. Western statesmen and soldiers, especially continental and more recently British, have forgotten the important role of sea power, but it was the dominant factor in the rise of European power. Although various European states, at one time or another, represented the foremost land power, if land power were superior to sea power, then they would in the end have been overshadowed by the rise of Russia. Only by the conquest of Russia or an alliance with her could European land power have endured over a long period.

The supposed ascendancy of air power has been ephemeral. Although commercial air transport has been of great value, it has not made a major impact on ocean commerce except in passenger travel. The warplane, as an expression of the projectile cycle in warfare, has run its course and is destined for a lesser role in the future. There have been many hints of this development which have been resisted, since so much has been invested in aviation in the past. It represented great financial interests, and even more important, it occupied the same emotional place as sea power once had in the scheme of things. The belief in air power became an article of faith much like the

Englishman's reverence for the Royal Navy. To question this faith, to suggest that the aeroplane might be an obsolete species, seemed heresy. Liddell Hart said that a battleship to an admiral was like a cathedral to a bishop – and one might stretch the analogy further, to say that a bomber to an aviator has been like a cathedral to a bishop. All represented salvation in various ways.

In asserting that land power would become superior to sea power, it was necessary to make the implicit assumption that the development of sea transport had attained a plateau. It was, after all, the relationship between land and sea power which was at the core of the Heartland theory. If land transport had improved in relative efficiency and sea movement remained much the same as in 1919, then the arguments set forward would have great meaning. But it is not as simple as that. There have been great strides in land mobility and because they are essentially new developments, interest is directed towards them. Sea power, on the other hand, has been around for several centuries. It is natural that the same spirit which attracted men to the sea four hundred years ago should have waned. It could not be otherwise. The sailing ship was the most complicated machine in existence when first developed and was a magic carpet which enabled men to transport themselves to the most distant regions of the globe. It was part of a great and exciting enterprise. To be a sailor was to share in an adventure; it had inspiration. But this attitude is virtually non-existent today.

In the last half century if someone wanted to get into a young, dynamic atmosphere he would have done well to interest himself in air transport. A director of Rolls Royce once told me that he had visited the division of a firm which made aircraft and later the section where they were making a nuclear undersea ship. What impressed him was the complete difference in attitude – almost completely different worlds. The former was efficient and gave the impression of interest in the work, and he concluded that the air division should probably have been building the undersea ship. In the last decade the oceans have again beckoned with new frontiers, and it is quite natural that major aero-space companies are among the most prominent pioneers in the field of hydrospace, while the tired old surface sea dogs – in both naval and commercial circles – have been reluctant to take the jump literally into the sea.

With such a prevalent attitude towards shipping, any developments in sea transport were likely to be underrated or neglected. In fact, there have been a great many improvements since 1919. The real cost of transportation by sea has been falling. The most obvious development in merchant ships has been the building of super-tankers. Previously, the largest commercial ship had been the passenger liners *Queen Mary* and *Queen Elizabeth*, which were each about 80,000 tons. The super-tankers ran up to 300,000 tons and even larger ships are contemplated. For hauling bulk cargoes, the giant ships are much cheaper to use, though there will come a maximum size when the advantages are counteracted by other factors. There is also the aspect of security: larger ships mean fewer ships, and the loss of a handful of them might be disastrous for a country. A modern industrial state dependent upon oil could be particularly vulnerable.

Mackinder himself seems to have been aware of the strength which lay around and across the ocean in the future. Professors Harold and Margaret Sprout have pointed out that the ideas of Mackinder which constitute the Heartland theory were formulated in 1919 and that later he changed the basis of his thinking. He came to look upon Western Europe and North America as an oceanic heartland. As early as 1924, he wrote:

Western Europe and North America now constitute for many purposes a single community of nations . . . The victory of the oceanic nations has brought it about that the line between east and west, between the continental and the oceanic nations, runs along the Rhine and not through mid-Atlantic. In the United States the most abundant rainfall and the most productive coalfields are to be found in the east, but in Europe they are in the west. Thus the west of Europe and the east of North America are physical complements to one another and are rapidly becoming the balanced halves of a single great community.[1]

This has largely happened; nevertheless, it is his ideas of 1919 which have made the major and lasting impact. Six years later, Mackinder wrote of this new theory that North America and

Europe could be combined together in a '. . . total of four per cent of the globe surface, and . . . the main geographical habitat of Western civilization. Within this area are 600 million people . . . Notwithstanding the oceanic break, it may be regarded as a single area . . .' [2] The growth of this oceanic alliance was not fully apparent to Mackinder when he died. The strength of the West in the post-war period rests upon its dynamic economic energy and much of this in turn is dependent upon international trade. The Western powers lie strategically around the world's oceans. Their economic interdependence is a paramount feature of the latter half of the twentieth century.

Nations are now beginning to use the oceans in more extensive ways than ever before. Historically, the oceans have been extremely important, but only on their surface. The richest societies have usually flourished near the sea or other large bodies of water (even in the extensive area of the United States, the great majority of people live within a hundred miles of the sea, and the Great Lakes – around which there is another large concentration of population – are now accessible to ocean ships). One factor conducive to this prosperity was favourable opportunities for trade; another in the past was the wealth from overseas empires. Navies were necessary to protect this trade; they helped to create wealth, while armies tended to be a drain on national resources unless they were able to conquer quickly. But the fleets of the past touched only the surface of the waters, and this is now changing. Nations are going into the underseas in search of wealth; there, beneath the ocean waves, potentially great empires exist.

It will be in the underseas that the greatest development will take place in the future. In the United States, the National Commission on Marine Science, Engineering and Resources in 1968 projected the goals that 'within ten years the United States should possess the capability to occupy the US territorial sea, utilize the US continental shelf and slope to depths of 2,000 feet, and explore the depths of 20,000 feet'.[3] It goes on to state: 'Within 30 years the United States should be prepared to manage the shelf and slope to 2,000 feet depths and utilize the sea bed to 20,000 feet.' In fact, 98 per cent of the ocean floor lies above the 20,000-foot level. Since the oceans of the world cover three-fourths of the surface area of the globe, this is a vast area. The question is what use can be made of this territory? In the continental shelf regions great use is already being made of it in the search for oil and gas. However, these are not the only minerals being sought and mined in the shelf areas. Diamonds, iron ore, sulphur, magnesium, iodine, fluorine, tin, and salt are being taken from the sea bed in increasing quantities by commercial operations.

The most important activity on the sea bed at the present time is the search for oil and natural gas in the offshore or continental shelf areas of the world. 'By 1979 it is forecast that between 35 per cent and 50 per cent of petrol supplies will come from offshore – a production equal to total world production today.'[4] Already 16 per cent of the oil and gas in the West comes from offshore wells. The extent of the finds in the North Sea is particularly notable. According to the *Economist*:

> Sir John Eden, Minister for Industry, estimated the North Sea's potential output [of oil] at 25m. tons a year by 1975 and perhaps treble that by 1980. This compares with current consumption in Britain of approximately 100m. tons a year. But as recently as December, Sir John had already put potential output at 50m. tons by 1975, and his own officials have been saying privately that they would not be surprised if it hit 150m. tons by 1980 and 250m. tons five years later. Even these are regarded as conservative estimates. There are some, not necessarily optimists, who would double them. If these last figures are anywhere near right, it would make Britain one of the largest oil-producing nations in the world, and certainly self-sufficient . . .[5]

Purely commercial interests are now giving attention to designing and building new means of working on the sea bed; this is a significant point of departure, as previously most of the concern in underseas operations has come from either scientific or military interests. A number of British, American and French companies have launched projects to build various forms of underseas life-support systems. The present method employed for underseas oil operations is to use surface rigs, and divers may be sent into the sea when needed. But the trend is moving towards putting more and more of the operations beneath the surface. This could be more expensive in capital, but, in the long run, it should be cheaper. There are several conflicting views concerning how best to work on the sea bed. One idea is to use free divers working from habitats on or near the sea floor. This concept has resulted in the building of a number of different types of vehicle for such work. Another idea is exclusively to use submarine vehicles with remote control arms for work to be done on the bottom. So far this latter method has not been entirely satisfactory. With work going on at increasing depths however, this could be the solution. According to Mr Gregory Mott, of the Vickers shipbuilding group: 'It is the wrong philosophy to try to adapt man to working at these depths. The investment should be in a machine that allows an ordinary man to work at these depths. For the submersible, the problems of working at 2,000 feet are the same as those at 200 feet. But for the diver, the physiological problems are very different.'[6] None the less, there are people who believe that there is no limit to the depth and pressure at which man can be adapted to work if proper controls are maintained.

Some of the firms and individuals intensely interested in working at greater depths are studying the possibilities of mining on the sea bed at depths from 6,000 feet to 10,000 feet or more. There are on the sea floor nodules of high-grade ore, and already several operations to try to mine these ores are underway. These minerals are formed naturally by a continuing process of accretion, and the supply seems almost inexhaustible. Dr John Mero has been the leading light in the effort to develop these resources. He maintains that the nodules in the Pacific Ocean alone could supply the world with manganese for 400,000 years, cobalt for 200,000 years, copper for 6,000 years, aluminium for 70,000 years, nickel for 150,000 years and titanium for 2 million years; there are ten other elements with similar potential. The abundance of the supply will drastically lower the price of these metals and could extend their use. According to Mero: 'If copper costs a dollar a pound then copper from the sea will only cost 20 cents. Nickel will be so cheap that it will make stainless steel possible even for structural purposes. There will even be stainless bridges – no more painting.'[7]

The resource is self-renewing, and is accumulating at rates considerably faster than present world consumption. The same applies to deep-sea sediments; all the effectively inexhaustible oozes of the ocean floor have economic value, and Mero calculates that the delivered cost of the marine-mined materials, such as diatomite and lime-bearing deposits, will be less than the land-mined equivalent. Mero has written a book entitled *The Mineral Resources of the Sea* in which he states:

Ocean mining offers many advantages which are not possible with traditional land mining. We have, in the ocean, materials that are available without removing any overburden, without the use of explosives, and without expensive drilling operations for sampling and ore breakage. With cameras, the complete deposit can be explored prior to mining – every ton of ore can be directly accounted for before the mining starts. There will be no drifts to drive, shafts to sink, or town sites to construct in developing a deep-sea mine.[8]

It all sounds too easy to believe, though mining at these great depths presents other formidable problems and the time-scale for its development is uncertain. The operation itself involves new techniques for sweeping the potato-sized nodules off the sea floor with a giant vacuum-cleaner type of machine. But even this is an advantage, according to Mero.

An ocean-mining operation, because it would be a whole new concept in mining, can be designed for automation from the beginning, which would result in new equipment designs not bound by traditions. The equipment would be very flexible to move from one area to another for various types of nodules as the market demands. Sea transportation can be used to carry the mined materials to most of the world's markets with no other form of transportation involved. About 75 per cent of the material, and more in some cases, being mined and handled is saleable in contrast to the 2 per cent or so of today's copper and nickel ores. The grade and physical characteristics of the deposits are highly uniform over large areas. The non-abrasive character and low density of the nodules would allow the use of hydraulic systems for transferring of the nodules throughout the mining and processing operations.[9]

Tests in relatively shallow depths of about 2,000 feet have indicated that it is possible to mine the nodules. When such operations are possible at greater depths and on a larger scale, they will have serious repercussions upon the mineral markets of the world, and aggravate problems in the balance of economic life between nations, creating new political tensions. Most of the present supplies of minerals come from the underdeveloped countries of the world; the trend making the rich nations richer and the poor nations poorer could be reinforced.

Another great resource of the sea is food; at present the annual value of the sea fish catch is about three times the income obtained from all offshore oil and gas and marine minerals. Obtaining food from the sea by what are essentially hunting methods has of course been practised since primitive times; almost the entire catch of present-day sea fishing is based upon such methods. But we are now at the point where a new approach to harvesting the sea will be introduced: the production and collection of sea food will be managed in a more systematic and scientific manner. This is sometimes loosely called 'sea farming', though marine farms in a sense which is equivalent to farming in land will be confined to inshore areas.[10]

It is estimated that sea fishing can be increased to four times the present world catch without danger of over-fishing and without any new departures in fishing methods (already there have been a number of highly successful experiments in simply transplanting species of fish from their nursery grounds to new and favourable areas). The catch has in fact trebled within the last twenty years. It is true that fears are already expressed that nations are over-fishing; this is the case for certain areas and for certain species of fish. What is desperately needed is some agreement between the nations with fishing fleets, and a means for the enforcement of it. Food shortages, together with population increase and pollution, are among the greatest threats to the future, and the sea has an important place as a source of additional food supplies.

In the longer run, there are prospects of radically new developments for both increasing the fertility of the sea and gathering its food. The continental shelf regions will obviously be the first to be worked by some means involving true husbandry, but the harvest gathered from certain areas of the deep seas will eventually increase as well. There is a suggestion for sinking a nuclear reactor on to the sea bed; its heat would stir up the sea and extend the amount of primary fish food, thus increasing the population of fish. Another suggestion is for a 6,000-foot pipe to be lowered into the mid Atlantic, which would bring the plankton on which fish feed from the deeps to the surface, and support pelagic species over a new area; because of the physical and chemical properties of sea water at these different layers, the pipe would create a natural fountain with very little pumping.[11]

It is evident that in the next decade or two great strides will be made in the technology for underseas development – in undersea vehicles, life-support systems, and mobile equipment. This course will be continued to permanent installations on the sea floor. It needs little imagination to visualize that these could blossom into underwater 'cities' in the future – self-contained habitats with nuclear energy supplying the power needs. As it is today, more and more of the lives of people in the advanced countries are spent in closed air-conditioned environments in vehicles and buildings. The idea of a submerged city is practicable, although it may be that the step to an underwater naval base will be taken first.[12]

The option of moving into the marine environment is now open for mankind, and the motivation is also there, for reasons of defence and commerce and, perhaps not least, because it now presents the most substantial and adventurous opportunity for man to extend himself on this planet. The oceans and seas cover 71 per cent of the earth's surface, and in volume, that is, in cubic miles, they are of course many times greater than the land above sea level. Clearly, men will have the drive to conquer this world. However, we have now become aware that to do so is no longer a question of choice, but is fast becoming a necessity. The rate of consumption of resources on land seems to be inexorably set to outstrip the ability to meet it in production from the land. Sir Frederick Brundrett has stated the truth simply: 'A world which spends more in a single year on research into space than it has done since the beginning of the century on research into the sea is mad.'[13]

The growing interest in the sea bed means that the nations of the world must settle the question of who owns the great resources lying there. The answer at present is that the sea floor beyond the continental shelf belongs to no one, which means equally that it may belong to everyone or anyone. The waters above are of course free and international. It is because the oceans have now become potentially important in a totally novel way that we must suppose that there will be attempts to assert political control over portions of the sea floor; until the question is settled politically, it is open to private entrepreneurs to exploit the mineral riches where practical for them. The position is different with the continental shelf areas; these are an extension of the land under sea level, and take up 5 per cent of the earth's surface. The average width of the shelf is 45 miles, but its actual width varies greatly from one coast to another: off Northern Russia it extends for 800 miles, and off the west coast of South America it is virtually non-existent where the coastal sea plunges to thousands of feet beneath the Andes Mountains. About 90 per cent of the world's fish catch is taken from continental shelf areas. In 1964, the international Continental Shelf Convention came into force; this gives nations sovereign rights over the resources of their part of the continental shelf. At a stroke, some nations' territory was greatly extended; the United States, for instance, acquired an additional million square miles. The clause in the Convention which was intended to define the national continental shelf area was unhappily worded, as it did not foresee the rapid progress in oceanology which has taken place, and it has been the subject of some dispute.

All the land under the North Sea happens to be part of the continental shelf; when the search for minerals there was intensified it was necessary to map out this sea floor with precision. In this case, the national boundaries are drawn midway between the coastlines of the bordering states. The coasts of islands belonging to a country are treated as baselines in the same way as the nearest points of the mainland coast. Britain, by her unique position, has obtained the largest of these national zones. A curious situation has been created. In effect, countries have extended their national zones so that Britain now has common borders with continental countries such as France, Holland, and Norway, but the surface of the North Sea is still considered international waters. The interesting question arises as to where national jurisdiction ends and international waters begin. (As pipelines now criss-cross the North Sea, anchors can damage them, and have already done so. These lines carry natural gas at present, but in the future oil could cause serious pollution.) The present concept of 'sovereign rights' over the national continental shelf zones does not carry with it the concept of 'ownership' in the unequivocal way which territorial sovereignty on land does.

The limits of territorial waters are another matter, and one which has led to much dispute in recent years as many countries have claimed large extensions of them. By international convention, territorial waters give a nation exclusive rights to all the resources in them and under them and to the air space above them. The main purpose of nations extending their limits has been to assert control over the fishing in them. There is at the time of writing no international agreement on recognized limits; the traditional three-mile limit which was formerly in general use arose for reasons of military defence, not protection of resources, and was based on the range of early cannon.

As the development of the sea proceeds, it may prove difficult in practice to keep quite separate the questions of jurisdiction over territorial waters (the ocean surface and the waters below) and over the ocean bed and its subsoil. Mineral operations affect fishing; installations on the surface can affect shipping; fishing can affect mineral operations on the sea bed (the actions of trawls can even be a hazard to pipelines). This situation will provide a further reason, in addition to that of protecting fish stocks, for nations to extend their jurisdiction over the ocean surface. There is also, of course, the reason of nationalism, a factor which hardly needs a rational motive to impel it – the flag has its reasons of which reason knows nothing.

Historically, there has been a gradual enclosure of the common lands, and it is possible that a similar trend will occur over the continental shelf areas of the common seas; the water space itself will become divided up according to the borders of the sea bed below.

The Law of the Sea at present largely consists of what has been set out in four conventions adopted by the United Nations. These allow the rights of free passage through territorial waters and free fishing on the high seas. The future is likely to see more restrictions on both. The issue of rights and responsibilities could arise at any time through an accident involving shipping and mining operations. Another important problem will be that of pollution: pollution in the open seas does not recognize national boundaries. It should also be noted that jurisdiction, whether by international law or national sovereignty, must be enforceable to be meaningful.[14]

The questions of national boundaries and of rights in and under the sea are going to be a cause of strong controversy, and no doubt real friction between nations, in the coming years. There are conflicting interests which must become more vociferous as the rewards come closer and the exploitation of the oceans gathers momentum. The silent world of 'the sea bed beyond the limits of national jurisdiction' will create a great deal of noise. Jealousies and antagonisms will erupt as nations seek gain or simply a fair share; even land-locked countries have an interest, for by no stretch of reasoning can the sea floor beyond the continental shelf be considered an extension of territory on land. The Western powers are strategically placed by geography and skill to lead in this great ocean enterprise, but if they seek a happier and more peaceful world as well as riches, they will have to lead in political imagination as well as in entrepreneurial endeavour.

All the economic uses of the sea, together with the emergence of undersea cargo ships, will have a profound geopolitical influence for the future. The relationships between states will be greatly affected; international agencies will have a more conspicuous role, perhaps even supported by economic and financial power if any arrangement is made to give them custody of leases in the seas; and the so-called 'Third World' will be deeply concerned in whatever way the political questions are resolved. The balance of economic and political power will undergo disconcerting shifts, the aims of policy will be reorientated and the means of implementing them altered.

In the past, only the surface of the seas has been used, as a means of transport and of fishing from the surface. One of the central points which Mackinder made was that sea power must rest upon a firm land base, productive and secure.

Every characteristic of sea-power may be studied in British history during the last three centuries, but the home-base, productive and secure, is the one thing essential to which all things else have been added. We are told that we should thank God daily for our Channel, but as I looked out over the glorious harvest of this English plain in this critical year of 1918, it seemed to me that our thanksgiving as a seafaring people should be no less for our fruitful soil.[15]

But what happens when a country obtains much of its food sources from the sea, its minerals from the sea floor and natural gas and oil from its own underwater lands? We have an entirely new view of the world. It is a global view which provides a new concept for sea power in the future. More than ever, the Western powers may have a source of strength in the ocean.

Notes to Chapter 9

1. Mackinder, H. J., *Nations of the Modern World*, George Philip & Son, 1924, pp. 251–2.

2. Mackinder, H. J., 'The Human Habitat', *The Scottish Geographical Magazine*, November 1931.

3. *Our Nation and the Sea*, Report of the National Commission on Marine Science, Engineering and Resources, US Government Printing Office, Washington, 1969, p. 15.

4. *Sunday Times*, 12 March 1972. Tony Loftas has written: 'Geologists estimate that the continental shelf holds supplies of oil at least equal to those on the land – some 1,000,000,000,000 barrels' (*The Last Resource*, Hamish Hamilton, 1969, p. 107).

5. *Economist*, 13 March 1972.

6. *Financial Times*, 21 March 1972.

7. Horsfield, B., and Stone, P. B., *The Great Ocean Business*, Hodder & Stoughton, 1972, p. 255.

8. Mero, John, *Mineral Resources of the Sea*, Elsevier, New York, 1965, p. 280.

9. ibid., p. 280. Another rich source of minerals in the seas is what are known as brine sinks. The first brine sink was discovered in the Red Sea in 1964 at a depth of 5,000 feet. Since then other brine sinks have been discovered, and speculation about their origin has raised major questions for geologists. The deposits in brine sinks contain high percentages of valuable metals, including zinc, copper, lead and silver. It has been estimated that the sediments in the upper 30 feet on one of the Red Sea sinks are worth two billion dollars, and these sediments are at least 300 feet thick. Several companies have sought to establish exploration 'rights' for this area; one firm has done so by licence from the Sudanese Government, having persuaded the government to claim national jurisdiction over it. But at the moment the technology for mining brine sinks at these depths has not been developed, and it seems unlikely to be for some years to come.

10. In terms of cost effectiveness, sea farming would appear to have a tremendous advantage over land farming. The food conversion ratios for fish – that is, the amount of food consumed by a fish in relation to the gain in weight of the fish – are very much more favourable than in mammals. For a number of reasons, fish do not need to use so much energy just to stay alive; being cold-blooded, for instance, they do not expend energy maintaining a constant warm body temperature. 'Compared to cows, sheep and other land animals, fish are in an even more advantageous position. Cows need to grow big bones to hold themselves upright and consequently they need larger muscles and more energy to move about. If their body tissues were supported in the sea like those of fish much of the extra energy could go into making edible body weight. One estimate suggests that roughly speaking an acre of land will produce 100 pounds of beef but the same area would produce more than a ton of fish. To emphasize the point, shellfish, which do not move at all, grow even thicker on the ground; from one acre it should be possible to harvest 100 tons of mussels or oysters. American calculations suggest that if Long Island Sound could be given over to mussel fishing its 1,000 square miles could produce a quantity of protein equal to three times the total world fish catch' (Horsfield and Stone, op. cit., p. 275).

11. Underseas vehicles will eventually be used for some sea fishing. Wilbert MacLeod Chapman, marine resources director of the United States' Ralston-Purina Company, has commented on how the fisherman is popularly pictured, with a loincloth, a big smile and outrigger canoe in the tropics, and in higher latitudes 'as a grizzled veteran in

oilskins, with pipe in mouth, in a dory surrounded by high, green, white-tipped waves' (Barton, Robert, *Oceanology Today*, Aldus Books, 1970, p. 76). But fishing has already moved into a new technological era in surface vessels, with automated aids for detecting and netting fish, and factories on board for filleting and freezing them. (The Soviet fishing ship *Vostok*, for example, is 43,000 tons, and carries on board 14 catcher vessels each of 66 tons, and a helicopter for spotting shoals. The power plants on board generate enough electricity for a town of 10,000 people.) It is obvious that fishing from vessels above the waves for fish that live and feed on the sea floor is a crude approach. The species which live close to the sea bed are called demersal fish, and include the flatfish such as plaice and round fish such as cod and haddock. The method of catching them is known as bottom trawling; not only is it an inefficient means in principle, but it can also be damaging in practice to fishing grounds. As fishing moves into the stage where it involves some degree of husbandry or sea farming, it will become not only more efficient, but necessary, to use something like submersible craft, probably working in conjunction with a nuclear-powered undersea mother ship.

12. The development of underwater human habitats would be associated with special purposes, such as aquaculture or mining operations. Sea cities in the sense of complete human communities are likely to arise as floating cities, with their usual activities on the surface, but other facilities lying in submerged quarters perhaps fifty feet below. Though for a long time projects for floating cities are likely to exist only on the drawing board – as is already the case – they are already more than idle speculation; there are good reasons for predicting that some time in the twenty-first century they will make economic and social sense. What is likely to happen in the meantime is that some particular installations will be put in the sea. Nuclear power stations, for instance, might be thus put out of the way. For both recreational and commercial purposes, accessible shoreline land is at a premium, and developments in coastal and ocean engineering could eventually extend the available coastline. There are other local uses of the seas which will have some part to play in the future. One of these is tidal power stations, and pilot schemes have been built by the Russians on the coast of the Barents Sea in the Arctic and by the French in Brittany.

13. Brundrett, Sir Frederick, *TheNeglected Sea*, Haldane Memorial Lecture, March 1963. Sir Frederick is Chairman of the Research and Development Committee of the White Fish Authority in Britain. He went on to say: 'Unfortunately, the general attitude of the public

in this matter is reflected by the fact that whereas the newspapers of this country seem to find it obligatory to record in detail the most trivial event occurring at Cape Canaveral, there is practically no comment of any kind ... about major International Oceanographic Congresses and the extremely important matters they cover' (Barton, op. cit., p. 13). An upsurge of awareness will no doubt occur in coming years, but it is urgent for political leaders in the West to get their priorities right. Those countries which foresee what is happening and put present energy and money into development programmes in oceanology will obviously be in a more advantageous position in the future.

14. In one way, rights over sea fish are much more elusive to draw up than rights over marine minerals. Minerals stay put, but fish move about – in and out of national and international waters. If a country engages in some form of sea farming which improves the environment and increases the stock of fish in the open sea, it will obviously not be pleased if part of the result of its efforts is taken by a fishing vessel belonging to a country which has contributed nothing to the cost. The management or cultivation of the food resources of the open seas requires some quite subtle and comprehensive form of international agreement.

15. Mackinder, H. J., *Democratic Ideals and Reality*, Norton, New York, 1962, p. 55–6.

10. A New World Outlook

> ... Men must adopt systems of thought that sift
> and order the vast amount of communication
> that assaults their senses every day ... Such
> thought-filters are systems of evaluation as well
> as mere ordering, and therefore may cause
> distortion ... That distortion is inevitable when
> some aspect of the world is permitted to
> dominate our view of it. The world is much too
> complex to be evaluated in terms of a single
> aspect. There is a basic paradox here: the world
> is so complex that we must systematise our
> knowledge of it, but the very complexity of the
> world makes our systems necessarily imperfect.
> The important thing of course is to remember
> that our global views are imperfect, to use them
> as aids to thought but not as dogmas.
>
> S. B. Jones (*Global Strategic Views*)[1]

We have come to the point where we face a new world outlook.
It is not only in the pages of this book that we have reached that
point, but it was evident in the news of world events while these
pages were being written; it is apparent, however ambiguously,
in the motions of statesmen; it is acknowledged, however tenu-
ously, by the professional commentators. But what is really
evident from these sources is not what the new outlook of the
Western World is to be, nor on what global realities it should be
based; rather what is evident is the negative conclusion that the
old outlook, which provided the basis of Western policy for so
many years after the end of the Second World War and the
emergence of the Cold War, is in pieces.

This does not mean that this fact is explicitly recognized by
Western leaders. The emperor does not easily see that he has no
clothes on, and statesmen are among the least ready of people to
admit publicly that they have been grossly mistaken. Even patent
reversals of policy are somehow rationalized and presented as
continuations of previous policy. Nor are we suggesting that

yesterday's false ideas have been discarded; they persist to a dangerous extent. It is possible for us to see that the Western world outlook is falling to pieces in principle; this does not prevent Western statesmen from attempting to put the pieces into practice. However, events in the world have brought us to a point where it is so obvious that the former picture of the world is incoherent that any systematic pretence that it is still true must be given up. The cracks are too glaring.

All periods of time are periods of transition, but some are more transitional than others. With regard to international relations, most people concerned are now aware that the early 1970s is a period when radical changes have become apparent. Positions and policies which were believed to hold good for about twenty-five years are now considered to be in the melting-pot. Fewer people consider consciously and analytically the global outlook, but that there is a distinctive global outlook, which must differ from one point in time to another and which is also likely to differ from one geographical and political area to another, is an inevitable and undeniable fact. This is so whether such a global outlook is systematic or unreflectively presupposed, coherent or incoherent in its parts. The fundamental point to be understood is that it is the global outlook which is in a period of transition today, in the strongest sense; that is, it does not just require some adjustments, but the previously accepted premises cannot hold. We need a new map of the world, and, to extend the cartographical metaphor, it should be based upon a new projection.

Changes which appear drastic have generally been working their way over a long period of time in processes which are gradual and little observed. People tend to hold tenaciously to received ideas, until the accumulation of evidence is such that the whole framework breaks up with a disconcerting lack of warning. To select particular events as turning points is really often no more than a matter of inconvenience, providing a symbol by which to characterize a vividly complex and continuing development. Certain events are, of course, unique in their public impact, even if not necessarily so in their underlying significance. If we take the case of the United States, we can pick on Nixon's visit to China as an event which woke up the American public to a changed world.

Later in this chapter other political events will be noted which indicate new orientations in the global outlook, though they are in themselves symptoms rather than causes. Later generations will select other facts by which to represent the critical developments of our period, and it has been suggested that one date which will be prominent in the future chronicles is August 1958, when the *Nautilus* voyaged from the Bering Strait to the Greenland Sea.

We have said that our new map of the world needs to be based on a new projection. It is true, as Mackinder stated, that 'the physical facts of geography have remained substantially the same during the fifty or sixty centuries of recorded human history'. But the facts of geography as a science are recognized to include more than location, shape, and topography; such factors as resources and population, technology and movement, must be considered. Many factors go into forming a world outlook, including such cultural factors as ideology and a country's experience of its own history. For the purposes of the thesis in this book, we have concentrated upon certain geopolitical aspects of the contemporary world. It must be emphasized again that the premises for policy lie in geopolitical views, and a world outlook exists within a geopolitical framework. The political importance of the geographical dimension has been aptly stated by Professor Cohen. 'It is to geography that we turn for a true appreciation of political realities. The geographical setting, both that which is fixed and that which is dynamic, provides us with a basis for understanding today's political map and for anticipating change. Therefore the geopolitical map is more closely attuned to reality than the political map.'[2]

The more obvious indicators of change lie in the shifting field of politics, and it is natural that the most immediate matters get noticed, both by the public and by those in power. Beneath the political surface are other underlying factors. Policy is made in the minds of men; its contours may not concur with a true map of the world. It is on the interface between these two that the study of geopolitics throws its light.

Half of the argument of this book is that Western policy as it emerged in those formative years in the mid century was based upon a fallacy – and that this fallacy rested primarily upon geo-political misconceptions, reinforced by some cardinal contradic-tions and confusions in military thinking. In order to expose this fallacy, we had to go some way back into history, and then to consider certain key factors which have come about in more recent years and which are of far-reaching consequence for the coming years. If the importance which we have attached to these new factors is at all near the mark, then we have given at least some indication of the direction in which a different world outlook for the West should move, if it is to be in accordance with the realities of geography and power in the last decades of this century. This forms the other half of the argument of this book, and in this final chapter we turn our attention to some of the positive implications for Western policy.

Before doing so, a brief résumé of the conclusions already reached is advisable. The essential dilemma posed in the first chapter is that there has been a basic contradiction in Western defence philosophy. Central to this philosophy is the theory that the West has a need for nuclear arms, and that this imperative is so strong that these arms must dominate strategy; this theory arises out of the belief that the Soviet Union occupies a superior strategic position on the World Island, i.e. the acceptance of the Heartland view of the world. On the other hand, we are faced with the recent discovery of the obvious fact that nuclear arms cannot be considered a useful instrument of policy. The force of this paradox has been concealed by the confusion between 'policy' and 'strategy'.

In order to resolve this intellectual dilemma, it was necessary to re-examine the basis of the Heartland theory. Is the Heartland theory a fact today, embodying the significance that Mackinder attached to it? Does the Soviet Union occupy a position superior to any other nations? The Soviet Union is a vast land mass and has great defensive strength. The essential question in this con-text, however, is whether all the advantages of its position add up to make it potentially the most powerful state in the world, and to constitute a threat in the unique form which was seen through Western eyes and has determined the main direction of Western policy and strategy.

It was shown that the Heartland view of the world does not correspond with reality. This has been demonstrated by means of reference, in particular, to the ideas of Mackinder. As the case for the strength of the Heartland was first, most fully and force-fully set out by Mackinder, this was a convenient and suitable means of undertaking our analysis in a clear and simple way. But there are some students of strategy and international relations – especially in Britain – who minimize the influence of Mackinder and who maintain that it was not so great as this approach might imply. They argue, in a characteristically pragmatic British manner, that the West would have reacted in much the same way regardless of Mackinder's writings. While it may be true that the direct influence of Mackinder in Britain was not conspicuous in the mid forties, the same cannot be said about America, and it was in Washington that the final decisions were made. The Americans, without a fund of experience in world affairs, have tended to be more theoretical in their approach. But, apart from this, temperamentally the Americans are more receptive to the kind of sweeping and portentous generalizations which Mack-inder made, while the English intellectual temperament would be very dubious about flaunting them. The point is mainly of academic interest, as it can be shown that the dominant views in both countries over the critical period were tacitly in agreement with Mackinder, and supported his major premises.

There is no doubt that the underlying factors with which Mackinder was concerned were greatly reinforced in the minds of Western leaders by more immediate factors. Much of Europe at the close of the Second World War was in ruins and its recovery was uncertain. The impression of the offensive strength of the Red Army had been fortuitously magnified. The establishment of Soviet-controlled régimes in Eastern Europe was interpreted as a sign of Russian aggressive designs. In the following years, the size of the conventional forces which the Soviet Union could readily deploy in Europe far exceeded that of the NATO coun-tries; the idea that the Western countries could not match the Soviet Union in terms of land power, and that therefore they might as well shield themselves behind nuclear arms, was itself a contributing factor in this situation. Nuclear arms also appeared to offer a short cut to a solution – defence with less cost and less sweat. And of course all the factors became aggravated by the ideological division; anti-communist phobia made the Heartland still more of a threat, and gave to the Kremlin a conspiratorial power which could cross borders without movement.

There were many other immediate factors which played a part; however, when they are all added together, it is apparent that Western strategy still rested on the broad basis of the Heartland theory – or the Heartland theory by any other name. This strategy may have been wrong, as we have argued it was; the alternative to viewing it as formed on this geopolitical foundation is to see it as silly and lacking in any coherent rationale, which is far less plausible. George F. Kennan was one of the principal architects of the policy of containment; this doctrine could only have been put forward in relation to a Heartland theory. It became in fact part and parcel of the same world outlook, yet Kennan disclaimed any influence of Mackinder on him. He wrote, 'Our [the United States'] problem is to prevent the gathering together of the military-industrial potential of the entire Eurasian land mass under a single power threatening the interests of the insular and maritime portions of the globe.' These words might be said to be taken straight out of the Mackinder's Heartland theory, and it seems quibbling to inquire whether or not Kennan developed his doctrine independently of Mackinder (as a matter of fact, he notes elsewhere the great influence which the book *Makers of Modern Strategy* had on him – and Mackinder was a great influence in that book).[3]

So, in substance, the West, and most prominently the United States, believed in the essential propositions of the Heartland theory, in the terms in which these have been put before the reader in previous chapters. There is, however, no evidence to suggest that the Russians have ever accepted the idea that they possess a stronger strategic position than that of the United States. Indeed, all their reactions indicate the exact opposite. There is a telling illustration of this in Milovan Djilas's book *Conversations with Stalin*. According to Djilas, Stalin wanted to prevent the grave threat to the Western lines of communication from the communist uprising in Greece in 1947. Djilas recorded

Stalin as saying to Kardelj: 'If, if! No, they have no prospect of success at all. What, do you think that Great Britain and the United States – the United States, the most powerful state in the world – will permit you to break their line of communication in the Mediterranean? Nonsense. And we have no navy. The uprising in Greece must be stopped as quickly as possible.'⁴

If anyone looked with favour upon the Heartland theory, then obviously it should have been the Russians. But they did not; they in turn felt threatened by the strategic position of the Western powers. Into the Russian world outlook has gone a different theory, which may be called the Imperialist theory.

One by one we have examined certain key aspects of the Heartland theory in the past five chapters, and we have seen that the concepts are not true. They will not stand up to any realistic analysis on land, they are falling down in the air, they have been sunk at sea. Chronologically, the land-based premises were the first to be invalidated. In the future it is the great revival of maritime power and an entirely new dimension of oceanic interest which will be of paramount importance.

The alpha and omega of the Heartland theory lie in the ideas of land power supremacy. Mackinder was the first to put forward the idea of land power supremacy in a systematic way. The central premise of the Heartland theory is the power of the Heartland region to expand easily. If this is translated into terms of military power, it implies that in modern warfare the attack is stronger than the defence. This is simply not true, but it is an accepted dictum of Western defence thinking. The opposite view has not really proved persuasive, despite convincing evidence to support it. First impressions are the strongest, and our minds go back to the Battle of France in the summer of 1940. The feeling persists that the Red Army could easily launch a 'blitzkrieg' to overrun Western Europe, although contemporary military theorists are careful not to use the term 'blitzkrieg' in this connection. The reader may have got the impression from Chapter 5 that the difficulty is simply a matter of education. This is an oversimplification of the problem, which undoubtedly lies far deeper. It is a state of mind. Western people have lost their buoyancy of spirit and cannot bring themselves to believe in the future. This is a spiritual sickness of Western society which has been noted by many for more than a century. We are attached to mental pictures of impending doom, disaster, decay, disintegration; even though it is quite apparent that the problems in the world are real and objective, our response to them is subjective and is a symptom of a malaise, of a failure of nerve. The Cold War period in particular was 'the age of anxiety', but a defeatist attitude has taken root in the Western mind over a longer period. If we can bring ourselves to believe that the defence is stronger than the attack in conventional warfare, this would mean that we have gone some way to restoring our faith in ourselves and in our future. It is rational to believe this, but it is also important psychologically, for it means that the West would not be continually reacting to imaginary threats. It implies a secure base, and a secure base is as much a psychological condition as it is a military concept. One can never be secure if one must be looking out of the window, into the closet and under the bed every few minutes.

Belief in the superiority of the defence over the attack in land warfare, also entails a reversal of the Western view on guerrilla warfare. The accepted idea has been that insurgency warfare represents a direct threat to the West, but looked at from another standpoint, rather than posing a threat, it provides a reassurance. If it were the aim of a state to seize control over the World Island, guerrilla warfare would make it immensely more difficult. The power of the defence gives smaller states more freedom of action in resisting overt force from the giant powers. This will not always be true, depending upon the circumstances, but the client states of both the United States and Russia have shown a remarkable degree of independence. Even the North Vietnamese have shown considerable independence of both Moscow and Peking.

One might recall the historical analogy from the Napoleonic Wars, when the French tried unsuccessfully to unify Europe by force. Guerrilla warfare was used effectively by both the Spanish and the Russians in sapping the strength of the French forces. While technology has aided the forces of oppression in the past, it could now favour the guerrilla soldier at the expense of the regular. New light-weight equipment and rapid-fire arms enables these irregulars to disperse themselves over a wide area with considerable force. In the Vietnam War, the North Vietnamese and Viet Cong have demonstrated the potential power of guerrilla warfare under competent leadership (and the Russians and Chinese have not, in fact, supplied them with the latest equipment).

If an aggressive power, whether Russia, China, or even Germany or America, were to try to extend its influence over a large portion of the World Island by the direct use of force, then it would soon face a manpower shortage (even in the case of China). One can rely upon allies, but this has serious defects. These allies, without similar motivations, become a weak link. If the senior partner has delusions of grandeur, this naturally has an adverse influence on allies. If, on the other hand, a nation tried to assert its dominance alone, it would have to rely on methods of overwhelming cruelty and destruction, amounting to genocide. A land devoid of people is not so attractive a prospect for grandiose ambitions or dreams of empire.

The Middle East was another factor of great significance in the Heartland theory, on account of its strategic location as the great land and sea crossroads of the world. But this significance has waxed and waned with the dominant mode of transportation in different eras. Today, the Suez Canal has become relatively unimportant to the Western nations, but it would be of great value to the Russians – the Heartland country. Before 1967, when the canal was closed, the Russians had used this route to help link European and Asiatic Russia. This fact in itself undermines the theory of the Heartland concept by showing that sea transport is still of great importance. Thus, the Suez route, rather than being a sensitive lifeline for the West, has far greater meaning for the supposed Heartland power. This is Mackinder turned upside down.

Mackinder could not have predicted the eventual development of undersea ships. They constitute an entirely new class of ships and introduce a new era in sea power. The power of aircraft over the undersea ship is negligible. Western navies have spent much time and money on trying to find means to defeat undersea ships, quite without success; but the theory that the best answer is another, and better, undersea ship has yet to be accepted by them.

If modern strategists saw the true state of affairs clearly, as a clash between the thinking of Mahan and Mackinder, then it would be obvious to them that the undersea ship should be viewed as a friend rather than as an enemy, and Western navies would redirect their energies into trying to exploit the strength and usefulness of this new form of sea power. The undersea ship makes the land mass of the World Island truly an island for practical purposes. The Heartland was so named because it was supposedly inaccessible to the influence of sea power. Sea power can now be brought to bear at any point of its coastline. It is a Heartland region no more. This has meaning in peace as well as war. Ocean-going commerce can now use the Arctic regions of North America and Asia, and geographically speaking the Polar Mediterranean is the centre of the world.

Contrary to popular, and even some expert, opinion the Russians have a formidable defence problem. They have a huge country, but therefore more to defend and greater distances, with inadequate communications, over which to move troops. They must maintain defensive positions in the Far East against a possible conflict with the Chinese; the frontier between China and the Soviet Union stretches for 7,000 miles – longer than the distance from London to Buenos Aires. And 6,000 miles away in the West they have the potential problem of Germany. The great economic power of Germany could at some point in the future develop into a threat to Russian security. Attitudes can change with different generations and with shifts in economic conditions; it is not inconceivable that a future German government, with an eye on reunion with East Germany, might see fit to ally herself with China for this purpose. (Nor, on the other hand, is a union of interests between Germany and Russia beyond the pale of imagination – the lure of vast markets in Russia is certainly an attractive proposition for the Germans.) Russia's defence capacity would be stretched to the limit if, in addition to these threats on either border, she had to face a possible third front along her Northern coastline.[5]

Mackinder's Heartland theory did not conceive of the new economic uses of the sea. Nations are fast extending their interests far beyond their coastlines. Great Britain, for example, in her home island, has grown immensely in size; today she has common borders with France, Holland and Norway. These boundaries may be submerged under the North Sea and English Channel, but they exist. The potential wealth within the sea is tremendous, and as the mineral resources on land are gradually depleted, these marine minerals will become of great importance.

The conclusion is that the Heartland theory is not correct. Russia does not occupy a superior strategic position. In certain ways, her geopolitical position is in fact unfavourable. This does not imply that Russia is weak or could easily be conquered – far from it; but despite her strength, she lies in an exposed position in terms of limited war. The Russians could not realistically challenge the United States directly, except with the use of nuclear arms, or with the use of naval force. But Russia could never hope to out-build the US Navy, assuming that the latter clearly saw the threat. The Russians, by virtue of their geopolitical situation, must maintain a sizeable land force to protect their European and Asiatic borders, and their GNP is only about two-fifths that of the United States. There is no land threat to the continental United States. Just as a large army was not of great importance to Britain in the past, so today it is not of vital importance to the United States.

The strategy of the deterrent was only applicable in the event of direct Soviet attack, and even in regard to that, as has been shown, it was a quite mistaken strategy. The preoccupation of the United States for so many years with direct Soviet attack meant that the West neglected to develop systematically the means to respond to other forms of challenge to its interests. Much can happen under the umbrella of deterrence. A direct threat in itself is generally unable to deter indirect movements. In the case of the major powers in the contemporary world, any critical conflict between them is likely to be in the form of indirect conflict, or carried on by indirect means. If actual military conflict is involved, it is still more likely that the confrontation will be indirect. Such are the ways in which serious conflicts between major powers are conducted in an age when they command force beyond acceptable use; but behind this, among other things, still stand the facts of military power, and in the last analysis the pòssibility of direct war. This possibility has to be reckoned with; it exists as a fact with or without its actual occurrence. The West must therefore develop a strategy which, in the event of any direct military conflict between the major powers, can bring military force to bear in an effective way against its opponent and which can be realistically used with regard to the issue at stake and realistically related to the aims of policy.

The rejection of the Heartland theory means that the role of nuclear weapons must change. Western strategic doctrine, in assuming that the West is in an inferior geopolitical position, has called for nuclear arms to deter not only a nuclear attack, but also a possible conventional attack. In view of this, it was impossible for the United States to support the principle of a 'no first use' treaty with the Soviet Union, or to consider proposals for nuclear disarmament unless they also included related disarmament measures for conventional forces. The possibility of actually using nuclear arms in response to the threat of conventional warfare has been carried further by the reliance placed on tactical nuclear weapons in NATO's military thinking.

Nuclear arms are applicable to only one type of warfare – unlimited war. We have come to the realization that they are not legitimate instruments of policy; they bear little relation to any political aims of warfare. The rejection of the Heartland theory should have far-reaching implications for disarmament: it is the essential step towards rejecting the need for nuclear arms. They could not, of course, be eliminated in the short term, but it would transform the outlook for disarmament negotiations. Disarming is the reverse side of the coin from arming. In the 1950s, the United States were motivated by the fear of Russia threatening their security at every point around the world. American diplomacy was intent on seeking confrontation with the Russians, who, in turn, viewed American actions as threats to their own security. If the threat were seen to be of a lesser order, disarmament would be made very much easier, and the most obvious matter this would affect is those arms which are foremost in Western strategy – weapons which are unrealistic and unnecessary.

Since the end of the Second World War, world affairs have

appeared to be dominated by the opposing power blocs of the Soviet Union and the United States – though much of great importance has in fact been happening outside the political hegemony of these two states. As the relationship with the Heartland power, Russia, was the overriding concern of Western policy and strategy, it was necessary, according to the analysis put forward in this book, to concentrate on the West's position relative to the Soviet Union. This focus of attention is also obviously based on geopolitical realities – the Soviet Union is one of the two most powerful states in the world, and it has been, and remains, not just a rival, but an opponent of the United States. One of the main concerns of geopolitics is the planning of state security in a global context – that is, in terms of the geographical relationships of states as they affect the whole world.[6] This has sometimes been called geostrategy or 'defence geopolitics'. In considering a strategy for the West, it is inevitable that we should propose courses which give an advantage to the West and entail a disadvantage for the Soviet Union.

This should not be misinterpreted to imply that we are advocating a hawkish approach or an aggressive strategy. Far from it; one of the most important conclusions from our analysis is that it points the way to obtaining a more relaxed atmosphere among the major states on the troubled globe. Our argument has shown how vulnerable Russia has been, and how she will be still more exposed with undersea ships. It is true that the direction of the policy implied is aimed to some extent at Russia, and the strategy could be aimed *against* her: but this is not intended to mean that the West has any need to threaten Russia.

There is nothing to be said for underplaying the fact that what we are dealing with are matters of power. The availability of force, and the possibility of its application in measured and relevant ways, is one element in the equation of power. J. R. V. Prescott has summarized the situation in these general terms:

All the policies for the defence of the state are likely to have one or both of two primary aims – to make the state and its allies stronger, and to make the opponents of the state weaker. Policy decisions to strengthen the state will usually aim at either an improvement in the state's intrinsic power, or the acquisition of allies. Policies to weaken a hostile state will usually centre on attempts to increase their problems, truncate their military and economic bases, and deny them the assistance of allies.[7]

Though this is broadly true, it needs to be seen in the light of the fact that the real interests of states are seldom – or never, while rational aims are pursued – in total conflict; in addition, this power game can be played in many ways, according to various rules, and within different limits. It is, for instance, elementary that one nation does not threaten the really vital interests of another if there is any regard for coexistence. It is a general principle that the greater the sense of security, the less threats will be made or be thought to be made. It is also the case that a nation will be less likely to make actual threats to another nation at one point if the other nation has the possibility of readily activating a counter-threat at a different point.

The import of all this is that it points the way to policies of détente. It should be quite apparent that the United States and Russia have some real interests in common and some real interests in conflict. In fact, when the Heartland view of the world is seen for the illusion it is, what they have to quarrel about is not so overwhelmingly formidable – it is substantial in certain fields and areas only. It is possible that if the West abandoned the Heartland view, the Russians would abandon more quickly their own suspicious world outlook and adopt a more relaxed and realistic one; indeed, it is very likely, and the factor that makes it difficult to predict how readily this would happen is the distorting role of ideology. But in the long run, in these matters, ideology is the servant of a state's natural interests and of *realpolitik*, not the master; a more realistic Western approach would readily go some way towards toning down the ideological circuit which is fed into power politics.

Security from external threats is a real interest of every state, and it is not necessarily an objective which creates conflict between opposing states, as a superficial reading of the statement by Prescott just quoted might suggest. The Soviet Union is probably even more concerned than the United States about the enormous resources which the defence budget takes out of the domestic product. Both countries, for differing reasons, have an interest in stability and peace in Europe. A policy of détente is meant to remove threats. But, in order to be able to pursue realistically a policy of détente, one must have a strategy which fits in with it and supports it – that is, which is able to provide a sense of security for oneself, and which also does not create undue threats to the other side. The analysis of the previous chapters shows that such a strategy is available to the United States, and is applicable whether or not we 'trust the Russians'. It has been shown that sea power remains a viable strategy, and it is best suited for the dominant military role in support of foreign policy.

What is the new course for the future that our analysis suggests? In particular, what should be the guiding policy for the West? An answer to this question reflects the historical analogy of the role of Britain in relation to the continent. The policy of the West should be to ensure that no single nation, or coalition, could dominate the World Island. This is a course of action which would be compatible with the interests of the majority of the nations of the world today. In a sense, of course, this has been the policy of the West, but it has not been clear, and the feeling has always been that the threat could only originate from the Heartland. It emphasized a division of the world into two separate encampments, and led to the idea that stability could only be achieved by a system of fixed allegiances which would hold a preponderance of states in Eurasia in a Western bloc. The idea of the expansion of the Heartland was mirrored in the encirclement of the Heartland.

The former British policy of the balance of power in Europe worked well for centuries. It was a successful policy since it combined the self-interest of Britain with the aims of the majority of the European nations. As long as the various continental countries, with their different cultures, resisted unification either voluntarily or by force, then the mutual interests of the threatened nations in Europe coincided with the interests of Britain. If the bulk of the European nations wanted to join together in some quasi-political organization, for example the present EEC, then no country could prevent it.

Harold Nicolson wrote: 'My view is: (1) Our ancient traditions and principles were based upon the theory that we should protect the weak and defy the strong. (2) I know that this theory was founded upon our own security, and was a luxury offered to us by our invulnerability, and therefore certainty of ultimate victory.'[8] Britain had a measure of control through this seeming disinterest. It gave the British a certain detachment from Europe. They were both inside and outside the European system.

Such a policy could be carried out today with respect to the World Island. The leading exponent of such a policy must, of course, be the United States – a country which today occupies a geographical position similar to that which Great Britain had with respect to Europe. The continent of North America lies like an island off shore from the central landmass of the world. In this position, the United States is not directly threatened by land attack and, in theory, could provide a balance or a stabilizing element in the world.

This policy of maintaining a balance of power requires a recognition of, and belief in, the essential strength of the West – both in material advantages and in the cultural and spiritual aspects of civilization. It could only be carried out if the United States were rid of its schizoid fears of being attacked or threatened. It depends upon a belief in oneself, the inward feeling that the future is on one's side. There is no such thing as one hundred per cent security. 'Security is a relative not an absolute concept, and, as A. D. Lindsay remarked, "the search for perfect security ... defeats its own ends."'[9] Life means risks and the United States, as it has moved into the world arena, has been attracted to the ideas of total security which were current in the days of comparative isolation. Nuclear arms have given the illusion of total security, but they are in reality an index of the psychological feeling of insecurity.

It is extremely unfortunate that people in the United States who call themselves conservatives should look with favour upon nuclear arms. These 'radical conservatives' cannot be regarded as representing a truly conservative outlook. Sir Lewis Namier remarked that the tragedy of the Chamberlain period was that it was not a truly conservative government. One might make the same observation on the United States in the post-war world.

American conservative interests have yet to establish where their true interests lie and relate them to rational ways of thought.

Sir Herbert Butterfield said that the world could breathe easier whenever there were two opposing giants on the continent. We can now apply this to the World Island. Today there are two opposing giants on the World Island – Russia and China. And the world will be able to breathe easier whenever a truly conservative element which clearly understands its own interests arises in the United States; only this can supply the stability which the world needs today. Instead the so-called conservative element has adopted the crusading spirit of trying to make all men good through a righteous war on communism. Hopefully this attitude is changing. It was Nixon, the arch-anti-communist, who visited China and Russia and opened the door for a realistic approach. Nixon's past record, however, which so typifies many of the flaws in the outlook of American conservatives, does not provide reassuring grounds for believing that American policy is in safe hands or that it will now be consistently guided by enlightened realism.

President Nixon's more flexible and level-headed foreign policy undoubtedly owes much to the influence of Dr Kissinger. It is highly desirable: Kissinger's approach is consciously well versed in geopolitics, and it demonstrates that geopolitics is not a matter of speculative theories, or airy-fairy ideas or grandiose designs, but can be very much linked to hard practical sense and a grasp of immediate issues. With Kissinger, the place of geopolitics is made explicit, though it must always be present in policy, if only implicitly; one may not agree with all of Kissinger's views, but his attitude is a welcome change from the geopolitical illiteracy of Dean Rusk and former Presidential aides. It is reflected in President Nixon's view, reported in *The Times*, that 'the United States should have no permanent enemies. Nations should be judged by their actions rather than by their ideologies.'[10] This is a step towards the policy of trying to maintain a balance of power on the World Island.

To ensure that no single country obtains dominance is an aim well within the capacity of the United States, because it is consistent with the desires of the majority of the people on the World

Island. There are far too many cultural and racial dissimilarities to believe that one country, no matter what ideology it may adopt, could effectively and easily seize control of this great landmass. With a powerful seafaring country in North America willing to aid the underdog, it would be virtually impossible. It is impossible for the United States to impose its own will upon even a small section of the World Island, as the Indo-China débâcle illustrates. Unfortunately, the Nixon administration has not had the moral courage to carry out a compatible policy in this region.

A policy of maintaining a balance of power means a more relaxed view of world affairs. It means that every perturbation must not be regarded as the signal for the end of civilization. There is evidence to suggest that Europeans, especially the British, played up the danger from the Soviet Union to Washington because of the possibility that the United States might return to the old policy of isolation. The sentiment was certainly present, and Britain realized that with the entry of Russia into Eastern Europe the balance of power was no longer possible; it was necessary to rely upon the United States. It was theoretically impossible for the United States to return to the policy of isolationism since this had been predicated upon the existence of a powerful British fleet, and it took very little encouragement from the British for the Americans to go from one extreme to the other. Undiscriminating and hot-headed interventionism ensued.

The policy of the United States became to contain Russia, and more recently China, under the impression that these countries had a superior geopolitical position. This view implied a defensive strategy, and a need to build a vast system of alliances around the fringes of the Heartland. It was a policy that was typical of the American temperament, which tends to see things in black and white and swings from one naïve simplification to a contrary one just as extravagant. It believed in an East–West struggle between the communist bloc and the Free World – though the Free World included many countries which had no regard for political liberty, and the communist world was not a unified bloc. (Vietnam affords a particularly ironic illustration: had Ho Chi Minh and Marshal Ky been invited separately to the White House, an appropriate memento for the President of North

Vietnam would have been a portrait of Abraham Lincoln, as Ho had testified that he had been greatly influenced by him; a similar memento for the President of South Vietnam would have been a portrait of his chief hero – Adolf Hitler.) The assumption of the monolithic nature of communism and Soviet hegemony in support of it tied in with the Heartland theory. Formerly the United States had abhorred alliances with other nations, and suddenly they felt impelled to buy as many friends as they could. The result was unfortunate and predictable. It was natural that any tin dictator who wanted funds from the US treasury could receive them by aping the true anti-communist faith. It is doubtful whether any security worthy of the name was ever purchased in this manner. It was money largely wasted, and it would have been better spent on relieving some more deserving problems.

In principle, the United States is the one nation in the world which can afford to take a detached view of events. This does not mean ignorance of the world, or lack of compassion. It does mean that the United States is the natural arbiter of the world's problems, within realistic limits. One cannot maintain a judicious adjustment of a balance if one is easily thrown off balance oneself in the attempt. Maintaining a balance of power is a delicate operation since it is not always possible to know which side has the greatest weight, or to interpret the significance of an event. Timing is of utmost importance. One must not be too hasty or too late in taking action. Historically Britain, like the United States today, had a favoured position which meant that she could afford to be conservative in judgement and deliberative in action. This prevented costly errors and erratic behaviour. In the atmosphere of supposed danger there is a special risk of making costly strategic mistakes. A cool head is necessary. Errors in tactics can usually be rectified in time, but mistakes in grand strategy can lose the situation irreversibly. At times the enemy might be Spain, the Dutch, France, or Germany, but the object was the same. When the weight was shifting between these countries it was important to reserve judgement.

Western, and especially American, attitudes and doctrines have been greatly influenced by the emotional content of the Cold War. Feelings of tension and danger can give rise to a flood of rumours and half-truths; this was true of the Cold War, which produced hysteria usually associated with a war-time situation. But this is not inevitable: it is instructive to note the difference between American reactions and the attitude of the Israelis, who have real reason for apprehensions of a quite different degree. Napoleon said, 'The first quality of a good general-in-chief is to have a cool head which receives exact impressions of things, which never gets heated, which never allows itself to be dazzled, or intoxicated, by good or bad news.' The North Vietnamese have also not panicked, and one reason is obviously that they believe in themselves. Of course the Americans believed in 'the American way of life', but when one considers their reactions, and such extreme manifestations as arose in the early 1950s at the time of McCarthyism, it is obvious that their high opinion of themselves goes together with a lack of confidence that is so irrational that it requires a psychological as well as a political analysis. Richard Hofstadter put a finger on this in the apt title of an essay, 'The Paranoid Style in American Politics'.

The determination of policy by emotion can be clearly seen in the American attitude towards China. There was a desire to side with the Russians in the Sino–Soviet quarrel.[11] This is totally irrational. The consequence of American policy was to push China into closer association with Russia. The cement which still binds them, even loosely, together is primarily fear of the United States. Ideology alone is an uncertain cement. An intelligent reading of the situation would have made it obvious that China would eventually break away from the Soviet Union; there were far too many factors contributing to disunity. Even ideological considerations pointed to communism splitting into different and rival factions, as Christianity had done. But there would have been serious sources of contention between China and Russia no matter who were the particular rulers in Moscow and Peking. The Chinese and the Russians look upon each other as their chief enemy, while the grounds for quarrelling between the West and China are not nearly so compelling.

The Russians are acutely concerned over the possibility that the United States may, at some point, ally themselves with China against Russia. Despite disclaimers from the Nixon administration, it is at least possible that the United States will align themselves with China in some matters. This would appear to be one of the most effective means to put indirect pressure on the Russians, in order to engage in more fruitful negotiations. The idea of bargaining from a position of strength, which was a dominant theme of the John Foster Dulles period, could effect nothing when 'strength' meant nuclear arms. One of the main problems from the Western viewpoint is that Russia holds most of Eastern Europe, but the diplomatic–strategic approach of the West did not help one jot to 'roll back the Iron Curtain'. One of the advantages of a flexible balance of power situation is that moves are not seen simply as black and white, nor options just one-sided; problems are interlinked and multi-faceted, and if the United States had better relations with China, it might well encourage Russia to have better relations with the United States. A balance of power policy would give America the initiative, rather than keeping her the prisoner of a defensive strategy.

There are countless lesser occasions where emotion has distorted American policy out of any relation to true national interest. It would obviously be in the interests of the United States to have friendly relations with Castro. In October 1970 Washington made the surprise announcement that the Russians were building a submarine base in Cuba, probably for undersea ships and not for submarines. One way of avoiding this eventuality would have been through diplomatic action, but that is impossible when there are no relations.

What we see here is a demonology which has become part of the American political consciousness. It produces a bizarre picture of the world, and absurd inconsistencies in policy. The essential contradiction has become more striking since the entry into public eminence of President Nixon's advisor in foreign affairs, Henry Kissinger. The alleged policy of Kissinger is contrary to the real direction to which the administration is committed by practical policies – that is, the course dictated by internal political pressures in America. This is a problem which goes to the very soul of the American Republic. It is a dilemma which cannot easily be resolved.

The difficulty about a new world outlook in the West is that the atmosphere within the United States is not adequately conducive to it. The American Midwest seems to have partially got over its period of pathological anti-communism, but it still persists in the South. In time they will get over it too. Unfortunately Southerners are less receptive to the changing world than others, not because they are any less intelligent as a group, but because they feel more threatened. They feel threatened by internal social changes in America, and this feeling is inevitably projected into views of the world. The most obvious, but far from the only, development which has created a feeling of tension is the militant emergence of the American Negro. 'When our identity is in danger, we feel certain that we have made a mandate for war. The old image must be recovered at any cost. But, as in the case of "referred pain", the symptom against which we lash out may quite likely be caused by something about which we know nothing.'[12]

The regional struggle between the North and South in the United States has never been truly resolved. Both regions have different conceptions of what they mean by the 'United States'. Although Southern politicians may wrap themselves in the Stars and Stripes and loudly sing the national anthem, many have the Stars and Bars in their minds and hearts while their feet are tapping out *Dixie*. It is no accident that opposition to and support for the Vietnam War was largely divided along regional lines. A Northern Republic Senator has far more in common with his Northern Democratic colleague than with most Southern Senators of either party. There are, of course, many in the North who identify with the Southerners – first- or second-generation immigrants who have yet to be assimilated.

Patience is not one of the notable virtues of Americans, but the position of the United States calls for it not only to learn patience in international affairs, but to educate itself internally in patience. This is not an easy task; it is one for leadership, and it is part of the process towards maturity.

This raises another important point. We have seen how both Mackinder and Mahan emphasized the importance of a secure base. Internal security is a factor in this. A curious illustration of this has appeared in press reports: some vessels of the American fleet are reported to have been prevented from sailing by political dissension among the crews. We need hardly point out that more attention should have been devoted to unifying America at home and healing its divisive sores; but what is specially pertinent is that a foreign policy which is internally divisive of a nation saps the strength of that nation both at home and abroad. Yet, in the name of national 'security', that is what successive administrations have done. The need for an approach to foreign policy which would in the long run be acceptable to the people of the United States could not have been made more obvious than by the disenchantment of Vietnam. Not the least costly element has been the moral damage within America, and the moral danger to America abroad is another element; yet the United States has had the opportunity to pursue realistic policies which would have been patently in her own interests and those of most other peoples.

The military instrument to enforce such a balance of power policy must be a navy – and in the future this would mean an underseas navy. The undersea ship has far greater freedom of action than any other class of ships has ever had. The West, and the United States in particular, should look upon their navies as the dominant service. Unfortunately, naval leaders in the West do not have the necessary belief in the strength of sea power. If American policy itself were clear, then they would come to see that it was possible to have a sea power strategy capable of backing up this goal.

It might also be noted that navies are more conducive to the rise of liberal democratic government and institutions than are armies. A fleet cannot be used as a force in internal affairs. As Orwell pointed out, no one has ever heard of a naval dictatorship, but army dictatorships exist all over the world. Moreover, the very fact that a navy is the dominant service implies that a country is not directly threatened by attack from a foreign country. The sea frontier provides a measure of security for the seafaring nation which other countries lack. Such a nation is less likely to suffer from a widespread paranoid fear of attack. Thus dissenting elements and opposition to a government can exist without the fear that such opposition will be treated as treason. Fear of attack encourages totalitarianism. Even in the United States, the large defence establishment has unbalanced its institutional structure.

This fact is connected with another which should be an asset in America's relations with other countries, and without which it would be impossible for a country to pursue a balance of power policy. In its strongest political ideals, from its founding to the present day, the United States has stood for concepts such as political freedom and self-determination. It need not impose its ways on other countries. It can afford to appear, and be, flexible and tolerant towards lesser states. These philosophical values, beside its strategic position, should facilitate its actions in the world arena; yet in practice American policy has often operated to the opposite effect. On the other hand, it is difficult for the Soviet Union not to appear committed to expanding Sovietization, and it can only be in the interests of the West for the Soviet Union to try to overcome this handicap. There are, of course, many more factors than this in the ways in which ideas contribute to, or interfere with, the influence of the great powers. But what is very noticeable is that whereas the Russians have often skilfully exploited their claims, the amateurish leadership of America, hypnotized by the Soviet threat, has responded in ways damaging to American leadership and even contrary to what is valid in the Western tradition.

There are many people who look upon any return to a balance of power policy or to traditional diplomacy as a retrograde step. But a balance of power system is already a considerable feature of the global picture, and it would be wishful thinking to imagine that there are any means available to replace it in the foreseeable future. In theory, the only ways in which it would be possible to do without a balance of power would be by international agency, world empire, or a Soviet–American coalition.

In practice, the maintenence of a balance of power should not move in a direction contrary to the development of other means of adjustment in the international system. There is no question of returning simply to an eighteenth-century kind of system. Ours is a very different world. Perhaps the most overriding apparent difference is the existence of a balance of terror – the ultimate power of annihilation which is in the hands of nations with nuclear armaments. For a time, when the world appeared to be more simply polarized between the Soviet Union and the United States, it was mistakenly thought that this was the only power which really counted. It can now be seen that in some ways, paradoxically, it has given non-nuclear powers more freedom of action in relation to the great powers. It is a power which has little effective use in policy and therefore bakes no bread.

Maintaining a balance of power is not a concept which embraces all policy objectives, though for the West it is compatible with them. Max Beloff has said of the concept: 'It matters vastly that the balance be maintained at the lowest possible level of armaments.'[13] This interest is shared by the major powers. Nor does a balance of power policy preclude seeking limits to the power of national sovereignty through other means, such as international law. Historically, national sovereignty and territorial possession have been in essential association. Chapter 9 suggested that the new world outlook on the oceans was bound to affect this situation quite profoundly. The utilization of the wealth of the underseas provides a challenge to the idea of sovereignty, and the decisions on how this vast domain is carved up, shared out, or managed are going to be made within the lifetime of most of us. Whatever part conventional power politics play in the final resolution of the questions of the oceans, there must come a historic debate of what is equitable in circumstances which have no precedent. It seems likely that it will mark a great watershed in political theory, apart from the material changes it will bring. The community of nations is indeed entering new territory in more than the physical sense. Not unrelated to that debate will be the increasing international concern about conservation of resources on land and about the environment. It seems inevitable that there will be tremendous pressure for some limits to be put on wild and reckless consumption, and some control on pollution. It is difficult to see how the idea of the orderly development of natural wealth can be entertained without supranational implications in the political field.

Another problem which must provoke increasing concern in the coming years, and which is again not unrelated to the coming debate, is the division of the world into advanced industrial countries and less developed countries. That it would be wrong to ignore this is obvious without discussion here; that it would also be short-sighted and dangerous in terms of the national self-interest of the Western powers is worth emphasizing in order to put this salient feature of the global outlook in perspective. This is not an East–West division; in so far as it has a general geographical line, it is more a North–South division. We have already noticed how American sympathies tended to side with her foremost foe – in terms of both power and conflicting interests – in the Soviet–Chinese quarrel, and one reason for this is undoubtedly emotional identification with the less primitive country, which had, for example, also entered outer space. As advanced industrial countries, the Soviet Union and the United States have some interests in common – not the least of which is simply to maintain the conditions for advanced industrial society to develop in an orderly way. But the West has its own particular reasons for concern about the Third World. It has become the main area of competition between the great powers, and the West has an interest in seeing that this does not create explosive tensions, and that rival super-powers do not extend domination over parts of it. But Western policy in this regard has been based on a misconception which has resulted in the opposite of what was hoped for. It has been obsessed with international communism, without recognizing the fact that international communism has not been able to break down nationalist barriers, let alone dissolve racial and cultural differences. One of the most obvious characteristics of the Third World countries is their independence of outlook; the West's role is much easier once it accepts that these countries positively want to resist domination by the super-powers. Nowhere is this more striking than in the most open of all areas, Africa. Communist governments themselves have proved to be so varied and independent as to invalidate completely any direct association between the mere fact of being communist and danger to Western security; the strongest unifying factor among them is American, not Soviet, pressure. One of the latest examples is Chile, where Western interests have again been severely damaged by the demands of American domestic politics.[14]

Another reason why the West must be concerned with the

Third World is that uneven distribution of power makes the problems of maintaining a balance of power more difficult. It is not only military force that is at issue. Max Beloff has pointed out that 'the alternative to the diffusion of power through industrial and other forms of economic development is an excessive burden upon the countries that have it'. The health and strength of the Third World is in every way a Western interest. This is even more evident in view of the fact that the West is an oceanic alliance and its prosperity is dependent on trade. Commercial considerations can be notoriously short-sighted, and in the international sphere they need to be aligned with long-term policy. An outstanding feature of trade is that, in principle, it is supposed to be of mutual benefit. This could also have an increasing part to play in relations between the major communist powers and the West. The value which Russia and China attach to trade, and to economic and technological agreements with the West, was made apparent in the course of President Nixon's visits to Peking and Moscow. This should prove a useful means of lowering the political temperature.

But almost anything which can be grounds for cooperation or exchange can also be grounds for conflict. The Soviet Union, and in a rival way the Chinese, have tended to have an immediate interest in dissidence and instability in the Third World, and the United States an interest in order and stability. But no great power exerts a controlling influence over these. Cooperation between the major powers would certainly aid peace and stable conditions in local areas. Nevertheless, all the indications are that we are living in a period in which there will be a very considerable degree of instability and anarchic disorder in the Third World. The United States can live with this, without feeling impelled to intervene at every point. As we have noted, insurgency is not an ultimate threat to the security of the United States, though it may sometimes be a considerable local inconvenience. This does not diminish the role of the United States as a stabilizing element in world affairs; it means that she can, and should, carry out her policy with skill and flexibility and apparent disinterest. In doing so, she should not demand gratitude or be hypersensitive, as she has in the past. Such hypersensitivity is a natural characteristic of the most vulnerable countries in the Third World; it ill becomes the United States' position in world affairs.

We said at the outset of this chapter that the former world outlook of the West was in the process of disintegration before our eyes. One of the factors in this is that the bipolarization in world affairs between the United States and the Soviet Union has been severely attenuated. China, the European Common Market countries, and potentially Japan are emerging as powers to be increasingly reckoned with on the world scale. The world is now being commonly described as multipolar. Looking more generally at the distribution of interest and power, with the particular associations formed by the positions of countries in less developed regions, such as the Arab world, Africa, and South America, the political structure of the whole world displays a growing characteristic of polycentrism. But the dividing lines are not tidy; we must expect to live in a world where nations combine for some reasons and compete for others.

Two things follow from this. The first is that the prospects for negotiation have enlarged. This means that the place for diplomacy, in the conventional sense, is being re-established as something of prime importance; and such diplomacy is necessarily closely interrelated with strategy. The art of diplomatic-strategic management should again become considerably more subtle and flexible. The second point is that the influence of lesser states on the international scene is of some significance, and is likely to develop. This is something which can occur independently of the military power of the weaker countries. There is also a moral in this for the major powers. Non-military forms of influence will have a relatively larger part to play in the determination of power among the nations of the world.

The balance of economic power is obviously of critical importance. But the patterns of international politics will be affected by other interests, which do not have such clear roots in geopolitics. Social factors are one determinant of change, and they can interact with the international political system. This points to another difference from the classical balance-of-power period. Mahan thought that sea power needed an overseas empire. But the day of colonial empires has passed; the problem for the

Western powers has indeed been to divest themselves of colonial involvements while retaining the good will of people who had experienced colonial rule. Economically, colonial empires can no longer be a source of strength; but Mahan saw them as necessary primarily for strategic purposes, because of the limited cruising range of ships. But even in the Second World War the development of techniques for refuelling oil-fired ships at sea gave the United States a commanding position in the Pacific against Japan, without dependence on bases. With nuclear-powered ships the need for a string of overseas bases has greatly diminished.

In the new balance of power, relationships with the Third World have displaced the question of overseas empires. In this matter, non-military means of promoting Western interests will usually be of far greater immediate consequence than military power. This is outside the scope of this book; however, we may observe that the strategy we have outlined would aid a more sensitive approach to the Third World.

There is, however, one element on which we might specifically comment. Movement is one major consideration in geopolitics – the movement of military force, the movement of patterns of trade, the movement of population, and changes in the means of movement because of technological developments. We must add to this the movement of ideas. It used to be said that trade follows the flag; similarly, it has sometimes been true, but with much less certainty, that ideas follow the flag. Conquest, however, which is what this notion of 'the flag' practically supposed, is a course of action which has become far less feasible for a major power. The movement of ideas follows other routes. It is an aspect of communications which can have political consequences as concretely as the movement of goods. Though many ideas are volatile and transient, and may even be assumed like new clothes for the sake of expediency, there are deeper levels to the distribution of ideas in the world which could be brought within the scope of geopolitical analysis. The mobility of both technological and socio-political ideas has an impact on the society of nations today which inevitably gives them relevance to policy. Their role in domestic politics can affect foreign policy; but, apart from being a condition of policy, they are used today as instruments of policy.

The world is now one world, in the sense that events in one part are consciously noted in all other parts.

We have come so far in indicating the outlines of a new global view. The analysis of this book has shown that a new world outlook must be formed to replace the former one which has guided, or misguided, the West for so many years. Even on the immediate surface of current events, the old outlook is now beginning to look so inapplicable that some of the tenets associated with it are being abandoned in practice, notably by the Nixon administration, and before that by the idiosyncratic policies of France under de Gaulle.

The study of geopolitics is only a tool towards the shaping of policy. Though it can provide a map of the world more in accordance with reality, policy, as we have noted, is made in the minds of men. An optimum policy must be based on geopolitical considerations, but it also will be informed by aims which extend beyond security and power to other values. Strategy itself, it should again be noted, is only the means to an end – that of a realistic policy. Any system of thought concerning geopolitics cannot exist independently of the spirit of a society. The intellectual arguments produced in these pages are meaningless if people cannot bring themselves to believe inwardly in them. It is a matter of faith in the long run – confidence in the essential vitality of a society. For this one cannot use reason alone; indeed, it goes beyond intellect. One can only observe that Western society, while it has much to learn, has also much to offer to the world, is worth preserving and strengthening. As Albert Camus wrote:

> The defects of the West are innumerable, its crimes and errors very real. But in the end, let us not forget that we are the only ones to have the possibility of improvement and emancipation that lies in free genius. Let us not forget that when totalitarian society, by its very principles, forces friend to denounce friend, Western society, despite its wanderings from the path of virtue, always produces a race of men who uphold honour in life – I mean men who stretch out their hands even to their enemies to save them from suffering or death.[15]

The point need hardly be laboured that there are distinctive characteristics of Western society, which are shared by Western

countries across national differences, and which broadly belong
to the nations of the oceanic alliance. There are, of course, many
inconsistencies in this picture, and even very alien developments
in some parts. Looking at it in full perspective, however, we can
see modern Western society as representing one phase, the latest
and not the least worthy, in the history of Western civilization.
We can properly speak of Western values, not implying by this
that the West has a monopoly of them, but that the most articulate
expression of certain values has come out of the Western tradition.
In the political field, the concept of democracy is very real, with
all the complex of attendant beliefs in toleration, freedom, and an
open society. Though it is common enough to deride modern
Western society, the very terms by which our society is criticized
are likely to be taken from ideals which have been formed in the
Western mind – and one of these is the inviolable claim of the
critical spirit.

Ideals can leave the door open to idealism, and in no Western
society has untempered idealism been more in evidence than in
the United States. Anthony Howard has said, 'For me the great
overriding attraction of America has always been its sense of
idealism; it may sometimes have been naïve, certainly often it
turned out to be sadly misplaced . . .'[16] It is an idealism which
has at times been its own worst enemy. For idealism is a dubious,
and even dangerous, motive force when not in common harness
with a corresponding realism. 'Much could have been saved in
human lives, in human freedom and contentment throughout
the world, if only the US policies had been guided by less
elevated and more practical goals, had they been instructed less
by a moralistic rhetoric and more by a realistic calculation of what
assets this country disposed of to help its friends and frustrate
the designs of its adversaries.'[17]

There are indeed challenging purposes for the West to fulfil in
the world. There are limitations on them in the nature of things,
but the prospects also are great. It should steer a course unswayed
by either illusion or disillusion. The new world outlook which is
necessary for the West, and for the sake of the other countries of
the world, is a coalescence of democratic ideals and reality.

Notes to Chapter 10

1. Jones, S. B., 'Global Strategic Views', in *Military Aspects of World Political Geography*, United States Air Force, Alabama, 1959, p. 67.

2. Cohen, S. B., *Geography and Politics in a Divided World*, Methuen, 1964, p. 62.

3. The quotation is from Kennan, George F., *Realities of American Foreign Policy*, Norton, New York, 1966, p. 65. Kennan's comment on *Makers of Modern Strategy* is in his *Memoirs, 1925 to 1950*, Atlantic, Boston, 1967, p. 308.

Without some qualification, the impression given by Kennan's identification with the policy of containment would be unjust to him. He has said that his original proposals were distorted. 'The sterile and dangerous effort to excel the Russians in the nuclear arms race ... had no place in my scheme of things,' he wrote in *Foreign Policy*, Spring 1972.

Certainly Kennan was more politically sophisticated than the governments he served, and wished to counter the expansion of the communist 'bloc' more by emphasis on political means than by the strategy of military deterrence which took over the thinking of Western leaders.

4. Djilas, Milovan, *Conversations with Stalin*, Rupert Hart Davis, 1962, p. 164.

5. Historically, of course, the Russians have a great defence problem, and this potential third front pushes it into view once more. The lateral communications across Russia are not good and it would be difficult for the Russians to move forces to counter such threats. One might assume that any such danger would be met with nuclear force. This might be the case, but it would not necessarily be so. It would depend upon the nature of the threat and how it was viewed by the Kremlin leaders. If the move was looked upon as a Hitler-type effort to destroy the Slavs then, unless they were confident that the move could be contained with conventional force, there would be strong motives for using nuclear force. If the threat were clearly of a limited nature, such as that associated with border clashes, then the Russians would be unlikely to escalate the force, and so the political aims, by rashly introducing nuclear arms.

In any direct military conflict on the World Island between Russia and the West, sea power would be operating in conjunction with some large World Island land power. The Arctic lands offer sea power a possible front for action, and they would have to be defended, against either invasion or more restricted operations.

6. See East, W. G., and Moodie, A. E., eds., *The Changing World*, Harrap, 1956, p. 23. J. R. V. Prescott draws attention to Professor East's recommendation on the use of the term in *The Geography of State Politics*, Hutchinson, 1968, p. 39.

7. Prescott, op. cit., p. 58.

8. Nicolson, Harold, *Diaries and Letters 1930–1939*, Collins, 1966, p. 345.

9. Buchan, Alastair, *War in Modern Society*, Watts, 1966, p. 26.

10. *The Times*, 22 December 1969. Compare this with the plaintive naïveté of Dean Rusk, Secretary of State in the Kennedy and Johnson administrations, who said to Louis Heren, *The Times* Washington correspondent: 'All we needed was one regiment. The Black Watch would have done. Just one regiment, but you wouldn't. Well don't expect us to save you again. They can invade Sussex, and we wouldn't do a damn thing about it.' But President Nixon's petulant reaction when he was criticized by the Swedish Prime Minister for resuming the bombing of North Vietnam in December 1972 should be recorded too: the newly appointed Swedish ambassador was banned from taking up his appointment. Many indications give one little confidence that American policy will settle down into a reasonable maturity during Nixon's second term of office; some very significant and sensible adjustments, which were long overdue, have been made, but a temperamental flaw in Nixon's American outlook threatens seriously to vitiate the United States' response to world events in other ways.

11. William F. Buckley, the editor of the *National Review*, and other American neo-conservatives, suggested in 1967 that the United States should bomb Chinese nuclear installations. The Russians would have been only too pleased, and might have made Buckley a Hero of the Soviet Union for his services. It could even have presented them with the opportunity to extend their borders further into Sinkiang and Manchuria.

12. McLuhan, Marshall, *War and Peace in the Global Village*, Bantam, New York, 1969, p. 97.

13. Beloff, Max, *The Balance of Power*, Allen & Unwin, 1968, p. 67.

14. The Chinese have put forward the concept that each nation must follow its own doctrine tailored to its own needs. 'It was the Chinese who put forward the doctrine that decisions of national parties are binding only within the area over which the party has jurisdiction. But, as Benjamin Schwartz has elegantly pointed out, in doing so Peking has not merely undercut Moscow's claims to ideological and

political authority but damaged, perhaps irretrievably, its claims to be the reconstruction of a central communist authority under its own aegis' (Gelber, Harry G., 'Strategic Arms Limitations and the Sino-Soviet Relationship', *Asia Survey*, April 1970). The ideological declaration of independence which Peking aimed at Moscow is of a boomerang nature.

15. Camus, Albert, 'Reply to Shepilov' in *Resistance, Rebellion and Death*, trans. O'Brien, Justin, Hamish Hamilton, 1964, p. 117.

16. Howard, Anthony, *New Statesman*, 14 April 1972.

17. Ulman, Adam B., *The Rivals: America and Russia since World War II*, Viking Press, New York, 1972, p. 386.

Index